4923

.95

# NUM

# AS SYMBOLS
# FOR SELF-DISCOVERY

## Richard Vaughan

**CRCS PUBLICATIONS**
Post Office Box 1460
Sebastopol, California 95472
U.S.A.

**Library of Congress Cataloging-in-Publication Data**

Vaughan, Richard B. (Richard Blackmore), 1916–
   Numbers as symbols for self-discovery.

   Rev. ed. of: Numbers as symbols of self-discovery
1973.
   1. Symbolism of numbers.  I. Vaughan, Richard B.
(Richard Blackmore), 1916–     .  Numbers as symbols
of self-discovery.  II. Title.
BF1623.P9V38  1985        133.3'35              85-29961
ISBN 0-916360-31-8 (pbk.)

FIRST PAPERBACK EDITION
INTERNATIONAL STANDARD BOOK NUMBER: 0-916360-31-8

Published simultaneously in the United States and Canada by:
CRCS Publications
*Distributed in the United States and internationally by*
CRCS Publications
(Write for current list of worldwide distributors.)

# Contents

*The glory of the future is but a reflection of the past in all its truth and the only key that is needed is the wisdom to understand . . . .*

**Richard Blackmore Vaughan**

# INTRODUCTION

## *THE IMPORTANCE OF NUMBERS*

Numbers go back to the dawn of history when man first began to think and identify various factors in his environment with an aim for some manipulative control over his affairs. Along with his discovery of numbers, man first came to distinguish one quality in nature from another. In addition to being conceived as simple digits or units of measurement in a quantitative sense, individual numbers were considered to have a distinctive character of their own on a qualitative level. Furthermore, these qualitative characteristics were believed to reflect both the laws of nature and the human spirit itself as evidence of eternal principles.

For example, the NUMBER ONE as a single object stood out in the mind as a dominant force which clearly held leadership, sway and influence over everything else. It also represented a force of aggressive assertion like a club or spear; and like the phallus which it resembled, it represented the male quality in nature as it stands alone. NUMBER TWO, on the other hand, reflects a duality in nature where one element is counterbalanced against another as a current between two magnetic poles. The presence of one produces consideration, allowance or adjustment for the other. The channel

11

between the two came to be thought of as receptivity or the female element of response. And so forth. . . . In this connection the reader is directed to the fascinating presentation of the primitive association of numbers with qualities of thought in *Io Unveiled by Bozena Brydlova*, Macoy Masonic Publishing Co., 1922 . . . or the more scholarly treatment by the great 18th century scholar, Thomas Taylor, in his *Theoretic Arithmetic of the Pythagoreans*, Phoenix Press edition, Los Angeles, 1934.

The descriptive characteristics or qualities associated with number values emerged at the same time as man's first discovery of their significance. Thus number ONE (however it was drawn or pictured graphically) became a symbol for "oneness" which referred to a quality or idea force in nature itself which man discovered as he first started to extract meanings or ideas from the reality of his daily experience.

With the extended development of more complex varieties of symbolic communication, man has become more and more removed from the rudimentary beginnings and primitive association of his basic thinking. Today in the complexity of our communication systems man is able to think and dream whole realms of creativity by the mathematics of numbers in their arithmetic, algebraic or trigonometric relationships to each other. This is a decided step forward in abstract symbolism, but it cannot be said to deny to number the primary conceptual or quality association from which number first evolved.

It is with the re-affirmation of this primitive and basic relationship between symbol and meaning PLUS the personal application of number values to ourselves as individuals that the present system of NUMBER ANALYSIS concerns itself.

The sophistication of our present scientifically orientated culture is loath to allow any philosophical or spiritual meanings to numbers as such. Such associations are not denied, but rather disregarded or ignored. Any connection of numbers with individuals in a personal way is hotly contended, however, just as the materialist philosophy resists any concept of Fate in our lives.

This concept of applying numbers to our personal lives is a PSYCHIC ASSUMPTION based on a spiritual link between ourselves and certain number patterns which are intimately connected with our lives.

The possibility of such a link tends to be denied by those who do not give any allowance for the validity of spiritual implications or hidden occult values. But then there are others, like myself, who accept such possibilities quite naturally and eagerly follow up whatever help such remarkable knowledge can reveal to us.

This occult or hidden value application presupposes a certain spiritual philosophy which is actually quite similar to that found in most religious beliefs — or as all religious beliefs were in their mystical beginnings. That is to say, this philosophy believes that THERE IS A SPIRITUAL PURPOSE IN LIFE AND THAT EACH OF US HAS A PART IN THIS PURPOSE.

An extension or development of this belief conceives that the individual spirit does not die and to some degree repeats itself in various forms which gives rise to the concept of reincarnation or the transition of the spirit through various lessons or stages of development. Our individual purpose in this life, then, becomes a challenge in SOME SPECIFIC DIRECTION.

If one does not accept this philosophical or spiritual position then there is no need to go further because the link which makes this possible is a hidden (occult) spiritual connection and not a material scientific fact.

As with religion, you either feel this is so or you do not. There is no way of knowing or proving it by sheer rationalization or material logic.

In occult language this association of human nature with personal number values has been called Numerology but Number Analysis is the term I prefer to use in this book.

Number analysis considers that there are two sources of number values which intimately relate to our personal lives. Neither of these sources happens by accident and their relationship to our life pattern is considered to be a matter of Fate.

One source is the DATE OF OUR BIRTH which is recorded in numbers and the other is OUR NAME which can also be expressed in numbers.

The belief in Number Analysis is that we are not just given a name. Rather, we are what we are and by psychic force we attract the name to ourselves which exactly labels and describes what we are. The person who bestows our name (whoever they may be) is not therefore giving us a name but is psychically expressing what they know us to be. The name, in Number Analysis, reveals what we are and conversely what we are not (which implies a great deal).

In Number Analysis the date of birth reflects our Fate and identifies our direction in life. It foreshadows all that will happen to us and it contains our over-all time table of points along the way.

The judgment or key for developing this special kind of information about ourselves comes from comparing the compatability or incompatability of ourselves as we ARE with our FATE which is our challenge. Out of this interaction comes the predictability of our present position.

Personal analysis such as suggested above is a two-edged sword. It can conquer or it can kill. A half way effort in self-analysis is apt to provide more difficulties than no effort at all. After all, our personal fate unfolds whether we are aware of it or not and whether we welcome it or fight it. One should have a predisposition and a talent for analysis or it may be said that it is better to leave it alone.

One should also be a seeker of truth and appreciate that the truth about one's self is ultimately constructive. If you can't face the truth about yourself or about life (and there are a great many people who cannot), then any presentation of this kind will hardly be appreciated.

One of the most difficult things to understand in life is those people who take the position (after granting that perhaps numbers can reflect such things) ... what good does it do to know the answers to questions such as; Who Am I?, or Where Am I Going?

I find such a position is like the attitude of mind that feels the best way to cross a busy intersection at the peak of traffic is to close one's eyes and plunge blindly forward. It has always seemed to me that the chances of making a successful crossing in this manner are not only doubtful but likely to be foolishly disastrous. And yet there are people, where the awareness of fate is concerned, who choose to go through life with exactly this attitude of mind.

But for those who would seek knowledge and guidance about themselves, number analysis can provide fascinating information and extend the potentials of a successful and happy adjustment as we go forward in life to meet the challenge of our fate.

14

# PART 1
## *ALL ABOUT YOU*
## *THE MEANING OF YOUR NAME*

### *Chapter I*
### *YOUR CHARACTER: WHO YOU ARE*

The numbers in your life that identify WHO YOU ARE come from your name. Who you are might also be expressed as ... WHAT'S IN A NAME? The answer in number analysis is obviously everything!

As already stated in the introduction, the belief in number analysis is that you are not just given a name but rather you are what you are and you psychically attract the label to yourself which correctly identifies you. The name distinguishes one person from another. If two people have the exact same name then they are basically alike even though this may not be immediately apparent on the surface. Even though two persons are basically alike (as a father and his namesake), each may be greatly modified by the conditioning of his fate pattern. Unless each also had the same NUMBER PATTERN in their birthdate (obviously they could not have the same date of birth), they would develop differently because they were exposed and challenged by different opportunities.

It makes no difference who actually calls forth the name (parent or otherwise). But it does make a difference that the name which correctly labels you is THE FIRST FULL ORIGINAL NAME WHICH YOU FORMALLY RECEIVE. If the father formally names you one day and the mother renames you the next, the first label is what counts. Usually there is a concurrence between those responsible and no formality is observed until together they come up with the proper identification.

An interesting but subtle aspect of naming children is a feeling within the one selecting a name (or fishing for the correct label) that there should be a coincidence of FITNESS. This feeling of fitness is something which is sensed on a psychic level before it is expressed in the consciousness.

Often one name is considered and then another UNTIL THOSE RESPONSIBLE FEEL THAT A CERTAIN NAME IS INDEED SUITABLE. Thus responsibility and suitability enter into the fitness of the label. This is always true regardless of the individual circumstances involved. Sometimes parents name their children before they are born. Sometimes they have mentally selected a name for their child, but when the child is born for some compelling reason they change their minds and call the child something else BECAUSE IT SEEMS MORE SUITABLE AS THEY SENSE THE CHILD TO BE AS A PERSON.

The whole point here is this very subtle distinction of suitability which as a psychic force generally falls only on the shoulders of those actually responsible for naming the child.

Naturally to bystanders or relatives this seems like an arbitrary or obvious selection. But to those entrusted with this assignment it is indeed much more than that, although few people think about it in this light.

An interesting sidelight on this is the naming of pets. Here we seem quite aware of the suitability of what we select as a name. One name seems to fit a certain pet and another name seems not to fit at all AS WE SENSE THAT PET TO BE. It is quite true that to someome else our pet should perhaps have another name. But it is OUR PET and this is important, just as it is important to the parent (or those otherwise responsible) in the naming of the child. It is only to those bystanders WHO ARE NOT RESPONSIBLE that the naming process seems arbitrary and relatively insignificant.

So in evoking or calling forth a name we are in effect using psychic force to bestow a label which suits or corresponds to HOW WE SENSE that object to be.

Even when we give the child the exact same name of the parent, as in junior, there is still this feeling of fitness as opposed to just

16

tradition. Sometimes the first child may be named the junior, but not necessarily so. There is much more subtle psychic interplay involved here than one would casually suppose.

The word 'junior' in a name is an adjective used to designate the younger of two persons of the same name — as a father and a son. In number analysis do not include the junior or any other appendages such as the 3rd or 4th of the same name. And of course do not include prefixes such as Mr., Miss or Mrs. or Duke or Princess in the case of titles.

Of frequent occurrence is the addition of further names at the time of christening to favor a relative or religious saint, or in the case of adoption a complete change of name by the new parents.

IN NUMBER ANALYSIS ONE MUST ALWAYS USE THE FULL ORIGINAL NAME AS FORMALLY GIVEN. In today's mechanics this is usually what appears on the birth certificate since hospitals usually ask for a name as soon as possible so the necessary forms can be recorded. People and even parents are often surprised to later find out that the name that was first formally given somehow got changed or was even spelled differently than they remember.

Since the numbers in our name derive their numeric value from the letters in the alphabet, THE ORIGINAL SPELLING IS ABSO-LUTELY IMPORTANT. In the case of misspellings it is important to determine who misspelled the name. If it was the parent who later found the error, then the correct name to use in analysis is the name originally given whether misspelled or not. If the parent knew the spelling but a recording clerk or the hospital copied it down wrong, then the name would be as the parent intended it. The criteria here is the INTENTION AT THE TIME, as this is what expresses the psychic force.

Although it is not usually considered in this light, people who misspell words are suffering from some sort of "psychic inter-ference" or "psychic static" in their daily life. People's inability to spell some words correctly comes from a blind spot in their perspective. It is not unlike color blindness. They really feel certain words the way they spell them whether it happens to be the normal spelling or not.

In the case of persons who know they had a prior name but do not know what it is, then it is impossible to use number analysis to know who you are. This in itself is an act of fate and for some reason or other fate did not intend that you should have this information.

At this point the subject and question which most often comes to mind about names is. . . . If it is true that you are what your name reveals you to be, can you change this by changing your name?

The answer is NO.

You can change the way you look or seem to others by changing your name; this is often done by people in the theater or others who have a broad public audience, BUT IT DOESN'T CHANGE THE BASIC YOU.

Changing your name changes the message or quality of your image, but this is only effective with those members of an impersonal audience who can't get close enough to sense you as you really are. The general public can and will react to your assumed name and this may prove more profitable or rewarding in special ways providing you happen to live the kind of life that functions in this manner — that is, before a wide impersonal audience. Show business personalities give us an obvious example of the merchandising results of name change for box office appeal.

Betty June Thornburg became BETTY HUTTON

Alexander Archibald Leach became CARY GRANT

Nicholas Ulman became DOUGLAS FAIRBANKS

William Henry Pratt became BORIS KARLOFF

Lucille Fay LeSueur became JOAN CRAWFORD

Frances Ethel Gumm became JUDY GARLAND

Leslie Townes Hope became BOB HOPE

To name a few. . . .

But with the small circle of everyday contact where most people operate, any such change of name WILL NOT HAVE THIS KIND OF BOX OFFICE EFFECT.

Since the straight route between two points is to take what you HONESTLY ARE and meet what MUST BE DONE, this change of names in order to make things seem easier or in some way more fortunate for yourself is rather impossible.

Although it seems redundant to repeat, in the case of married women the maiden name must be used. And the same applies even though some of your name is never used or dropped completely.

Undoubtedly the most difficult thing for students to comprehend about number analysis is the validity of people's names as symbols and focus of meaning. And yet it is perfectly true. You are what you are and the name you attract invariably labels your product.

Some say sugar, some say salt and some say poison. And that's the way it is.

There is no point in asking how this happens or why it works. It is a fact of life as inevitable as water is $H_2O$ and that $H_2O$ is labeled water.

Your name in number analysis identifies you in all your complexities as we shall soon see.

To transfer the name into numbers we substitute numbers for letters of the alphabet. EACH LETTER OF THE ALPHABET BEARS THE NUMBER VIBRATION OF ITS SEQUENCE IN THE ALPHABET. Thus A is ONE because it is the first letter of our alphabet. B is TWO because it is the second letter of our alphabet.

Double numbers are reduced to a single digit by addition. K is the eleventh letter of our alphabet and reduces to TWO. X is the twenty fourth letter of our alphabet and reduces to SIX.

The following table easily enables you to tell at a glance the number value of all the letters.

$$1 \quad 2 \quad 3 \quad 4 \quad 5 \quad 6 \quad 7 \quad 8 \quad 9$$

$$A \quad B \quad C \quad D \quad E \quad F \quad G \quad H \quad I$$

$$J \quad K \quad L \quad M \quad N \quad O \quad P \quad Q \quad R$$

$$S \quad T \quad U \quad V \quad W \quad X \quad Y \quad Z$$

The nine primary numbers represent nine basic qualities of human nature.

Numbers on the first line represented by "A" through "I" are said to be the PHYSICAL manifestation of that quality or element.

Numbers on the second line represented by "J" through "R" are said to be the MENTAL manifestation of that quality or element.

Numbers on the third line represented by "S" through "Z" are said to be the SPIRITUAL manifestation of that quality or element.

The first distinction to be made in the numbers of a name is between the individual numbers themselves (which come from the separate letters in the spelling of the name) and an index number which is derived as a total.

The individual numbers in a name comprise the subconscious warehouse of the individual. These are the qualities in which the individual has talent, subconscious awareness, inherent know-how and instinctive reliance. In every sense of the word these are the individual's assets — the tools he has been given to do the job at hand.

Not every name contains each of the nine basic numbers. When a number is missing from the name the individual is considered to have a blind spot in the over-all perspective and function of that element of behavior. In the philosophy of number analysis a missing number is said to represent a karmic link with a past life in which the use or function of that quality was somehow mismanaged and certain unfortunate conditions in this life are regarded as evidence of a debt that must somehow be paid or overcome with CONSCIOUS EFFORT.

Missing numbers in the name are the individual's liabilities — in every sense of the word.

Just as some numbers are missing altogether, the individual may have an excess of a number which distorts the over-all balance in another way. Such accents are called PASSIONS and indicate the area where the individual is prone to over-do or over-play a certain quality to the detriment of SOUND BALANCE.

In an average name composed of 14 letters the usual distribution would be as follows:

3    ONES

1    TWO

1    THREE

| 1  | FOUR   |
| 3  | FIVES  |
| 1  | SIX    |
| N0 | SEVENS |
| 1  | EIGHT  |
| 3  | NINES  |

Research has proved this to be so — that the average person has the above average qualities of the nine basic elements or idea forces.

The individual number qualities are only warehouse items until the individual has conscious need or specific purpose for putting such assets or tools to use. In the case of missing numbers, or too many of one number (by proportion), the individual may be said to have a liability situation in that department of life.

In contrast to the subconscious condition of qualities there are THREE POINTS OF CONSCIOUS FOCUS which together pattern the individual's nature. Together these comprise HIS CHARACTER, HIS PERSONALITY and HIS MOTIVATION. The numbers which symbolize each of these points of concentration derive from NUMBERS IN TOTAL.

The character as the most important index of all is symbolized by the number total of all the numbers in the name. Again double numbers are added together (and together again if necessary) to reduce the total to a single digit. This index number reflects WHO YOU ARE and the type pattern you represent. It symbolizes the eventual way you get things done since it describes the technique and form of expression which is native to the individual. We call this the native's CHARACTER.

The first consideration in appraising the effectiveness of the character is the degree to which this same quality or pattern is backed up or supported by any warehouse talents for this type of expression. If the number is well supported in this quality then the individual is a POSITIVE EXPRESSION of that quality and is generally able to effectively deal with any and all situations to which he is ideally matched. That is, confronted with a situation or condition whose nature is the same as this number.

If, on the other hand, this number is not supported by having at least one of this same number in the individual numbers (letters) of his name, then appearances are not what they seem. Many important qualifications must be made in evaluating and dealing with this type of person.

Under the above karmic condition the individual's conscious focus is in one direction, but his subconscious awareness of all that this quality implies is reduced, impaired, hampered and deflected in some subtle but significant way.

He is what he is, but he lacks the depth and understanding to effectively deal with all situations to which he is matched. Generally speaking, the individual will perform effectively in the quality or category of this number WHEN HE IS DEALING WITH MATTERS OR CONDITIONS THAT DO NOT DIRECTLY AFFECT HIS PERSONAL LIFE. In dealing with others on the matter at hand he tends to behave as any other normal representative of this quality would act. His "lack", such as it is, is less apparent. But in dealing with his own personal affairs he tends to falter, behave less effectively and consequently less true to his pattern type.

When one has no number symbols to back up what he is (in total), then the individual tends not to accept himself or even like himself or behave constructively in the very pattern of his nature. In many cases he will act in a negative and contrary fashion to the more positive expression of this quality.

All number categories tend to have both a positive and negative side to their expression. Whether the individual tends towards the positive or negative side is shown in the over-all judgment of the pattern. But one rather clear cut example of negative expression is when the individual has no subconscious support of the very qualities of his conscious focus. He will then IN HIS PERSONAL AFFAIRS tend to express himself negatively while in more objective situations he will tend to express normally (or positively) according to the nature of his pattern.

The more talent there is (coming from the individual numbers on the three planes of manifestation — physical on the first line, mental on the second line and spiritual on the third line — to back up the conscious focus, coming from the name total) the more positive and constructive the expression.

The above distinction is a vital consideration in number analysis because it universally accounts for the glaring contradictions in life when people are credited for one thing but fail to consistently produce or perform in the FULL IMPLICATION of their pattern.

To summarize: WHAT YOU ARE IN GENERAL IS THE TOTAL OF YOUR NAME.

# NUMBER *1* CHARACTER

A number ONE character is a person who is independent, resourceful, aggressive, strong, domineering and pushy. ONES are also inclined to be original, inventive, pioneering, ambitious, determined and uncooperative. They generally work best alone or in a sufficiently independent capacity as the person in charge or command. They find it very difficult to operate effectively under the control or management of others. Self-interest is, of course, their natural frame of reference, as it should be. In dealing with children who are ONES, their ONENESS should be encouraged for to do otherwise would be contrary and harmful to the development of their basic nature. It would obviously be wrong to encourage a ONE to behave differently or discourage their ONENESS just because someone did not like ONES.

ONES naturally strive for leadership and individuality in all things. ONE symbolizes the "spirit" and "will" acting through decision. ONE people tend to establish their own individuality regardless of how this may effect others and it should be remembered that this self-justifying ego is right and natural for them.

There is always a necessity for ONES to be first in something they do. They obviously can't be first at everything, but some situation should be found and encouraged which will enable them to shine and thus sense their accomplishment on their terms.

ONES are not designed to listen or follow. They must instead dig within themselves to convince others that they have the right to take over and lead.

Since ONENESS reflects the masculine principle in nature, it is obviously more suitable for men than women but this depends on the larger framework of social patterns in terms of what is currently expected of the individual. If the current social framework expects that only male members are expected to reflect the masculine principle in nature then ONE is certainly more suitable for men. But the demands or views of social patterns may differ between cultural cycles and it may become equally acceptable and desirable for women to also reflect ONENESS.

The essence of a ONE tends to be a spontaneous push, therefore qualities or circumstances which prevent or hinder this spontaneous thrust must be resisted and overcome in order for the individual to be himself. When a number is obviously successful in what they are doing we tend to think of them as a positive or constructive manifestation of that quality. Unfortunately when a person is less impressive with what he seems to accomplish, we tend to think of him as negative or nonconstructive. Thus a ONE is sometimes thought of as vain, egotistical, selfish, conceited and overbearing which is undoubtedly true at various times for all ONES. But if the individual is also an outstanding leader of prominent distinction we tend to overlook these less laudable qualities of ONENESS. Success becomes the cover-up.

In being yourself, whatever your vibration, it is inevitable that some people will consider you in a negative light because that is how you effect them (and their numbers). This should not, however, become the guiding principle as to whether you are acting positively or negatively. The individual must be himself no matter how his vibration effects others. There is in nature something of all qualities. Just as their are individuals who are born to lead, there are individuals who are born to follow. Each must find his own level of operation. The challenge here is to be yourself and let others find their own level without you interfering or destroying their function.

If an individual is out of step with most of his environment then the thing to do, if at all possible, is to seek an environment or situation where he may not be so out of step. People should somehow appreciate and realize that there is an ideal place for everyone in this world. Nature is universal and somewhere there is a place and reason for all its parts. Too often we forget this and are defeated by too narrow an experience or too limited a vision or too shallow a faith. Incidently, each of these qualities in our nature is symbolized by some specific number which in turn explains why we do or do not do certain things.

The ONE type of character is supported in his consciousness by the amount and quality of ONENESS which resides in his subconscious. He is supported on the physical level by any A's in his name, on the mental level by any J's in and on the spiritual level by any S's.

To have no letter symbols for ONE in the name is unusual because the average name has at least 3. With no ONES the individual tends not to accept or like himself as the type of character he is. Nevertheless, since he is a ONE he ends up acting like a ONE but in a more negative than positive expression of his type. But when he is acting on a more objective (less personal) matter then he will tend to act more constructively as a true ONE.

# NUMBER *2* CHARACTER

A number TWO character is a person who is in most respects just the opposite from a ONE. TWOS are dependent, nonaggressive, vascillating, gentle and receptive. Their strength lies in their understanding, inspiration, helpfulness, consideration, sensitivity, patience, tact, diplomacy, timing and rhythm. They are particularly adept at the so-called constructive compromise. Naturally they are cooperative and sympathetic. They make good followers and listeners. They are often careful, deliberate and have high regard for small details and the "little things" in life which to them are always valid indications of larger more important things to follow. Where standing alone as a leader is important to ONE, TWOS need companionship and someone who will intercede on their behalf. They are imitative, reflective, quiet, unassuming and frequently fond of music and the arts.

Just as the rhythm of two alternating beats represents the balance between two poles, TWOS are the adjusters of differences. They represent the law of duality, the principle of give and take and blending opposing views into a common interest. A TWO can see and appreciate both sides at once. They have great powers of analysis and the ability to break things down to their component parts yet remember the whole from which they came. With acute powers of observation, they are very sensitive to the lack of balance or harmony between opposite sides. Honesty in the literal unqualified sense or taking a definite stand on issues is not their chief virtue because they dislike to favor one side against another. They always prefer to straddle the issue and give a little consideration to both sides. Nothing to them is ever just black or white but preferably shades in between.

In terms of ONE which is strong, TWO is inclined to be weak and needs protection, but each has its own virtue and function in the "whole" of life.

Since TWONESS reflects the feminine principle in nature it is obviously more suitable for women then men, but this also depends on what is expected of the individual by the larger framework of society. Current social patterns may find it equally acceptable for either sex to reflect TWONESS. But if it falls in a man's chart and he is (for some reason or other) trying to do a traditionally masculine job, then being a TWO type is a liability.

The TWO character is supported in his consciousness by the amount and quality of TWONESS at the warehouse level of the subconscious. He is supported on the physical level by any B's in his name, on the mental level by any K's in his name and on the spiritual level by any T's.

With no individual letter symbols for TWO at all in the name this individual does not accept or appreciate himself even though he can only act as a TWO.

# NUMBER 3 CHARACTER

The number THREE character is one who in some respects combines a little of ONE and TWO in a joyous combination that results in some form of creative self-expression. As ONE is the spirit force of "beginning" and TWO is the sensitive reflection of what "might be", THREE is the composite "whole" which gives justification of what went before in ONE and TWO. THREE is the happy child product of the union of ONE and TWO.

THREES are generally enthusiastic, optimistic, entertaining, imaginative, talented, decorative and happy-go-lucky. Their special quality is for synthesis — putting miscellaneous items together so they somehow form a coherent whole and creates a "picture". They have a gift for making others "see" which often bypasses the necessity of taking each step separately. THREE is a youthful quality which is naive, unsophisticated, childish, immature and petulent, but it also has all the freshness and spontaneity of a totally "new creation". The qualities of THREE stand up best when responsibility, practicality and endurance need not be considered. THREE is the "window dressing" approach to life and should be valued for just what it appears to be as of "that moment" with little concern for what went before or what may come after. It is a suggestion and a fantasy rather than the substance and reality of what may be intended. The function of criticism is very important to THREE for they tend to have an opinion or reaction to everything. Naturally they are frank and outspoken, as they should be, but they tend to scatter their interests so it is difficult to keep them focused on any one point for very long. They have a talent for persuasive salesmanship and so make excellent salesmen if the subject or product has captured their interest and enthusiasm. Fear is their worst enemy. Fear, pessimism and ill humor are all negative to the best that THREE has to contribute. On the positive side their charm is the picture making facility for their life is the world colored by make-believe. Their solution is always through capitalizing on their heightened imagination. They should strive to mentally visualize what they desire and then pretend it is already a reality. Intensity and accent are part of their palette. Since THREE is the natural vibration of childhood, the THREE type tends to retain youthfulness even in mature life.

For a healthy vindication of the artist he is, the THREE character should be supported in his consciousness by some amount and quality of THREENESS in his subconscious. This is manifested on the physical level by any C's in his name, on the mental level by L's and on the spiritual by any U's.

With no individual number symbol for THREE in the name the individual is sadly lacking a true appreciation of what he himself is and should be. He may say and do many funny, amusing, captivating things, but he seldom sees or understands it that way himself.

# NUMBER 4 CHARACTER

Where the THREE type is born young (and remains youthful) the FOUR type is born old and serious. Their feet at all times are planted firmly on the ground and they speak for the facts and material realities of life rather than decorative values. Generally speaking they are sound, practical, economical, down-to-earth realists. They have a talent for common sense, physical effort, endurance, order, regimentation and discipline. They also have a very high threshold for pain, discomfort and hardships. In fact, they can be a little hard and even cruel on others, but they justify this by being just as demanding of themselves. They rely on logic and what they can detect from the material facts in front of them. They are also apt to be stubborn, pigheaded, difficult to persuade and in some respects a trifle blind. Certain matters may have to be proven to them again and again as they are sometimes slow to learn. If anything their feet are planted too firmly on the ground. The physical and practical side of life is the area they are best designed to serve. They are generally reliable and can invariably be counted on to hold fast, dig in and see a job through to the bitter end. This "bitter" quality is something they do not mind as much as other number types; in fact, it seems they sometimes take a perverse delight in making things harder for themselves and others.

Since FOURNESS reflects the hardening to life through direct awareness of material realities, FOURS are more effective in maturity when such values seem more natural than in the ideality of youth when one should sense the totality of experience. FOURNESS is a quality which hardens and therefore enhances the traditional masculine strengths but generally disfigures the more pliant sensitivity of traditional feminine values.

The FOUR character is supported in his consciousness (and therefore in his particular sense of reality) by the amount and quality of FOURNESS which he has in his subconscious. He is fortified on the physical level by any D's in his name, on the mental level by any M's in his name and on the higher plane by any V's in his name.

Without any individual number symbol for FOUR in the name, the individual tends to cheat on himself, demanding more from others than he is willing or prepared to supply himself. Although he expects complete conformity to his own regimentation of values, he personally generally fails to comply. In the case of the karmic FOUR (no subconscious support of the Character Number) the results are inclined to be socially unfortunate for others. This is because the hardness they demand (but do not apply to themselves) can be cruel and even sadistic/masochistic.

# NUMBER *5* CHARACTER

The number FIVE character is one who represents a fundamental departure from standard pattern. His aim and objective is to be different in some way from everyone else. As the ONE needs to stand out (generally by development of some resource within himself), the FIVE needs to gain the advantage over others in contest. FIVES are particularly alive to all the five physical senses of touch, sight, sound, taste and smell. They have a talent for finding new and often improved ways for doing things.

Where FOURS are at their best when sticking to one regimented formula, FIVES excell in changing things around in order to gain some kind of manipulative advantage. Opportunism for FIVES is a natural asset and they should not be hesitant to make full use of it for whatever seems important at the time since their best opportunities come and go quickly. FIVES are much concerned with speed and generally consider that anything is improved by speeding it up or heightening its sensory effect. They make very good drum beaters, bally-hoo artists and carnival promoters.

FIVE is generally considered the sexual vibration and all FIVES have a strong appreciation of sexual potentialities.

The essence of FIVE is change which is often misunderstood by others who see a constant switching back and forth as a sign of weakness rather than strength. FIVES are often criticized as restless, unreliable, careless of responsibility and too eager to give up sound situations for something new and different. The fallacy of this judgment against FIVE lies in judging others by our standards rather than by their own. To FIVE there is an advantage for him in his sudden change of position. When one person gains a sudden advantage it usually means that someone else has fallen to a disadvantage. There can be a valid and desirable reason for this which is usually proven in time but as of the moment the limitations of our individual perspective usually means we only resent the one gaining the advantage. FIVES are specifically designed to somehow instrument these sudden shifts in position and without their compliance there could be a general state of inertia, deterioration and decay. Since the world is subtly in a state of constant movement, change is needed in order to more fully reflect the total reality of the moment and FIVES are ideally programmed to push this change along.

Since FIVES are always searching and seeking for something they themselves may not be fully aware of, they take naturally to adventure, investigations and undercover work of all kinds. As instigators of change certain things become possible only because of something which they do or start. It must be remembered that FIVES are often innocent parties to what finally emerges and surprise plays a large and exciting factor in their response to life's adventure. There is no doubt that all FIVES have some talent which is rather special and not shared by most people. This talent may be the depth and range to which they can react on sudden demand which far exceeds normal capabilities. Or the way they differ from others may be in the variety and uniqueness of something they do — like running the world's fastest mile. Whatever it is, it involves or includes some heightened exaggerated use of the five physical senses.

Freedom is imperative to FIVES since they must be able to respond on short notice to whatever compels them to sudden shifts of interest. If they are not given this freedom naturally, they will invariably create it for themselves. Others who are closely involved with fives should always make allowance for their need for freedom; otherwise serious misunderstandings are apt to result. Generally speaking, it is others who must make allowances for or adjustments to FIVE and not the other way around. FIVE has automatically sized up each and every situation and instinctively knows which direction might be best for himself should development provoke a change. It is exactly this instinctive awareness of "potentiality" that gives FIVES their advantage over others. There is a tendency to resent their advantages and FIVES often acquire an unfortunate reputation which may not be wholly deserving. It depends on whose rules one is following as to who may be right and who may be wrong. FIVES are usually not concerned with such moralizing as they make their own laws and from their standpoint this is the right way for them to behave.

The native instincts of FIVE are supported on the physical level by any E's in the name, on the mental level by any N's and on the spiritual level by any W's.

With no individual number symbol for FIVE to support the conscious, the native not only does not like himself and pretends he isn't the kind of person he is, but he eventually defeats the best of the FIVE potential by behaving in a negative manner towards the positive values of FIVE.

Since FIVE is the sex vibration, FIVES who have no number symbol for FIVE in their name would tend to take an unnatural or unhealthy attitude towards sexual matters. One way in which this can manifest is that there is a substitute of sexual objects out of their normal context. In other words, this type of FIVE would respond sexually to objects which would not normally be considered as bearing a sexual connotation.

# NUMBER 6 CHARACTER

The number SIX character is one who easily relates to others in a natural, friendly, conscientious manner. In number SIX the requirements of the personal ego are modified to show an increased appreciation of other egos in the same situation. Thus the essence of SIXNESS is adjustment, curtailment and possible elimination or renunciation of certain personal factors in order to more fully appreciate a group composite. SIXS are more group minded than individual orientated. The stress is less on the individual "I am" than on what "we are" or "could be together" acting as a team. SIX is the vibration of ideal partnership where one voluntarily gives up in favor of another, or in favor of a revised entity which is an amalgamation of more than one.

To number SIX it is perfectly natural to be as interested in what others are doing as in what he himself is doing. Teaching is one of SIX's talents because they are so easily able to put themselves in the other person's position and see through "their eyes".

In the formation of partnerships the individual members must all give up the independence of their own position in favor of a collective ideal. It is from the concept of such social commitments that moral structures evolve — hence group values, moralizing codes of behavior and the community of interests. SIXS believe strongly in all these matters and they tend to expect that others should naturally do likewise. SIXS are highly protective and usually conventional in terms of conformity to what is currently expected by the social structure as a whole. They are responsibility conscious and strong advocates of whole hearted team-work. They have a natural concern for all matters of a domestic nature and they usually tend to

37

domesticate all issues by putting everything into an inter-personal context as though society were but a large reflection of the individual family kind of partnership. They appreciate receiving advice and like to give advice. They also believe strongly in talking things over and coming to agreements which can be expressed in words or codes. They believe less in what is suggested or imagined than in what is actually said and expressed.

Where certain number vibrations may be said to represent the value of the individual as supreme, number SIX tends to regard the COLLECTIVE MAJORITY as being of greater importance. Since any group association must by necessity undergo a certain "averaging out" process in order to reach a common denominator, it seems obvious that the "under" and "over" extremes have to undergo considerable modification in order to fit into the "average". And this is exactly the valuation process that SIXS employ to determine the group values which they will acknowledge and support. There is some danger, of course, of averages becoming only mediocrities, which is always a probability with SIX.

If there is any number which might be said to be representative of the "average" type of person, that number is SIX. But it is just this factor which makes them friendly, congenial, responsible and therefore generally well qualified to carry out the bulk of life's assignments. If they might be said to lack some of the extremes of individuality, they certainly comprise the fiber and substance of man as a social animal. They are sympathetic but also require appreciation. Service is their honor and they make wonderful hosts and usually have very good speaking voices. They stand for education, the home, community, guardianship, stability and protective values. They are burden-bearing, trusting and reliable. They seem to have a special sense of color and can usually be very creative with color or music. In some ways SIX is the most fortunate of vibrations because the characteristics are the most evenly divided. They sometimes have poor business ability, however, because they tend to feel that the ends do not alone justify the means. And they can refuse to join causes because they are opposed to some minor matter of little importance. They are usually not competitive but can take care of themselves. They tend to delay decisive action, preferring a more placid, quiet, loving home atmosphere and domestic responsibilities to bring out their best contribution. Being born advisers they need an audience or someone to tell what to do. They also seem to have a natural understanding of most health matters which probably stems from their sense of inter-personal relationships — how one thing supports another.

To be fully productive SIXS must be supported in their SIX kind of consciousness by some individual number symbol for SIX in their name. Any F's in their name give understanding on the physical level, any O's give understanding on the mental level and any X's give a special comprehension of SIX matters on the higher or spiritual level.

With no individual number symbols at all for SIX in the name there is a considerable disparagement between what one professes publicly and at the same time exemplifies personally. This is of course less apparent in matters of an objective (less personalized) nature in which instances the native usually functions as an average SIX type. But on matters in which he is more personally involved, then his lack of subconscious support of the collective values which constitute his SIX character is apt to prove a contradiction and even denial of all the best which SIX represents.

# NUMBER 7 CHARACTER

In SEVEN we have a type of person who in most respects is entirely the opposite of a SIX as indeed all contiguous number vibrations bear a contradiction and slight antagonism towards the qualities which the other may represent. Contiguous numbers are numbers which stand next to each other in the normal sequence as FIVE stands next to FOUR on one side and SIX on the other, or as NINE stands next to EIGHT on one side and ONE on the other as we begin again in a new dimension.

Where the SIX type represents the desirability of a collective ideal, the SEVEN represents the refinement of a speciality which evolves through the "withdrawal" of the individual from the normal channels of contact rather than through any increase in social commitments.

SEVEN is therefore a lonely vibration and symbolizes perfection through a kind of self purification. This usually means elimination of most standard and mundane matters in favor of something more select and spiritually elevating.

The number SEVEN character is one who has a very special view of life not shared or particularly appreciated by ordinary people. SEVENS seem to possess a kind of double vision which enables them to react from two perspectives at the same time. An example would be the type of person who senses things from both a man's and woman's point of view as indeed SEVEN symbolizes a certain bi-sexuality of the qualities traditionally attributed exclusively to just one sex. SEVEN tends to combine the strength of the masculine with the sensitivity of the feminine.

This double vision or bi-focus undoubtedly lends an added depth to the insight but it also results in a specialized awareness which cannot be communicated easily to others unless they also share a potentiality (or subconscious awareness) of this same unique faculty. This in itself tends to cut them off from ordinary everyday matters so that their attitudes and interests become a "specialized" view of life rather than in any way a reflection of the "whole" of nature which does not especially interest them anyway.

SEVEN is likely to be the most misunderstood of all number vibrations. It suggests withdrawal, introspection, self-analysis, self-appraisal, perfection, mysticism, spiritual values and a belief and faith in what lies beyond the material evidence of the everyday world. To some number types the material evidence of the everyday world is all that matters. To number SEVEN it tends to be their least concern.

SEVEN symbolizes a point of view, or a time in life, when man must look beyond the physical world for what may concern him most. To do this effectively he must withdraw into the realm of the "spirit" (or intuition) rather than work through the "body" (or just material facts) to seek whatever eternal principles he will need to face a world which to SEVEN is only an outer shell of material instability. SEVEN is the Sunday time of life. It represents study, analysis, research, wisdom, occultism and spirituality. It gives people peace, poise, dignity, refinement, inner beauty, stoic self-sufficiency, character and distinction. It should lead to a position of technical authority and professional polish. SEVEN is absolute and firm but also retiring and unassuming. All SEVENS stand apart and generally above the crowd. For effective operation their best approach is obliquely from the side or hidden from behind rather than fully exposed as head on or face to face. They should imply rather than command. To others the SEVEN frequently seems haughty and aloof as though they were superior in some way to everybody else. This is because SEVENS do feel closely allied with a mysterious force outside themselves and it gives them additional strength and conviction in whatever they do or represent.

To some people SEVEN may seem like a lonely position but SEVENS like it this way. They often prefer their own company or their own thoughts to that which is going on around them. This inner communication is one of the factors that helps to make them

41

different. They sometimes have strange and uncanny powers of perception. They also have a peculiar type of valor or strength of character which is sometimes more effective than ordinary physical bravery. Having a certain inner resolve and dreaminess they cannot be imitated or especially intimidated by persons not of this vibration. Sometimes their love of solitude leads to a lack of general communication and they have to be brought back into the main stream of social relationships. Shrewdness is one of their talents and if highly developed their very shrewdness can outwit others who may be situated more advantageously from a material or factual point of view. This is because SEVEN usually knows how to get around or behind a point where others may be dealing only with the obvious.

Even when the SEVEN character is unsupported in the subconscious (by an individual letter symbol for SEVEN) the SEVEN type shows unusual mannerisms. In fact there is a tendency to possess even more uncontrollable Extra Sensory Powers than when the SEVEN consciousness is well fortified, understood and controlled.

The SEVEN is fortified on the physical level by any G's in the name, on the mental level by any P'S in the name and on the highest level by any Y's in the name.

# NUMBER 8 CHARACTER

EIGHT symbolizes confrontation with important deisions, passing judgment, administrative control and executive perogatives. Therefore an EIGHT type is one who is invariably tough minded, of mature (though somewhat hardened) sentiments and is generally prepared to go all the way to get what he wants. EIGHTS should be extremely efficient to the point of complete ruthlessness. For EIGHT the ends invariably justify the means no matter what amount of disruption this may cause with those who must comply. This EIGHTNESS may be considerably softened or watered down by other factors in the overall analysis (as indeed all numbers are modified) but nevertheless the EIGHTNESS when fully developed behaves in exactly this manner.

Since the qualities of executive leadership tend to be involved one way or another with all types of power structures, EIGHT is generally considered to be the highest evidence of material power and control. And since power is what society pays for, EIGHT is also considered to be the money vibration. Usually power and money go together, but not always. Some individuals want and seek power and don't particularly care about the money involved. Others prefer the money and are only indirectly interested in the power it brings.

Scale is very important to EIGHT. They usually want everything to be on a sufficiently grand and impressive scale because it matches the material splendor they potentially control.

Actually the power of EIGHTNESS derives from a very delicate sense of balance. This is the center point of the scales where just a fraction one way or the other can reverse the whole picture. It is this awareness of both the gravity and the implication of unbalance that gives EIGHTS their power edge over others for they have an instinctive sense when something lacks this delicate sense of balance. They can also generally come up with some practical suggestion which shifts the situation or problem back to its proper balance and results in increased efficiency all around. To effect this powerful shift of balace EIGHTS must usually employ some kind of "shock technique" or shock therapy.

To perform their function properly EIGHTS must pass judgment (which may be either for or against something). To give up this perogative is fatal to the inherent power of EIGHT. All judges make themselves unpopular with those judged against, but this cannot be allowed to stand in the way of performing their proper function. Foolish or unfounded sentiment has little place in the purpose of EIGHT. That is why EIGHTS are so hard-nosed and they have to be because they have a very tough job to do in life and it takes all their particular kind of strength to carry through their job as it should be done. The compensation for this sort of talent in our society is usually money which is itself an impersonal medium of exchange. As the 'Dolly Levis' of this world would say about ending up with only the cash register . . . "On winter nights it may be a little cold, but at least it rings." . . .

The EIGHTNESS should be supported in the consciousness by some amount and quality in the subconsious warehouse. It is fortified on the physical level by any H's in the name, on the mental level by any Q's in the name and on the spiritual level by any Z's in the name.

With no individual letter symbol at all in the name for EIGHT the individual tends to be overly hardboiled and heartless when dealing with others and inwardly insecure when trying to make important decisions in his own life.

# NUMBER *9* CHARACTER

As number NINE is the highest and final primary digit, it represents the close of a complete cycle of development before the ongoing spirit begins over again in the position of ONE for a new cycle of growth. In terms of human character NINE can symbolize the ultimate in human achievement as opposed to just material (or other) advantages as evidenced in lower or lesser stages of development. In NINE materiality has somehow dropped out of the picture and what we are left with is the human spirit elevated to the possible position of ultimate tolerance, universal goodwill, compassionate charity, selfless service, impersonal love and supposedly complete understanding of the "totality" of life. NINE retains, however, a good deal of emotional wallop and intense dramatic impact.

NINES can sometimes be very destructive to other numbers (and qualities) as they rise up to wipe out what they sense threatens something they are trying to put over. The essence of NINENESS should be objectivity but since NINES are almost over committed to whatever captures their interest they sometimes mistake objectivity for their own intense dedication. NINE is indeed a dangerous vibration in that consciousness has reached a point at which it is felt there is a natural right to take over on their own without further checking or verification. NINES are in fact more than a little paranoid and some are apt to have other mental abberations as well. Since this type works on such an elevated level of emotional maturity and supposed objectivity, they often find themselves in a position of influence and control over others. But when they make a mistake, as they can do, many others may have to pay for this disaster as well as themselves.

Since NINE can be all things to all people (hence the universality of their appeal) they can by seizing the emotional leadership of the moment (as a politician) dramatically stir up the primal instincts of the mob (hence NINES are born dictators and rabble rousers). They also tend to be self-appointed messiahs who may or may not be on the right track. Since the NINE character lacks many of the normally built-in brakes that other vibrations have, it is often possible for them to be completely wrong in their assessment of a situation yet be totally unaware of just how wrong they are. When other number vibrations go haywire they tend to destroy only themselves, but NINE because it has this following based on a primal affinity (usually in the name of spiritual or political uplift as in evangelism or communism) when they go off the deep end they can also take a number of devoted and fanatical followers with them. History is indeed dotted and blotted with many such examples.

NINE is supported in the consciousness on the physical level by any I's in the name and on the mental level by any R's in the name. There is no higher spiritual level on the NINE vibration since NINES are supposed to have encompassed that in their own nature.

It is most unusual when there are no individual letter symbols for NINE in the name but such a person would tend to be overly fanatical and unrestrained on general issues yet totally without any sense of personal objectivity when dealing with his own affairs.

# Chapter II

# YOUR PERSONALITY: HOW YOU APPEAR TO OTHERS

The number vibration which symbolizes your character type identifies you in a "total" perspective. As already explained in Chapter I, this number is derived from adding up all the digits in your name and reducing this total to a single number.

While the character is the single most important consideration in evaluating yourself, or others, it is not the most obvious point of reference.

That which stands out most clearly when dealing with people in general is the quality of their personality. This is a pattern of behavior which the individual assumes most naturally about himself and he reflects this on an instinctive level of consciousness. Thus the "outer" impression or personality image is something which you express automatically without conscious thought or effort. It is so automatic that often many of us are totally unaware of the kind of impression we are making except as it begins to react back on us in fundamental ways.

THAT WHICH IDENTIFIES THIS INSTINCTIVE FOCUS OF REFERENCE IS SYMBOLIZED BY THE NUMBER WHICH DERIVES FROM THE TOTAL OF ONLY THE CONSONANT LETTERS IN THE NAME.

The individual letters in our alphabet are classified according to their function in speech as either vowels or consonants.

All words (names are word labels) are composed of phonetic units called syllables. According to phonetics, which has to do with speech sounds and their production of the spoken word, syllables constitute a segment or element of speech uttered with a single impulse of breath and consist of one sound each. Eacy syllable in order to be sounded as an individual element of speech must contain one or more vowels. The vowels are considered to be the primary or "sound" core of the syllable. In the English language we have five such letters acting as vowels: "A", "E", "I", "O" and "U". In addition we sometimes make use of the letter "Y" as a vowel. THE LETTER "Y" IS FUNCTIONING PHONETICALLY AS A VOWEL WHEN THERE IS NO OTHER VOWEL IN THE SYLLABLE. In number analysis "Y" is therefore considered a vowel in the one syllable name Lynn and in the two syllable name Mary.

Fleshing out the syllable in order to give it "full" sonority are the other letters which are subordinate to the vowel "core". These are called consonants.

It is the consonants by themselves alone that reflect the "outer" and therefore somewhat superficial impression that you make on your immediate environment. They represent that part of you limited to outward appearances or superficial impression as opposed to the total impact of the character. This impression you make is obviously important because for most general purposes this is all the world sees, or has need of, in making an adjustment or allowance for you as an individual.

The degree to which this image of the personality behaves in a positive, true pattern is again determined by the subconscious support from the individual's source of supply. If the personality quality is well supported the native is what he seems to be on the surface and will generally behave in all matters as might be expected from positive and constructively patterned personalities of this type. But if there are no individual number symbols in the name to match this personality index, then that person only superficially seems to have that type of personality. Instinctively he will still seem to act this way in dealing with others on impersonal matters, but he is rather prone on provocation to easily switch to a negative expression of this quality which at its worst would deny the quality itself. That

48

person will particularly do this when challenged, threatened or in any way driven to discard his mask for purely personal motivations.

BASIC COMPATABILITY AMONG THE NUMBERS THEMSELVES, AS PERTAINS TO THE QUALITIES WHICH EACH ONE SYMBOLIZES, IS THE PRIMARY KEY IN ALL NUMBER ANALYSIS.

The qualities of the number symbols which are a reflection of nature itself happen to be mutually incompatable when contrasted or aligned to contiguous numbers. Thus the qualities which go to make up ONENESS are incompatable with number TWO or with number NINE just as number FIVE is incompatable with number FOUR or number SIX. This will be more understandable as we continue to explore the qualities and idea forces of the numbers themselves as they relate to each other in example patterns of behavior. I mention it here when considering the implication of contiguous number totals falling on any of the three conscious points of focus which pattern the individual's nature such as HIS CHARACTER, HIS PERSONALITY or HIS MOTIVATION (yet to be considered). If the character total is a contiguous number to the personality total, this puts the individual's personality image at considerable variance and disadvantage with his character pattern. The public which superficially reacts to the obvious personality is unprepared for the ultimate impact of the individual's character which only becomes apparent after long and intimate association (that is getting to really know the individual, in this case, in spite of his personality). This consideration to be taken into account is irrespective of the talent back up from the warehouse supply which largely determines positive or negative expressions of that quality. In other words, if the personality is a TWO type with a ONE character those who do not like TWOS and are in fact somewhat repulsed by them (as are all individuals who have a TWO karma) then they are unprepared for the ultimate ONE character which will emerge eventually if others can take the time to know this person in total. If the example individual also has a TWO karma in his personality number this reflects whether he is a positive or negative TWO personality which is another consideration than where certain people do not like a TWO PERSONALITY (whether positive or negatively expressed).

The contradiction from contiguous numbers between the personality and the character arises from the public on superficial observation expecting one thing while the individual himself ends up programming an idea force in an opposite direction.

In casual hurried matters or situations which are not really fundamental to your larger purpose, the treatment and effect which you express follows the tone of your personality. In matters of greater importance where more of your personal interests are involved (where more of you is "turned on"), then the final outcome follows the pattern of your character. For most everyday matters our personality format is what solves and dispatches the situation, but in the broader perspective the ultimate character is what counts and the final outcome is as the "total" character requires it to be. The character number acts as a guiding but UNSEEN PRINCIPLE. The personality vibration is only the more obvious.

# NUMBER 1 PERSONALITY

Number ONE on the personality makes a person appear pushy, determined, aggressive, self-centered, selfish, egotistical and forthright. They may also exhibit strong evidence of courage, leadership, resourcefulness, independence and general self-reliance. They would not appear to be ideal as followers or likely to take kindly when others order them around or try to tell them what to do. Since ONE symbolizes the traditional masculine virtues, the ONE personality always appears highly masculinized which may not be quite suitable for women if society expects all women to behave in a more traditionally feminine image.

The number ONE personality usually comes right to the point with little or no beating around the bush. You generally know exactly where they stand, right from the start. They strive to simplify matters and get right to the core of the problem. It is perfectly natural for them to place themselves at the center of consideration and they generally do exactly what they see as most beneficial for themselves. What helps others (if anything) is a secondary consideration which is seldom (if ever) allowed to take precidence over what they themselves require.

They have a highly developed sense of honor and integrity and they are quick to react if any disparagement is cast on the purity of their intentions.

The number ONE personality is supported on the physical level by any A's in the name, on the mental level by any J's in the name and on the spiritual side by any S's in the name. Thus the self-reliance of the ONE personality is able to prove itself in physical ways if there are A's in the name. They are able to express this with mental

51

know-how if there are J's in the name and they are able to impress their spiritual courage on others if they have S's in the name.

Remember the personality total gives CONSCIOUS FOCUS OF THAT QUALITY (as do the other two index numbers of character and motivation). In line with the above, any name with S's reflects an individual who has a potential for spiritual courage, but when you have a ONE personality this spiritual courage is obvious to others because it is the image which you instinctively express (it is no longer just a potential but by conscious focus becomes a constant reality).

With no individual letter symbol for ONE in the name the individual tends to appear more negative on ONE and their selfishness and self-centered interests are more overbearing. Remembering how automatically we assume the posture of our personality image, a ONE personality cannot help but appear as his self-centered self, but with no constructive support of this quality in his make up then others will always suffer the more unfortunate consequences which this number symbolizes. When dealing with a negative number ONE they tend towards extreme selfishness coupled with a decided lack of personal integrity on private matters.

# NUMBER *2* PERSONALITY

Number TWO on the personality makes a person appear shy, sensitive, condescending, gentle, sympathetic, understanding, cooperative and helpful. Naturally they make good followers for their instinctive inclination is to wait for someone else to take the initiative or tell them what to do. They appear patient and considerate and even somewhat helpless. They also exhibit motherly tendencies and can become quite possessive with all those with whom they come in contact. In men the number TWO on the personality is definitely effeminate no matter how much they may try to cover this up because of pressures from society. In women, of course, it is generally considered beguiling and attractively feminine but they may turn out to have a much tougher character pattern underneath their personality.

For the more constructive expression of the TWO personality there should be some support for this quality in the individual letter symbols of the name. With B's in the name one is considerate in physical ways. With K's in the name one is capable in their understanding of more mental comprehension and with T's in the name one is able to convey a deeper sense of sympathy which lends a spiritual implication to their sensitivity.

With no individual number symbols for TWO in the name at all, the person pretends not to be as he in fact appears and he does not like or appreciate the very qualities which others give him credit for. There can be a certain all around negativism to all the qualities which are symbolized by TWO.

# NUMBER *3* PERSONALITY

Number THREE on the personality gives the impression of one who is talented in some form of self expression whether they capitalize on it or not. They seldom hold back their feelings and are rarely at a loss for word, comment or opinion. On the whole they present a happy, carefree disposition as indeed they seem to take things more lightly than most. They can appear childish, naive and unsophisticated but invariably charming and persuasive when they turn on their enthusiasm or try to win others over to their point of view.

THREE gives them a natural sense of youthfulness which also makes them seem amusing and witty. They are the type that invariably tries to soften things up by a joke even at their own expense. They want to be happy and they try to bring happiness and enthusiasm to others. Their nature is, however, not to push consistently hard and they may need encouragement to stay on the bright side and not become victims of their own fears and imagination.

Just like children they can be delightfully nice or they can be exasperatingly spoiled when they can't have their own way. THREE is essentially not a vibration of maturity but it is very attractive to most people because they are so decorative.

C's in the name give obvious talent for self expression on the physical level. L's give facility on the mental level and U's give a command of higher or more spiritual levels of suggestiveness.

No individual number symbols for THREE at all in the name gives a confusing picture where the person is not nearly as sold on his own talents or opinions as he might appear to others. Since THREES

54

create comedy and humor as part of their typical sales's persuasion, with no back up support on THREE they may still do funny, amusing things but will seldom see them that way themselves. But more important, with no THREES they are somehow unable to laugh at themselves which may sometimes be the only escape valve possible.

# NUMBER 4 PERSONALITY

Number FOUR on the personality gives the obvious impression that the person is a practical, down-to-earth type who is generally willing to put his shoulder to the wheel and do whatever is necessary in terms of effort and persistence to get the job done. They appear to have more than average strength and endurance and to be able to put up with hardships and privations that others could not stand. They exhibit a very high threshold for pain and they discipline themselves easily so as not to complain or expect something without effort or struggle. They often seem blunt and outspoken with a proclivity for laying the unvarnished truth right on the line. They firmly believe that the only way to get going is to face the facts early and not try to pretend or fool themselves or others that things are any different from the way they know them to be. FOUR personalities are the workers of the world and they can always be counted on for more than their share. They are invariably fair and square in all their material dealings as they try to show everybody that honesty is after all the best policy. They seem happiest when they are engaged in some form of routine activity which is not only good for their general health but improves their emotional stability as well. The FOUR personality is generally robust and sound in construction (or appears that way) and their health is undoubtedly better than average. They can certainly stand up under more trying condition than most everybody else.

D's in the name give special qualities for endurance (as well as other qualities which FOUR symbolizes) on the physical level. M's in the name give a tenacity for solving practical problems on the mental level and V's give a mastery over practical affairs calling for a broader perspective as in a higher or "master" plan.

56

No individual letter symbols for FOUR in the name mean that while the personality reflects a certain physical soundness, at times and under certain conditions, it may not live up to the practical demands made upon it. All those who lack a letter symbol for FOUR in their name tend not to face facts squarely, try to avoid the truth when it does not please them and at times expect from the world something for nothing. This is complicated when they have a FOUR personality image because they are credited with living up to just these very demands which others assume they exemplify. In this case they always demand these things of others but seldom of themselves.

# NUMBER 5 PERSONALITY

The number FIVE on the personality gives the obvious impression of one who invariably gets out of line in one way or another and insists on doing things differently from everyone else. At times and under certain conditions this ability to improvise and seek new solutions leads to constructive change and a fundamental break-through for everyone concerned. But in the very young the FIVE personality is generally considered difficult to handle and train because they feel they know so much better what is best for themselves, which is undoubtedly true, but parents are somewhat unable or unwilling to concede that their children can know their best advantages better than they do. The FIVE personality needs exercise and physical activity in order to feel right even though this may not go as far as competitive sports all FIVES need some kind of physical action.

Since FIVE is also the sex vibration, the FIVE personality manages in some way, no matter how subtle, to give some impression or suggestion of sexual potentiality. If others are not keyed to notice this sort of thing they may not be at all aware of this suggestiveness. Of course giving an appearance of sexual talent and having an above average talent for it are two different things. EVERYONE'S BACKUP FOR SEXUAL INTENSITY IS SHOWN IN THE ANALYSIS BY THE AMOUNT AND QUALITY OF FIVES THEY HAVE IN THEIR NAME. Having a FIVE in one of the index numbers (Character, Personality or Motivation) brings the matter to conscious concern. The number FIVE personality is definitely sexually suggestive. There are, of course, all manners and ways in which this sexuality can be utilized. When one is sexually intense or keyed to a

58

high degree of sexual interest in matters which they undertake (as evidenced by a conscious attitude of FIVE) this need not follow the usual stereotype examples of sexuality which may become a social problem or lead to social misconduct. Sublimation of sexual energy into other fields of creative effort often accounts for that extra, passionate stroke of genius which bestows distinction rather than mediocrity in achievement.

The essence of the FIVE personality is adaptability to situations that suddenly appear, demanding some change or adjustment to the situation. This leads to a certain versatility (particularly under stress) and a resourceful improvisation that can amount to inventive genius.

Since FIVE is the number of action and physical motion, the FIVE personality is invariably restless, somewhat irritable, frequently nervous and apprehensive but generally with good reason. They like speed and freedom and are generally found in unusual walks of life such as detective work or exploration.

E's in the name give adaptability on the physical level. This is also indicative of strong regenerative sexual powers. N's in the name give versatility on the mental level and W's in the name give a greater intensity of sensual awareness on a broader perspective or more spiritual level.

It is unusual to find no individual number symbols for FIVE at all in the name since the average 14 letter name has at least 3 FIVES. No FIVES in the name tends to fix the native on normally nonsexual objects but with a certain sexual reaction; thus cause and effect seem somewhat out of perspective. With an index number of FIVE, such as on the personality image, the person may be quite capable of sexually satisfying others but may not himself be particularly gratified by the experience.

# NUMBER 6 PERSONALITY

The number SIX on the personality makes the person seem obviously friendly and congenial in spite of how they may otherwise feel. They give the impression that they are even more concerned with the reaction value of others in a social context than they are of their own motivations. They have a talent for mixing and mingling and seeing problems from the other person's point of view. Since people are generally flattered when anyone seems more interested in them than they are in themselves, the number SIX is invariably well liked and welcome to have around. They seem to make natural teachers and instructors. They are also frequently seen to be talking or gossiping about their neighbors' affairs which is quite natural since they sincerely feel they have everybody's best interest at heart. Very often what number SIX considers to be your best interest is a composite of moral values which he has gathered from numerous sources which may or may not fit the actual case at hand. When it doesn't fit, SIX has a habit of trying to force the "over" and "under" average into the composite which he regards as socially desirable. SIX is the social vibration and the SIX personality appears to have an obvious talent for socializing, playing the host and in general making others feel at ease.

Since the essence of SIXNESS is communication, having a good speaking voice or some special effectiveness through the voice is symbolized by this number. This could include musical talents as well as just a pleasing and impressive speech delivery. Response to color tones and a talent for knowing how to mix or use colors is also one of their assets.

F's in the name support the attractive socializing talents on a physical level. O's in the name contribute a sensitivity to the reaction value of social groups on a mental level and X's in the name give a command of social awareness as it relates to a broader perspective of idealized community relationships.

No individual letter symbols for SIX in the name suggest that on personal matters the individual is not nearly as friendly or as socially prepared to appreciate your point of view as you give him credit for. Lacking a SIX also frequently indicates some sort of lack of persuasiveness in the voice mechanism such as a thin or shallow resonance or having the kind of voice that just wouldn't command a crowd or carry a tune. The lack of SIX also indicates a reluctance on the individual's part to easily assume responsibility for others. This usually has to be proved to him or forced on him in some way.

# NUMBER 7 PERSONALITY

Number SEVEN on the personality immediately sets that person apart from the crowd. This may appear as a notable distinction or just an eccentricity that hinders easy social intercourse. Quite frequently, as it turns out, the individual has something to hide or something he feels reluctant to share or disclose to others so he may adopt an air of aloofness or a social reluctance to let others get to know him better.

In the SEVEN we have the quality of the specialist, the social deviant and the perfectionist. As an attitude of behavior all SEVENS view the world from a somewhat rarefied point of view. Whether this is right or wrong or desirable or undesirable is all beside the point and relative to some idealized scale as to how one should act. It is their view and it is natural to them and when finally understood by others their contribution lends a definite quality or depth which was never there before. This specialized viewpoint is considerably more appreciated by persons of culture and refinement than it is by rough and ready types who are naturally more concerned with the rudiments of survival in an everyday world. Thus SEVENS are a Sunday kind of person who, like Sunday clothes, are somewhat over dressed for regular days of the week.

Among the qualities of distinction which SEVENS often express is an air of elegance, superiority and professional grace, none of which can be easily copied by others who do not naturally fit this exclusive mold. Many people, of course, do not care for this brand of exclusiveness, in fact oppose it. But some people consider it an enviable position not unlike some type of spiritual perfection.

As an attitude of mind, which the SEVEN personality automatically presents, the fundamentals of their position are above personalities or sexual bias. This is true for all numbers above SIX (which represents the highest vibration of social involvement on the personal level). In SEVEN we have the beginning of detachment which evolves from both a masculine and feminine point of view. Thus, SEVEN in point of attitude might be said to be bi-sexual which contributes considerably to their separation from the crowd as a whole which is mostly masculine (dominating) or feminine (receptive) in their approach. SEVEN symbolizes a position which is not so much neither as a little of both which contributes to an attitude of mind that is at least somewhat more aware of the complexities of life.

G's in the name lend a distinction on the physical level. P's in the name raise the concepts of perfection to systems of mental proficiency and Y's in the name give a concentration on the more idealized forms of spiritual perfection.

With no individual letter symbols for SEVEN at all in the name (an average name of 14 letters has no SEVENS) the individual is confused as to the spiritual foundations of his professed and conscious attitudes. SEVEN on the personality does focus a conscious attitude in that direction which others observe but which the individual tends to deny to himself. In the extremes to which the individual may go to nullify this aspect of himself there may be some sexual indulgences which alternate between excessive sexual behavior of a deviant nature or total repression of all natural sexual appetites, neither of which may be considered healthy or balanced behavior. All people who lack a seven in their name tend to lack a sense of philosophical faith which would in ordinary circumstances enable them to rise above and beyond the physical limitations of any immediate situation. With a SEVEN personality the individual may encourage others to profess this faith but they themselves would be sadly lacking it just when they might need it most.

# NUMBER 8 PERSONALITY

Number EIGHT on the personality, like the SEVEN and all numbers above the SIX, accents a point of attitude in human behavior which rises above personal bias. In the EIGHT we have the apex of human relationships which delicately balance themselves around a hypothetical point of equilibrium. At this point of balance, the EIGHT is concerned with the weight of physical or material matters against the probability of mental or nonmaterial considerations. Thus EIGHTNESS equates or redistributes the forces of materiality against the principles or guide lines which these forces should serve or instrument. Therefore in EIGHT we have the quality of judgment, making decisions and the influence of power manipulations in order to bring these two elements more into line with each other. All EIGHTS must invariably resort to somewhat violent tactics in order to shift these forces of power when they are out of line. EIGHT has a talent for sensing when things are out of line or balance and they are invariably right although they may be unable or reluctant to assume the consequences of doing something about it. Therefore an obvious aspect of the EIGHT personality is this tough ability to deal effectively with all types of power structures. Any area of activity which deals with matters having control or influence over others (such as in matters of superior judgment) is a potential position of power control. When systemized or ritualized on a sufficiently broad plane so that many similar types are equally effected then you have a source of definite power manipulation.

EIGHTNESS, it should be remembered, is an attitude of mind (or in this case, type of personality) that reflects this talent for power manipulation. It is not indicative as to exactly what kind of material is involved. Thus an individual can be challenged on EIGHTNESS in the field of music or art or literature or business or politics since all of these fields are matters of interest which hold potential influence over human nature in commanding ways.

The essence of EIGHTNESS is both toughness and ruthlessness. Those who are ruthless, by the way, assume an attitude wherein they are loathe to let anything stand in the way of what they have set out to achieve. Any exhibition of this quality seems to make most people shudder, but in the higher echelons of human behavior it is almost mandatory in order to accomplish anything of real and enduring value.

H's in the name support this balanced toughness on physical matters. Q's contribute an insight on complex mental problems of balance and inbalance. Z's give an unique comprehension of eternal principles of balance which are not sensed, or even dreamed of, by ordinary people.

No individual letter symbols for EIGHT at all in the name creates a confused situation in the individual's own affairs. He is, of course, credited with a great deal more EIGHT "know-how" than he really deserves. Usually in the judgments which he is called upon to make, if anything he will invariably short change himself only to be forced later to rejudge the situation again, and again, if necessary. With or without the required talent for it, all EIGHT personalities are obviously power minded and behave accordingly.

# NUMBER *9* PERSONALITY

Number NINE on the personality is supposed to reflect the highest court of sympathetic appeal. While the tolerance and lack of prejudice should open all avenues for the compassionate understanding of one's fellowmen, at the same time it tends to detract from a more intimate approach to life such as found in other numbers which are also understanding (like TWO) and socially responsive (like (SIX). Apparently in NINE, in order to cope with the "totality" of life with which they are constantly subject, this clinical objectivity amounting in some cases to a downright coldness and clinical detachment is almost mandatory. Thus while NINENESS can mean all things to all people, or a little something for everyone, in some respects it can also be not quite "everyday human". They seem to be aware of everything around them but also they can be disposed not to do too much about it either. NINES are like the proverbial politician who promises everything under the sun but ends up doing nothing whatsoever except ride at the head of the parade as the dramatic spearhead of some emotional catch-all.

NINES do have a way of being in the center of all kinds of activity but their significance lies not so much in themselves but in how they capture the force of some movement and focus it through themselves. Thus a NINE without a cause (worthy or not) is completely lost or ends up a zero.

The average person is easily impressed with NINENESS so it is not too difficult to find some group somewhere who can use an effective and dramatic focus. This is exactly what NINES have a talent for providing.

Much of the drawing power of NINENESS seems to reside in some return or appeal to primal base instincts which can often lead to results not originally forseen.

As NINE represents a form of idealized love it can also represent a very compelling dedication to hate. As NINE stands at the climax of a complete cycle of growth and development from ONE through NINE, it also presides at the disintegration of form as one cycle ends and another begins to form again in a new cycle of ONENESS. Anyone with a conscious focus on NINE can apparently be just as much for the final build up as for the destruction preparatory to new programs.

Not all number vibrations stand up to NINENESS with equal calm. NINE, among other characteristics, acts as a great leveler which can be totally nullifying to other numbers which are trying in their own way to build up a more individual point of view. SEVEN and EIGHT are less affected by this leveling function and so are more compatable and less competitive because they too have risen above the personal bias of strict individualism in favor of a more specialized point of view in SEVEN and the judgment of balance in EIGHT.

I's in the name supply the NINES with a command of universality in ordinary matters. R's supply the same competence on matters of extraordinary importance. Familiarity on both planes would be desirable for complete understanding.

No individual letter symbols for NINE at all in the name is somewhat unusual according to the average distribution of names. Any negativism on NINE would promote the emotions of Hate rather than Love and there is a marked inability to forget or FORGIVE, both of which are essential in the full maturity of NINENESS.

*Chapter III*

# YOUR MOTIVATION:
# THE INNER DRIVE

As the consonant letters in the name dictate the outer appearance of what I have labeled the personality image, the TOTAL OF ALL THE VOWELS IN THE NAME COMPRISE THE INNER DRIVE OR MOTIVATION.

Again, as with all index totals (Character, Personality and Motivation) these numbers symbolize POINTS OF CONSCIOUS ORIENTATION as opposed to any supporting talents in the individual's subconscious warehouse (symbolized by the individual letter symbols in the name).

Of the three index totals, the individual FROM HIS PERSONAL POINT OF VIEW is most immediately concerned with the gratification and achievement of his motivation. This is what he feels he wants and needs. This is what he enjoys doing best and when this number vibration is expressed he feels an inner sense of satisfaction. Whatever he tries, he wants to present it in this format.

The law of incompatability (with the qualities of contiguous numbers) is again a primary consideration in assessing the over-all harmony of the individual as between his three conscious points of reference.

For example, the FOUR motivation which wants the hard core truth is a considerable contradiction to a THREE personality which seems decorative, relaxed and carefree, or to a TWO personality which appears sensitive to the point of covering up anything they want to protect. Similarly the SIX motivation which wants to be friendly and become socially involved is in basic contrast to a SEVEN character whose ultimate behavior is to remain aloof and aim for professional perfection, or to a FIVE character who must seek advantages by capitalizing on differences or excelling through active competition. However, it should be noted that the incompatability contradiction in itself sets up a certain rhythm or tempo which produces a certain flavor or distinction as opposed to lack of intensity or "nothingness". Thus people strongly at cross purposes within themselves, as individuals, create more vibrations and hence stand out from the crowd as opposed to melting into the vast glob of human indifference. If you are the type of person who admires, respects and seeks examples of outstanding individuals, then such cases would always be found to constitute such prime patterns of strong contrasts and/or contradictions. It is in the challenge of overcoming or melding such opposing forces that the tone of our character is formed. Therefore, strong contrasts in the index points makes for something more outstanding than where only harmony, ease and compatability prevail.

The individual's Character is, of course, his ultimate and total format. His Personality is what others casually observe him to be on the automatic or instinctive level of ordinary behavior. His Motivation is what he is trying to satisfy in order to secure some degree of personal satisfaction from the situation.

Just how any number on the motivation fits in or modifies any of the NINE character types is examined in Chapter VII The Perspective Of The Whole. It is here pointed out, however, since the end result tends to be how the individual affects others in the social context, that it is the Motivation which is initially dominant and the Character tends to be modified accordingly. But as will be examined later, each Motivation number is itself mated with a specific Personality vibration in order to result in a specific Character index. Example, if we are considering the 9 varieties of the SIX Character, those with a ONE motivation would all have a FIVE Personality (obviously for the total to come up a SIX). The sum of the vowels (Motivation) plus the sum of the consonants (Personality) must always equal the sum of all the letters in the name (Character). And a

TWO Motivation with a SIX Character would all have a FOUR Personality.

In dealing with very young children one is immediately more aware of their inner Motivations than of their personality affect which develops somewhat later, or their ultimate Character pattern which emerges still later. All concerned parents would be wise to make allowance for the normal expression of the child's Motivation urge rather than suppress it just because it may conflict with the parent's preferences.

Rather aside, but still an interesting point which bears on allowing for early development of the natural motivation urges in young children, would be the bestowing of names in accordance with the parents personal bias in respect to numbers. The point here is that this is in no way the normal course of events in naming or calling forth psychic reactions in the labeling or naming process. Very few people, if any, select their children's names on the basis of number preference. It is certainly not the way I think it should be done. One's own feelings in the matter of the name (the name which feels right to those responsible) is what should govern here. I would also suggest that if we stopped naming our children in the "normal" manner and started naming them in a pre-selected way according to the way society wanted them to be that Number Analysis might just stop working because one would destroy this delicate chain of psychic awareness and substitute a personal and unnatural bias.

The challenge for all parents is to encourage the growing child, when at all possible, to cultivate and expand the full possibilities of their inner motivation. This is what makes them happy and happy children tend to grow up into constructive and responsible adults. There are, however, definition limitations on what the parent can do as opposed to what Fate has in store for that child irrespective of what the parent may hope for. This is examined at length in Chapter V The Pattern Of Your Destiny.

Just as the child starts to work immediately on developing his motivational impulses, older people, as they begin to get a little senile, also tend just to harp on their inner motivation drive. During the span of our mature years motivational drives can be suppressed in favor of some advantage gained in meeting the challenge of one's Destiny pattern (see Chapter V) but in the more primal state of general human behavior the motivation drive is nearly always in their constantly demanding to be satisfied.

# NUMBER *1* MOTIVATION

Number ONE on the motivation demands that the individual assert himself in any way that will place him over or ahead of others. He has to be first in everything he tries. Being first obviously holds him back in giving much consideration for anyone else until his own needs have been definitely satisfied.

It should be pointed out that since the Personality number is both automatic and obvious and the Motivation number is what the individual is trying to put across, whenever he can make it work, that number ONE on the personality is obviously more aggressive and pushy than number ONE on the motivation. Actually the motivation is a drive which the individual can and does turn on and off according to other considerations in the situation. But the motivation quality is something the individual will push whenever he can get away with it just because he likes it.

Just as numbers symbolize qualities in general, so they also represent people who are in a sense prototypes of these qualities. The ONE motivation therefore admires and respects the traditionally masculine virtues and people who fit these qualifications, namely certain hard driving men or in some cases very dominating women who obviously display this same type of traditional masculine aggression. The most obvious type of women in this category would be women with a ONE personality.

Since ONE symbolizes aggression of all types, ONE on the motivation indicates that aggression (and all the other ONE qualities) are considered valid and indispensible tools for any purpose which the individual may wish to pursue. It may not always be possible, or permissable, but they will try these pushy tactics whenever they can.

ONES want to lead; they want to take over; they want to be self-reliant; they want to persevere; they want to dominate; they want to pioneer and they want to be independent. They may not feel up to all the demands required, but they will try it if they can. ONE on the personality is an instinctive reaction and has nothing to do with whether the individuals likes to be that way or not. ONE on the character is the way the individual will have to program himself eventually as that is the way he is designed to be, but again this has nothing to do with whether he likes it or not or whether he can do it automatically.

A's in the name give courage and determination in physical matters. J's give mental independence in pursuing ONE'S motivations and S's in the name give a high comprehension of the true "spirit" needed to push ONE'S way to the top.

Since the motivation index is not automatic like the personality focus, when there are no individual letter symbols in the name to support the motivation number it is considerably more difficult to effectively satisfy the motivation. With no ONES the individual lacks some degree of all the qualities necessary to do that which HE WANTS TO DO EFFECTIVELY. Since the motivation persists, that which comes out tumbles in erratic fashion with no real integrity or courage behind it. The effect seems like the determination of ONE without its full impact.

# NUMBER *2* MOTIVATION

Number TWO on the motivation means that whenever these individuals can, they want to be kind; they want to be sympathetic; they want to be understanding; they want to be considerate; they want to be helpful; they want to offer a compromise. When they are able they will try to be patient, tactful and sensitive to matters of timing, harmony and rhythm.

In terms of types of people who are prototypes of TWO, these individuals appreciate people who are gentle, sensitive, feminized, soft, yielding and compliant. This is also to imply that they do not care for people who are directly the opposite of the TWO type, such as the aggressive, masculinized ONES. A CONSCIOUS PREFERENCE FOR ANY TYPE IN THE MOTIVATIONALWAYS IMPLIES A REJECTION TO SOME DEGREE OF ITS OPPOSITE TYPE AS WELL.

B's in the name make it easy to be emotionally sympathetic on an intimate level. K's in the name contribute a mental rapport on sensitive matters of feeling and T's in the name give a spiritual grace to what has already been extended as a helping hand.

With no letter symbols for TWO in the name the individual, try as he might, will always find it very difficult to control his emotions sufficiently in order to convey the spirit of understanding he desires. In terms of liking the prototype symbolized by TWO, he seeks them but then rejects them because they also offend him in some sensitive way.

# NUMBER 3 MOTIVATION

Number THREE on the motivation means these persons like to express themselves and seek the responsive appreciation of an audience. They want to voice their opinion; they want to be creative; they want to cultivate talent; they want to admire decorative values. As a tool for effective expression they believe in the "window dressing" approach to life; they want to exploit the "here and now" rather than the past or future.

In prototypes they admire all talented people, creative artists and anyone who speaks out and registers some kind of "reaction" rather than the type who just sits there like a bump on a log, taking it all in buy conveying nothing.

They enjoy being optimistic and enthusiastic but they can also become the victums of unfounded fears.

C's in the name give a talent for self expression when dealing with physical forms or material media. L's in the name give a mental facility when dealing with creative matters and U's in the name lend a certain spiritual suggestiveness with creative forms.

With no letter symbols for THREE in the name, and in spite of the desire to be creative, the individual has difficulty in readily finding the right words, ideas or forms to effectively express what he has in mind. Anyone who lacks a THREE in the name has an unability to laugh at himself or see the natural humor in a ridiculous situation. They may appreciate a good joke but they can seldom make one themselves.

# NUMBER 4 MOTIVATION

Number FOUR on the motivation shows a person who really wants the bare facts and unvarnished truth which also makes them better prepared than most to do something constructive about it. A number of people ask for the truth but few are really prepared to accept it as the FOUR is. They want to be fair and square in all their relationships; they enjoy working hard for what they want; they even enjoy going without in order to save something or to put up with inconveniences for the sake of future advantages. They want to be economical, practical, down-to-earth, common sense realists.

In prototypes they admire older, mature people who take most matters seriously, which is also to imply that they tend to downgrade or disparage younger, frivolous, happy-go-lucky, carefree types (such as the THREE).

D's in the name enable them to withstand the difficult pressures of material and physical hardships. M's in the name give them a capacity for bridging trying situations through a mental grasp of the realities involved and V's in the name give them an awareness of some over-all "master plan" which may provide a reason for things even though they may not understand it fully at the time.

With no individual letter symbols for FOUR in the name it is difficult to assimilate the real truth behind all the facts they want to collect. They also try in some way to pretend that reality is not quite as they find it. Their desire to return again and again to the same old facts can amount to some form of self inflicted punishment or downright masochism.

# NUMBER **5** MOTIVATION

Number FIVE on the motivation insures that one will go on searching and seeking until they finally find an ingenious solution which most likely no one ever thought of before. FIVE on the motivation definitely keeps a person on his toes and alive and responsive to all matters directly related to the five senses. They manage to regard everything with a certain sexual intensity which may not always take the form of sexual expression or actual sexual gratification. Anything that seems interestingly different catches their eye for it is this departure or variation from the usual which intrigues them most. They like speed, adventure, excitement, thrills and the freedom to pursue all these matters whenever they feel like it.

In prototype they admire anything that is sexually suggestive for it arouses their own appetites in that direction. They like active, competitive people and they enjoy being able to gain an advantage over others whether this advantage be real or only a bluff. They like to take chances and always admire a certain bravado and bluff in others.

E's in the name give them a talent for exploiting the physical advantages in a situation. N's in the name give them an ability to devise more complicated maneuvers on a mental level which can outwit their opponents and W's in the name give them a type of extended vision which conceives solutions for improving methods that most people would pass right by.

With no individual letter symbols for FIVE in the name that person is considerably hampered in the full use of his physical senses which he requires to physically gratify the motivations he desires. He will often place a sensory accent on qualities or situations which would normally not be considered in this sensory context.

# NUMBER 6 MOTIVATION

Number SIX on the motivation describes a type of person who wants to be friendly, gracious and as consciously concerned with your problems as though they were his own. They want to become involved; they want to assume a sense of social responsibility and even in some cases share a sense of collective guilt (if necessary) for what others do in group cooperation. They believe in team work and getting together with others on any project which they have in mind. By the same token they do not want to do things on their own or go off on some independent venture which would in any way separate them from the "crowd" or group as idealized by them in their own social context.

In their admiration for prototypes of the SIX quality they respect average, typical individuals who seem to easily fit in with others around them. They would obviously avoid the unique individualists who might stand out from the crowd as all SIXS prefer to consider atypical behavior more harmful to the greater good of the larger social community.

They can be busybodies because they love to gossip and carry tales back and forth; they consider this sort of behavior as helping to cement the bonds of a common morality. They tend to stand firm on middle class values, as we define such values today, and while they might on occasion overstep these limitations themselves, they never do so without some sense of guilt.

F's in the name give a talent for socializing and "fitting in" on the average level in most situations. O's in the name give a sense of rapport with persons of like mind and values even though they may not be obviously associated in the same group or have identical

78

backgrounds — hence a sense of mental rapport on moral issues. X's in the name (which are not often found since comparatively few names contain the letter X) would lend a sense of warm brotherhood on a more spiritual level in spite of obvious physical or material differences which might be present because this individual senses a compatability with moral issues before they may even be expressed.

With no individual letter symbols for SIX in the name the individual is considerably hampered in his conscious desire for mutual compatability with others because something is inwardly lacking which would make these relationships gratifying. They are drawn to others in a friendly fashion but are somehow unable to convince everyone concerned of the mutuality of their interests, or on closer contact they no longer even see themselves as suitably compatable with the group. Rather than cementing the bonds of friendship in the social exchange of news and views, they also tend to expose unbridgeable gaps in the very loyalty which is supposed to cement average people together. Lacking the SIX, what they say boomerangs as offensive gossip rather than an act of intended good will.

# NUMBER 7 MOTIVATION

Number SEVEN on the motivation identifies the type of person who enjoys being alone in order to plumb the depths of his own spirit as opposed to leveling off in an exchange of social relationships which seek a common denominator. The SEVEN motivation wants to perfect himself in all the uniqueness of his being so that he stands out (at least in his own estimation) as the last word of professional distinction. They seek expressions of depth and rare insight rather than that which is just easily communicated to average people. In fact by their motivation for "specialization" they tend to dislike average or, as they would label them, mediocre individuals. They admire refinement, exclusiveness, wisdom (as opposed to just lengthy experience), specialized authority, unique distinction, professional perfection, inner values, a sense of spirituality, a consciousness of philosophical faith (as opposed to just emotional superstition) and an appreciation for cultural heritage. They also enjoy a certain mysterious, mystical suggestiveness.

As prototypes of SEVENNESS they admire any individual who even subtly suggests a talent in any or all of the above qualities which they themselves seek for inner gratification. They are always aware of "rare" types who stand apart from the crowd because of some refined distinction which may not be at all apparent to average people but is invariably sensed by those who are motivated by SEVEN. The SEVEN motivation always collects a very miscellaneous "bag" of friends most of whom may be quite "odd". I should add that subtlety is always an ingredient of SEVENNESS which automatically avoids the obvious and commonplace. Their friends seem odd to others because their virtues are generally quite hidden.

G's in the name give a talent for the gratification of perfection on the physical and material level. P's in the name contribute an appreciation of more complex manifestations of the refined exclusiveness associated with SEVEN and Y's in the name place the motivations on a very high spiritual plane which may be quite difficult for others not on this wave length to fully understand.

With no letter symbols for SEVEN at all in the name, the individual is considerably limited in the variety and range of spiritual depth which he can really understand or handle. This person may be restricted to an eccentric form of superstition which is mysterious and mystical but which may fail to follow the main stream of cultural heritage which SEVEN really represents.

# NUMBER **8** MOTIVATION

Number EIGHT on the motivation signifies a person who really aspires to a position of power and influence in the world. Money and financial perogatives may or may not also be included. This is the kind of person who wants everything on the grand scale. Smallness or pettiness is generally something they can't abide. They generally have a facility for making important decisions easily because they know what they want in material terms and they can usually size up situations and people quite accurately as to how they might potentially meet their requirements in this important area. They want to believe in the efficacy of power tactics although other considerations may sometimes hold them back from an all out push in this direction. They want to be materially expansive and financially far-sighted. They always appreciate efficiency in any form and they learn to be good judges of value, particularly when important money considerations are involved. They always want to do the "just" thing even when this may alienate some position which they feel may deserve more consideration for sentimental reasons.

As prototypes of EIGHT, which these persons most admire, any individual who obviously possesses the trappings of power and position quickly catch their eye. It seems to matter less whether such privileges be the result of effort or just usurpation. The point which they openly admire is that such persons actually have some kind of power in their control. In keeping with their preference for things on a large scale, they like everything big and expensive like large homes, impressive possessions, elegant backgrounds and all the enviable things which power and prestige usually bestow. Diamonds in the rough or hiding your light under a bushel is hardly their idea of how to live effectively.

H's in the name give the individual a highly proficient "know-how" on most all material matters involving physical factors. Q's in the name signify a more intellectualized approach which because of its more highly developed speciality may not be easily understood by just average minds. Z's in the name (which are comparatively rare since so few common names contain Z) symbolize an even wider grasp of the potentials of power manipulation which, however, have their greatest area of application on more highly refined segments of human behavior such as man's ultimate spiritual purpose.

With no letter symbols for EIGHT at all in the name, that individual is considerably hampered in making the best use of his grandiose aspirations when his own personal affairs in any way become involved. This individual is invariably more equipped to be better at making decisions for others than he is at directing his own personal life in the very channels that would give him the most gratification. In the end he lacks a complete perspective on the techniques of effective justice and he may be very apt to act just as unjustly towards himself. He may also develop an overly hard-nosed manner which to others signifies a definite ruthlessness of attitude.

# NUMBER *9* MOTIVATION

Number NINE on the motivation represents a person who aims to find something in everyone with which he can identify. They want to view life in its broadest perspective and they continually strive to accent the ties that mankind has in common rather than in any way to emphasize the differences that distinguish one from another. Very often, in order to put over this "amalgamation" or universality of value structures they are led to extremes of behavior because the number NINE, wherever it may be found in the human character, encourages the right to take over or dictate in the interest of the greatest good for the greatest number AS THEY SEE IT. All NINES have a peculiar way of seeing things which leads to a certain fanaticism and such fanaticism without regard for "all" the factors in a situation can be a dangerous thing. NINES are capable, therefore, of a great deal of destruction and annihilation of anything that opposes their program as they want it to be. One reason for this is the cool, clinical objectivity of which all NINES are capable which, if carried far enough, would seem to drop the personal "human element" out of the picture altogether. The NINE motivation can easily justify this because they want to act in a selfless, dispassionate manner but they also lack the talents for realizing how or when they may be imposing a code or ethic on a situation which simply does not apply.

As prototypes of their motivation they admire selfless, supposedly dedicated people who give freely of themselves to causes or movements without apparent or obvious motivations for personal gain. They like anyone who immediately sees things in a broad expansive context rather than one who personalizes matters as petty examples. They themselves are easily moved or ignited by persons who can sway mobs or raise the public tempo to fever pitch in the name of some cause. The area of politics is often particularly attractive to them as are also the politicians who are riding the crest of the moment.

I's in the name give a sense of drama which is very effective in matters to which the more average person can easily respond. R's in the name lend an even further range of emotional wallop which digs even deeper into the primal instincts of the crowd. There are no letter symbols for NINE on the still higher level of expression (such as the other primary numbers have) because NINE in itself is supposed to convey a certain degree of universality on all levels.

With no letter symbol at all for NINE in the name the motivation is reluctant to pursue the charitable aspirations which it endorses in principle. On closer contact the individual tends to reject his commitments because they offend him in ways he cannot fully understand. His motivations become more theoretical than concrete applications of charitable intent and he is more likely to scarifice others for any destructive qualities to which he inadvertently contributes.

# Chapter IV

# MISSING NUMBERS
# AND KARMIC LINKS

When individual number symbols are missing in the name that person has a blind spot in his perspective on the full implication of the qualities which that number symbolizes. This lack of perspective acts as a stumbling block in all activities calling for the expression of that quality. This is an absolute law in the structure of Number Analysis.

Most people are missing at least one number in their name. Only a comparatively few individuals are fortunate enough to have at least one each of the nine primary numbers in their name. When a person has no missing numbers they may be considered to have some degree of talent in all categories. At least when they are called upon to handle a certain type of situation calling for certain attitudes of mind (such as a FOUR type situation calling for down-to-earth realism and facing facts squarely, or an EIGHT type situation demanding the individual face an important decision, or a NINE type situation calling for broad understanding and perhaps a little compassion to just forgive and forget the whole matter) then the individual at least does not have a blind spot in his perspective on those qualities. He may not particularly enjoy doing what must be done but at least he has a healthy sound approach to the situation, whatever it may be.

Perhaps the most unfortunate aspect about missing numbers (which symbolize character traits that are missing in our make up) is the angle that we either do not realize they are missing and thus make allowance for this "lack", or that we try to cover up, pretend we have more talent on the matter than we do, and botch the situation in such a way that only leads to more problems. Because we do not realize or admit that we may not know what we are doing we are much more likely to get into situations over our head. Very few people want to admit it when they are wrong and when a person has missing numbers in their name they are invariably wrong or twisted in their thinking on matters concerning these missing areas of experience. This matter becomes even more serious when this missing number also happens to be one of their focus points of conscious interest.

As already pointed out in the chapters on Character, Personality and Motivation, there is a very subtle qualification on these points when the individual has a conscious index on this same quality: for example, if his Motivation index is a THREE but he lacks an individual number symbol for THREE.

The distinction I am making here is perhaps the most difficult point to get across to all students of Numbers because it is one of those "YOU ARE AND YOU AREN'T" type of situations.

The general rule is: when one of your INDEX TOTALS calls for expression of a certain quality and you lack an individual number symbol in that same quality, you usually respond in kind in the more constructive aspect of that quality WHEN YOUR OWN PERSONAL INTERESTS ARE NOT INVOLVED. For example, if your Character index is a EIGHT you do act judiciously with material foresight and financial vision ON IMPERSONAL MATTERS, but you tend to act negatively on judicial matters in your own personal affairs. You may, for example, make hasty decisions on important matters which somehow create a situation of unjust proportions and invariably the matter will have to be taken up again and rectified. If you were called upon to pass juddgment on a impersonal matter, not affecting your own affairs, then your decision would be far more equitable and you would even be commended on having such sound judgment.

The following are rules of thumb about missing numbers in the name:

WITH NO ONES — the individual lacks integrity and courage and is apprehensive of the traditional masculinized drive in others. It could also be said that they do not like (or fear) strong aggressive men. They would be correspondingly more relaxed around weak, nonaggressive, gentle type men because their manner would not challenge or threaten this "lack" in their own make up.

WITH NO TWOS — the individual lacks sensitivity, tact, patience, consideration and an effective sense of timing and rhythm. It could also be said that they do not like (or fear) women (or gentle types which they see as an indication of weakness or something to be resented).

WITH NO THREES — the individual lacks a sense of humor. They also lack a facility for synthesis and fail to grasp a "picture" of the whole. They often find it difficult to express how they really feel in words suitable to the occasion. Articulation is a struggle. They lack a capacity to relax and enjoy things in a simple carefree manner. They would not particularly enjoy being around children or naive, unsophisticated types.

WITH NO FOURS — the individual dislikes the task of work. They invariably expect from the world something for nothing or the wrong things from the wrong people. They have a low threshold for pain, hardship, privation and endurance. They have a reluctance to face facts squarely or admit the truth (particularly about themselves). They would seem to have some difficulty with the effective manipulation or handling of "form". To them all forms would seem somewhat distorted, or they would distort them in some way because they do not appreciate the standard or normal forms.

WITH NO FIVES — the individual lacks the spirit of competition. Their sexual energy and regenerative powers in general are below average. They are reluctant to take chances or allow things to be changed even when such advantage is pointed out. They resist all changes which intrude in their lives. They are not adaptable or innovative and the challenge of discovery or adventure has little appeal. Their sensory reactions are poor.

WITH NO SIXS — the individual is unable to mix freely with groups because he resists the implied responsibility of the group members for each other and the yoke of collective values required. Domesticity, marriage, the responsibility of children and all the other factors arising from this type of cooperative effort are looked upon with some distaste. What they are resenting here is the necessity to adjust their side in order to put up with a "give and take" situation. They also suffer from an unfounded need for approval and in order to overcome this they invariably share too much of themselves with the wrong people trying to secure this approval they think they need. The wrong people invariably turn out to be those family members and old friends closest to them from whom approval has more value. They would be better advised to keep their mouths shut in the presence of intimate friends and relatives especially concerning their motivations or reasons pro and con for the things they do. The intimate friends and relatives of all individuals with a SIX karma are prepared to take the individual at his face value therefore too much personal disclosure only makes them begin to wonder and gives them ammunition to fire right back in an effort to put their own domination across. If all individuals with a SIX karma would be less open with intimate friends and close relatives they would gain the RESPECT THEY DESERVE because they will never secure the approval from this source they think they need. Idle talk and even the most innocent of gossip always gets them in trouble.

WITH NO SEVENS — the individual lacks a sense of natural refinement. They also lack of sense of faith in the form of a personal philosophy which might otherwise enable them to see above and beyond the physical and material limitations of whatever situation was confronting them at the moment. With no natural sense of "faith" they tend to consider that all there is or ever will be is just the way things are right now. It is almost impossible for them to feel things might be better tomorrow. For those individuals who are highly keyed to material vibrations like FOUR and EIGHT, as long as they are making material progress they feel they don't need faith. But when material progress slackens off and they run up against a stone wall they have no faith that they might be able to get things going again later. They are naturally distrustful of those who hold themselves apart from the crowd or who are different in some way from the average. Spiritual in the sense of mystical awareness, or a belief in the Fate concept in life is not part of their nature and they are suspect of those who feel otherwise.

WITH NO EIGHTS — the individual resists the necessity for making important decisions. They lack a sense of fundamental value structures, particularly where money is concerned. They tend, at one

90

point, to either overvalue money itself and undervalue it at another. Either way money and money fears distort their perspective. They make poor shoppers where price is concerned for they tend to be guided by price rather than a sense of "true value". It may be said in certain cases that they know the price of everything and the value of nothing. They lack of true sense of justice. Justice to them is siding with the position that pleases or pressures them the most. Efficiency is not one of their talents.

WITH NO NINES — the individual lacks the ability to forgive and forget. They are unable to let go even when they know full well that something has passed beyond their reach. They seem oblivious to the inherent natural drama of certain events and general affairs which extend beyond their own familiar circle have little significance. Charity, compassion and tolerance for those beyond their personal group are somewhat impossible.

*     *     *

In the philosophy inherent upon which the value of number symbolism relates to human life and destiny, it is regarded that missing numbers in the name represent karmic links with a past life experience. Since missing numbers essentially constitute a blind spot in our perspective and consequently a trouble spot in our behavior reactions, it is felt that these areas of "lack" arise from the improper handling of these qualities at some former point in our spiritual evolution. The individual's experience in this life will reflect a constant series of situations which provoke or call for added effort in these specific directions.

For apparently spiritual reasons, life seems to have a way of presenting us with an abundance of situations and/or opportunities which apparently call for or demand a response to the specific qualities of our karmas.

ONE karmas will have a great many chances in life to build and improve their sense of integrity, courage, originality, independence, push, aggression, determination and forceful leadership.

TWO karmas will have a great many chances in life to develop their sensitivity, understanding, consideration, observance of small details, tact, diplomacy, rhythm and timing.

THREE karmas will have a great many chances in life to express themselves before an audience or be called upon to give their opinion and criticism or to contribute to the decorative side of life.

FOUR karmas will have a great many chances in life to prove themselves through hard work, physical effort, self-discipline, enforced routine, application of common sense and logic, and learning to dig in and hold on.

FIVE karmas will have a great many chances in life to get out and investigate new, improved ways for effecting exciting changes. Sexual opportunities will be abundantly available as though their best opportunities invariably started from some sort of sexual experience. Their life is apt to be filled with more "real life" adventure than for the average and things will always seem to be happening to them which others might consider exciting but for them it is all just another challenge to adapt to a changing tempo different from their own.

SIX karmas will have a great many chances in life to become intimately involved with others. Responsibilities which must be shared (such as develop in romantic attachments) will be a frequent occurrence in order to teach them about their lack of social motivation which would otherwise be naturally avoided.

SEVEN karmas will have a great many chances in life to be alone in order to inventory themselves on a personal basis for life's deeper purpose. Unfortunately this also indicates a disproportionate number of losses, setbacks, disappointments and even some tragedy, all of which is trying to teach the individual the power of faith and the necessity of a philosophy which sees beyond the limitations of just the present.

EIGHT karmas will have a great many chances in life to handle money so as to learn its real purpose as a medium of exchange and not something you can "take with you". They will also be placed in frequent situations demanding executive authority and administrative perogatives just to develop the qualities they lack the most.

NINE karmas will have a great many chances in life to let go, give up, broaden out and wander the face of the earth so they can actually see that there is so much more to life than the narrow circle they would otherwise choose for themselves. Much of their life will seem to call for an extreme effort in the capacity for charity, compassion, tolerance and forgiveness.

92

There is a strong touch of irony here in the operation of karma because LIFE WILL SEEM TO OFFER THE MOST OPPORTUNITY TO PERFORM CERTAIN FUNCTIONS TO THOSE WHO ARE REALLY THE LEAST QUALIFIED (because they have misused or misapplied these functions in the past) AS OPPOSED TO THOSE WHO MIGHT BE THE BEST QUALIFIED OR HAVE THE STRONGEST DESIRES IN THIS DIRECTION.

Thus Fate through its program of so-called KARMIC REHABILI-TATION institutes ON THE JOB TRAINING for those individuals who would never choose or experience these qualities unless Fate forced them into a situation which demanded a DEVELOPMENT IN THIS KARMIC DIRECTION.

LEADERSHIP is offered most to ONE karmas.

CELEBRITY STATUS is offered most to TWO karmas.

CREATIVE ARTISTRY is offered most to THREE Karmas.

TO ACCUMULATE THROUGH WORK (including in some cases building an empire) is offered most to FOUR karmas.

ADVENTURE, EXCITEMENT, THRILLS AND SEXUAL IN-VITATIONS are offered most to FIVE karmas.

ROMANCE, COMPANIONSHIP and opportunity to SHARE THEIR LIVES are offered most to SIX karmas.

PROFESSIONAL STATUS and opportunity to excel through TECHNICAL REFINEMENTS and RELIGIOUS EMPLOY-MENT are offered most to SEVEN karmas.

MONEY, POWER and ADMINISTRATIVE AUTHORITY are offered most to EIGHT karmas.

TRAVEL, FREEDOM FROM PERSONAL RESPONSIBILITY and opportunity to really experience a WIDE VARIETY OF LIFE are offered most to NINE karmas.

However, our specific purpose in life and the subject that we should give our greatest concern is NOT THE AREA OF OUR KARMA (which will always remain a trouble spot and potential pain in the neck) but the AREA OF OUR DESTINY which is covered in YOUR FATE – Part II.

# PART 2
## *YOUR FATE*

## *Chapter V*
## *THE PATTERN OF DESTINY*
## *IN YOUR LIFE*

Part I described all about you — the you that exists before the external circumstances of Fate take over and mold you in the direction of your spiritual purpose in life.

In the philosophy of Numbers and the application of their symbolic values to our lives as individuals it is believed that each of us (in addition to being born a specific person) also faces a definite spiritual challenge which we call our personal Fate or Destiny.

Just as we psychically name ourselves with the label that identifies who and what we are, fate has ordained that we enter the world at a specific moment of time and it is the symbolic application of this date of birth that reveals the pattern of our destiny.

Just as INTENTION is the criteria of the psychic force that recognizes the label of who and what we are, intention is also the criteria which establishes the "true date" of our birth.

In a superficial sense the construction of calendars and the recording of dates is a man-made device to measure the passage of time. But so also is the discovery of numbers as symbols of qualities in nature as:

ONE represents UNITY
TWO reflects DUALITY
THREE symbolizes CREATIVITY
FOUR expresses BASIC FOUNDATIONS
FIVE suggests VARIETY AND CHANGE
SIX involves CORRESPONDENCE AND COHESIVENESS
SEVEN implies SPIRITUALITY
EIGHT demands BALANCE
NINE embraces UNIVERSAL TOLERANCE

Most of us are aware that the passage of the earth in its eliptical path around the sun determines the seasonal variations of climate and growth. As it completely revolves once each twenty four hours, the earth's movement on its axis accounts for the daily variations of light and darkness. So also does our calendar symbolize these same important qualities that comprise the external conditions outside our personal selves. Thus the dates of our man-made calendar are not as arbitrary as might be supposed.

Because calendars are a man-made device which is designed to reflect a true condition in nature (the actual passage of time, etc.) sometimes seemingly arbitrary adjustments are made to reflect this condition more accurately such as the allowance in the calendar for an extra day every four years (known as leap year) or the addition or subtraction of a second of time in a twenty four hour period because the greater unit of time does not always lend itself to mathematical division in exactly equal units.

Puzzling as its spiritual validity may seem, there is a seemingly arbitrary adjustment of comparatively recent times where we change actual clock time in order to adjust our daily habits to a longer span of daylight hours. This manipulation of time, for purposes of "daylight saving", at the moment of midnight as one day's date passes into another arbitrarily changes a date in time or history.

For example, a person born at 12:30 AM under daylight saving time is said to be born a date later than if he had been born on its equivalent under standard time of 11:30 PM of the day before.

Arbitrary as it may seem, the law of intent is what governs this psychic relationship. If the social machinery (such as it is) has provided for daylight saving at that time and place of birth THE DATE WHICH SYMBOLIZES THE PATTERN OF ONE'S FATE IS THE ACTUAL LEGAL DATE. That would be the date that may have been created by the use of daylight saving and not the date that would have been had daylight saving time not been in effect.

While our name which labels the qualities of our Character, Personality and Motivation is generated psychically, irrespective of time, the qualities and conditions of our Destiny are an EXTERNAL FORCE which is placed upon us exactly in relation to time and the social manipulations of those around us who pattern themselves in OUR LIVES in the very quality of OUR DESTINY.

So it isn't just happenstance that we enter this world as the child of specific conditions, parental, environmental and so forth including in some cases a manipulation of the actual date for economic reasons.

Looking back in history this would also apply to those cases where an individual was born under one calendar which was legally operative at this place and time in history even through a neighboring location or country was legally operating under another type of calendar.

When doing number analysis on historical figures who were born under one calendar system WE DO NOT CHANGE THE DATE to conform to the calendar system used by our area at that time or to a calendar system now in use. This is particularly applicable for the date of birth on our first four presidents of the United States. In 1750 by act of the British Parliament the Julian calendar was replaced by the Gregorian calendar by eliminating 11 days from September (september 3 to 13 inclusive) in the calendar of year 1752. This applied to Great Britain and the colonies. U.S. Presidents George Washington, John Adams, Thomas Jefferson and James Madison were all born when the Julian calendar was in effect but history now records their birthdates as though the Gregorian calendar had been in effect at that time. See data in Chapter XII on the Number Patterns of Celebrated People Of Our Time.

To determine the over-all pattern of your destiny add up all the digits in the date of birth and reduce this to a single number just as you did for the conscious indexes of the name.

This single digit symbolizes the spiritual demand that is made upon you in your personal confrontation with life AS YOU DISCOVER IT TO BE. This has nothing to do with your confrontation of life as anyone else may assume it to be because they may have felt that they (as for example, your parents) provided it for you.

As you walk down the street of life certain things happen to you (BECAUSE IT IS YOU AND THEY WERE INTENDED TO HAPPEN TO YOU) which do not happen to the person ahead of you or the person behind you (because these certain things were not intended to happen to them).

One so often hears the complaint ... "but why did it have to be me?" The answer is clearly that it has to be you because your fate pattern demanded that it be you and there is an overall spiritual purpose in what happens to you whether you are aware of it at the time or not.

According to our individual make up (as outlined in Part I) certain people can more naturally understand this spiritual implication than others. For example, all those individuals with a letter symbol for SEVEN in their name or (with qualifications) those whose Character, Personality or Motivation is SEVEN, have an instinctive awareness of such spiritual implications whether they have thought the matter through to its logical conclusion or not. This awareness is perhaps of even more concern to those persons whose Destiny vibration adds to SEVEN because these individuals are constantly learning day by day exactly what all of this implies in the shaping of their ENTIRE LIFE.

In this regard it is pertinent to point out that the number vibrations of TWO (on a more personal level) and NINE (on a wider, more universal level) are both sensitively attuned to UNDERSTANDING. But SEVEN is the vibration which gives spiritual depth to what is otherwise only AWARENESS. There is a considerable difference here.

It must be remembered that the pattern of one's Fate, or the challenge of Destiny, is a life long concern and is never entirely finished. Even though the individual may be attuned to and have talent for dealing with this exact frame of reference, IF IT IS ONE'S FATE, then there are still problems to be constantly solved in this specific direction.

The number vibration which symbolizes the pattern of one's Destiny sets the WHOLE TONE OF THE LIFE EXPERIENCE. It is therefore a constant challenge to the individual in the quality of this vibration BUT IT ALSO MEANS THAT ONE'S BEST AND ONLY OPPORTUNITIES THAT CONTRIBUTE TO THAT PERSON'S REAL PURPOSE IN LIFE ARE SUPPLIED TO HIM IN THIS SAME FORMAT AND DESIGN.

As expressed earlier, life also presents each of us with chances to work with and develop our so-called karmic debts (missing number areas). In fact as is so often the case, life seems to present so many chances for these karmic corrections (repayment of karmic debts) that the average individual is very apt to consider these karmic chances as his real spiritual opportunities.

This attitude (which is quite common) is an unfortunate mistake but it does account for so many people we know spending most of their life trying to correct or improve their liabilities (which always remain a liability) rather than seizing the potentiality of either their REAL ASSETS or THEIR PURPOSE in life. It is indeed the wise individual who can eventually sort this out for himself and see exactly wherein he should devote and concentrate his best efforts.

ONE'S MAIN EFFORTS IN LIFE SHOULD NOT BE CONCENTRATED ON ONE'S LIABILITIES OR PROBLEM AREAS. These are something that should be corrected IF AND WHEN OTHER CIRCUMSTANCES PERMIT. THE MAIN DIRECTION IN LIFE IS THE RESPONSE TO OUR INDIVIDUAL SPIRITUAL PURPOSE AS DEFINED BY OUR DESTINY PATTERN.

Since some people rather balk at the term "spiritual" it would perhaps be better to refer to one's individual Destiny as THE FUNCTION OR IDEAL SPECIALIZATION FOR WHICH THAT INDIVIDUAL IS BEST DESIGNED OR PROGRAMMED. It should be the accumulated experiences of his life, as he eventually discovers it to be, that will prove this to him in the long run.

The challenge of our Destiny is seldom proved on single individual matters. It is the accumulation and totality of our experience which patterns the long, detailed journey in this general direction. It is in the wisdom of maturity that one finally sees the "true path" along which they have been traveling but which they may not have always recognized as BEING DESIGNED FOR THEM. In some cases it is only at the very end of life that one fully appreciates the direction in which he has come. It is at such times that the individual pieces do fall into place and the "why?" (at the time unanswered) is finally self evident. The common rationality for this: " ... everything that happens is always for the best," or, even more common place " ... everything always comes out in the wash." Realization and acceptance that this might indeed be true is a matter of spiritual insight which to some people comes easily and to some, unfortunately, not at all.

Spiritual awareness, I might add, is not, by any means, the pattern of destiny for all of us. It most certainly is for those whose birthdate adds to SEVEN and to some extent for those whose birthdate adds to TWO or NINE since for them the "deeper understanding" of life also plays such a large part.

Spirituality, or the format of spirituality, can also play a significant role in the way in which one goes about meeting the pattern of his Destiny if spirituality (symbolized by SEVEN) is one of the conscious indexes of Character, Personality or Motivation for these are the specific tools AND THE ONLY TOOLS which he has been given to pursue life's adventure.

The answer or direction to which all this leads — the function or use to which one applies whatever he has been given to work with — is contained in the vibration of the birthdate.

# NUMBER *1* FATE

Number ONE on the destiny pattern means that the general direction for the entire lifetime is a never ending uphill struggle to outdo or better oneself at each step of the way. Nothing is intended, with this life pattern, to come too easily. The totality of life's experience is such as to force him on so that each success becomes merely the foundation for another effort in a new direction. The ideal solution for all the important situations in life with which this individual is constantly confronted is to fall back on his own resources and never to expect solutions from others. What is needed here is direction, courage, conviction, independence, self-reliance, drive, spirit, invention and leadership. Men and others who exhibit the traditional qualities of masculinized aggression will always hold some meaningful key to this individual's effort to raise his station in life. There will seldom be much time for extended periods of rest for once recovered from one's latest exploit the urgent desirability (which once seemed to be necessary and compelling) will have faded away, forcing one to look around for new goals to pursue. A ONE destiny is the life pattern of an individual who can never be permanently satisfied with what has gone before. There will always, in his eyes, be room for improvement whether or not he still has the energy to try again. In responding to the demands of each new situation the first consideration should be to strip appearances down to single units so each can be overcome one at a time. The spiritual eye should be focused on the unity of the whole rather than on the details which in his case would only cloud the picture. (A TWO destiny on the other hand must forget the unity and concentrate on the details.) The ONE must take each step at a time and give it his

101

best effort. Force may often be necessary to break down whatever opposes this person. In learning to muster all the strength one has in order to concentrate on a single objective, a certain selfishness in attitude of mind is absolutely essential. Since everyone somewhat resists the challenge of their Destiny pattern, no matter how much native talent the individual may have for the matter, he tends to ignore or play down the very qualities which are needed most. The pattern of our Fate is always a challenge. Although selfishness and egotistical supremacy are always needed for the number ONE fate pattern, there is invariably some reluctance to assume such peroga-tives. For those bystanders who are naturally concerned for this individual (such as parents) selfishness and making one's personal interests primary should in this case be encouraged. Even when this encouragement is missing circumstances on their own will tend to operate against the individual just to force these very qualities to the front.

It is very difficult, if not impossible, for others to correctly judge a situation as one might see it for himself because for that individual to whom the matter is a purposeful challenge he alone is acutely aware how he must respond irrespective of how others might evaluate the situation IF IT WAS UP TO THEM. The point is, it isn't up to them.

There is almost a universal lack of understanding by people everywhere on this important point. Each of us is prone to prescribe how we would have reacted in the same situation. But everyone fails to appreciate that no situation is the same to each of us unless of course there were such a basic similarity between our respective charts as to enable us to really see the situation through the other person's perspective. This is somewhat impossible to do without the use of Numbers.

This lack of "true" perspective is particularly true concerning situations of potential violence. Violence is something that certain people attract and there is some good reason for this. A situation may appear menacing to one person but not to another. This is not to say that either one misjudges what is called for, but it is to imply that each of us is destined to react differently to something which may from all superficial details appear to be exactly the same.

In the number ONE destiny pattern the individual is continually pushed to get ahead. If, for example, the parent by his own life experience has found that the best things for him come by patiently waiting his turn, then it is almost impossible for him to see the wisdom or necessity for the child with the ONE destiny to provoke an opposite stand. With a ONE destiny nothing of importance will ever come to that individual by patiently waiting. He must get out and take what he feels he needs. The reason for this, of course, is that it is this very quality that must be developed by that person in order to master what challenges him in life.

In the guidance of young children everyone should refrain from sitting on or trying to restrain a number ONE destiny. To do otherwise may only leave a permanent scar which will have future spiritual implications. Others should also keep in mind that those with a number ONE destiny also have a high sensitivity about their personal integrity and they of all types are less liable to overuse their ONENESS to the detriment of others. What they are trying to do is to exert all their potential strength just to put themselves on a par with the challenge they face. They are really not trying to exceed this level and indescriminately exert domination over everybody else. Once their immediate confrontation has been overcome then they tend to step down or ease off from this display of ONENESS.

# NUMBER *2* FATE

Number TWO on the destiny pattern means that the general direction for the entire lifetime is a constant encouragement to hold back and patiently wait for just the right moment in order to capitalize on the ideality of TIMING. Number TWO, among other things, is the essence of rhythm and timing. A natural sense of timing comes instinctively to some and is an impossibility for others. The presence and placement of TWO in the chart symbolizes one's natural talents on this matter. Having such a letter symbol for TWO in the name is one thing, but having a conscious concern about TWO is far more important and when number TWO is on the destiny it is the most compelling accent or emphasis of all.

Since number TWO stands for highly developed sensitivities, all those individuals, men or women, who clearly reflect this gentle quality are vitally important in life for the individual with the TWO destiny.

Number TWO has also come to be understood as representing the cycle of re-birth. Therefore number TWO on the destiny means that the individual will in some symbolic way die many times during his lifetime ONLY TO BE REBORN AGAIN LITERALLY IN SOME NEW IMAGE. Thus the TWO destiny is froth with emotional highs and lows like the crest and trough of waves. The number TWO destiny is apt to be storm tossed all through life in much the same manner, being up one moment only to sink down the next, but hopefully to rise again even higher than before.

There is also inherently symbolized in number TWO the quality of sacrifice or martyrdom. On the destiny pattern it means that many times in life the individual may be called upon to stand aside at the last moment so that someone else may step forward and achieve for themselves what otherwise may not have been possible.

At its highest potential (which in numbers is often spoken of as the ELEVEN vibration rather than the simple TWO) the individual life can take on the quality of THE GREAT EXAMPLE or the glow of inspiration which lights the darkness so that others may also find their way. It is a refinement of this application which gives number TWO the potential of the celebrity. the TWO destiny always holds promise of limelight attention at some time or another. Whether this will flower into fame of great proportions or just occasional prominence for small accomplishments is something else, but each shares in the same general pattern that TWONESS holds.

Just as the parents of a ONE destiny should encourage that child to push himself forward, they should allow the TWO destiny child to find his own level of participation even though that position may be much further in the background than the parent might prefer. The child here who is confronted and challenged by the TWO destiny is the one to judge the RIGHT TIME to emerge and claim what may be his due.

Naturally the TWO destiny has much to contribute in the way of diplomatic and tactful counseling. They can also, at the proper time, become an outstanding source of inspiration in the role of the perfect example, but their ideal function is to follow up or lend support rather than to seek the "lead" for themselves.

# NUMBER 3 FATE

Number THREE on the destiny pattern means that the general direction for the entire lifetime is towards conditions of ease and relaxation in order to contribute to the decorative aspects of living. These people are designed to express themselves and voice their opinions and criticisms for they have a talent for vision and picturization. They invariably have a heightened sense of imagination which may to some people assume the proportions of unreality or just not sticking to the facts as they are. As young children they may seem overly carefree and even listless and at times entirely too free with their comments and opinions.

Again, the point here for the concerned parent is to encourage the THREE destiny to follow where their imagination leads them and not try to judge them by material accomplishments of practical value. Practicality (and even so-called common sense) are not the guidelines of creative imagination.

Very often what is needed for the THREE destiny is to acquire some intermediary medium which can carry the message beyond their immediate frame of reference. Too often their spirits are discouraged because those immediately around them may fail to respond or appreciate what they consider creative. What they have accomplished may be in fact highly creative but requires just the right type of audience to appreciate this particular talent and it may be unlikely that this type is available in the immediate environment. If a medium is used to convey the creative message then the circle widens and the proper audience can be located more effectively.

The important thing to remember here in developing the individuality of creative expression is to DO YOUR THING AND LET IT

FIND ITS OWN AUDIENCE. Another axion for the THREE destiny is to avoid tailoring your creativity to fit the audience you already know or assume you should have. Let your creativity develop its own format and you might be quite surprised when you discover the true audience for what you have done.

Not all creativity makes use of a medium to convey one's message. Some artists must still do "their thing" on a personal face to face basis, but eventually in this case, it is the subject matter which becomes the medium and the personality is lost or minimized by the subject as in music or acting.

Since THREE symbolizes creativity of all kinds, talented and colorful individuals are immediately attractive to the THREE destiny and he can always learn from them as they stir his own imagination or provide material for his own embellishments.

Since creativity thrives best under conditions of ease and lack of the ordinary social responsibilities, any situation that would over-burden the THREE destiny in this direction should be avoided. Generally speaking the THREE destiny should be an easy sort of life. It may not add up to a great deal in terms of material accumulation but it should provide plenty of color, ornamentation, enthusiasm, entertainment and sparkling charm.

# NUMBER 4 FATE

Number FOUR on the destiny pattern means that the general direction for the entire life is a constant necessity to hold firm, dig in, hang on and continually work the same ground over and over again. Routine, regimentation, discipline, physical effort, common sense and logic are the key guides for making this arduous challenge into a practical reality of enduring value.

Since FOUR, among other things, symbolizes a certain amount of hardship, the total life experience is apt to be trying and difficult, calling for great effort and unbelievable endurance.

Through perhaps no fault of the parents intentions, the FOUR destiny child will be conditioned in some way along lines which lay down strict disciplines and careful adherence to hard core reality. The child will be well aware of these values on his own, but the parent may from time to time point out their advantages which will be surprisingly acknowledged in this case.

Like number TWO (which has a so-called higher vibration of ELEVEN) the simple number FOUR is said to have a master potential of TWENTY TWO which in essence means MASTER BUILDER. Too much importance should not, however, be placed on these glamourous labels because as number ELEVEN boils down to just simple understanding, number TWENTY TWO also resolves itself down to just plain hard work.

However, all FOURS should aspire to some type of construction where their accomplishments can endure and prove useful in many ways, like feats of engineering, gigantic construction complexes and technical scientific achievements which are all based on physical facts and mathematical measurements.

Although the FOUR destiny is essentially restricted in one respect or another there will emerge in life from time to time a compelling necessity to carry one's carefully laid plans just one step further and GAMBLE (which is itself a TWENTY TWO vibration word). The speculation involved here is not, however, just an idle game or one undertaken for the thrill of taking chances. The FOUR destiny when operating on the higher potential of TWENTY TWO will discover that after he has all the proper facts, figures and measurements that there is one more step which he must take in order to put his project or dream over the top and into the "big time". The results of such great undertakings can only achieve the status of the spectacular because of the soundness of their FOUR organization but their success becomes the TWENTY TWO vibration of the MASTER BUILDER because of this courage to undertake sound but daring risks.

To the FOUR destiny life is indeed real and earnest. As individuals they are naturally attracted to older, serious mature types whose experience before them on the same hard path can be instructive and helpful. The value of the routine and discipline which is developed from reworking the same material over and over again is sometimes discovered to be the most meaningful long after they have gone on to something else. It is later in life that they find the work patterns and mental discipline learned earlier to be the cornerstone of larger projects which could only have been mastered because of this difficult early training.

# NUMBER **5** FATE

Number FIVE on the destiny pattern means that the general direction for the entire life is a series of surprising turns where the best opportunities may appear suddenly and in such a manner that one is forced to undertake big risks and speculative attitudes in order to break away from the general pattern which really holds him back. Nothing is designed to last too long under the FIVE destiny less the individual becomes too attached or too spoiled to be willing to accept the call to adventure when once again it knocks.

Since FIVE, among other things, symbolizes sex and the regenerative power of sensory stimulation, that always plays a large role in the meaningful direction of the FIVE destiny pattern. Many of their best opportunities will seem to have their source or beginning in some sexual relationship or sensory suggestion which brings about things which otherwise might never have been possible. It would therefore be wise to understand the real purpose of this sexual attraction since it does lead, directly or indirectly, to many fine opportunities.

The FIVE destiny should never be loathe to drop something they may be doing, even at the expense of an accumulated investment of much time and effort, if something new and exciting makes its appearance, which clearly indicates potential in a new direction. One way or another the benefit from one experience contributes to another although the transition between the immediate steps may at the time seem unrelated. It may be that step six relates beautifully to step ten even though the transition from step six to seven seems more like an abrupt dislocation. The eventuality of these potential links is something that FIVE should keep in mind when trying to weigh the advisability of taking a chance or trying something new and different. It is only after one has made enough changes that he can begin to see the ultimate advantage and relatedness of steps which are somewhat removed from each other in time, as in the above example. This pattern quality primarily applies only to the FIVE destiny as they come to sense the profit for them in breaking away from established molds and discover the particular merit in the risks they assume.

As one grows older these risks are somewhat harder to undertake because one may feel less physically attuned for all the new adjustments involved in such adventuresome undertakings. The natural youthfulness of the FIVE and their seemingly endless source of regenerative powers should always help to carry them from one situation to another in an exciting fashion.

FIVE always symbolizes a certain amount of competition and the necessity of seeking advantages over situations and people. Most of their life is a constant struggle for survival because all FIVES are so basically keyed to just their five senses and their exploitation.

Sometimes the function of FIVE doesn't allow the individual himself to stay around long enough to actually see the good he may have done by the upsets and changes which he helped to instrument. But without their ground work and innovative contributions, many situations would never continue to grow or improve. For FIVE himself it is apt to be here today and gone tomorrow, but they should always be able to gather some sense of gratification just from the excitement involved.

Physically active people are always attractive to the FIVE destiny as they see how others are able to capitalize or improvise in ways that give them new ideas. Sex always plays an important role in their life even though they themselves might not be considered highly sexual.

# NUMBER 6 FATE

Number SIX on the destiny pattern means that the general direction for the entire life is to develop an appreciation of what is to be gained by giving something up, or particularly adjusting oneself in order to operate more effectively in a partnership or team. With number SIX something always has to give and this usually means some sort of independence such as in his own individuality. This loss of individuality, or social independence, is never as important to the SIX destiny as the satisfactions that are gained by joining with others in a cooperative effort. It may, however, take them some time before they can appreciate the wisdom of this compromise.

As might be appreciated, responsibility and group consciousness are the important guides for all effective expressions of SIX. With number SIX on the destiny (and all persons to some extent naturally resist the challenge of their fate) there is invariably trouble with the institution of marriage for it is in marriage that one is most intimately aware of all the lessons of SIXNESS. In fact, it is among people with a SIX destiny that you find the most unmarried or the most frequently married or the most unhappily married. Unfortunately whether the SIX is going to function or not is directly dependent on his intimate, social involvements with others, so when his efforts don't work out, or he has to make new social contacts in trying to follow his fate, others have to suffer for his failures. And there are plenty of failures in this area of life.

The SIX destiny reflects the life style of someone who, sooner or later, whatever they are doing, will have to take time out and correct the responsibility structure in their private lives. This tends to include the majority of average, homemaking people who are trying to make a go of it working things out together because this is just what SIX symbolizes.

Morality, middle class values and all the social complexities of group communal living are involved with the SIX destiny. Any individual may resist becoming a part of this type of program, but sooner or later with a SIX destiny that is the court where his problems must be worked out. Even though the SIX destiny may themselves resist making all the social adjustments required, they are prone to advocate that others follow these moral group codes because they realize that this is what holds together the program they must eventually support. Any dislocation of traditional family life will always be strongly opposed by the SIX destiny. SIXNESS would also be a natural breeding ground for male (or female) chauvinism and I dare say such movements as anti-legalization of the abortion laws are largely pursued by those with a SIX destiny. Until we have achieved a freer structure of society where more reliance is placed on the individuality of life (such as Plato discusses in his discourse on the Republic) those who are not average are likely to be more plagued than blessed with the operations of any group morality.

# NUMBER 7 FATE

Number SEVEN on the destiny pattern means that the general direction for the entire life is to remove oneself from the general flow of experience (particularly as evidenced in strong group commitments) and seek vindication and nourishment from the strength of the "inner spirit" as opposed to the physical and material elements of daily living. This need not, however, mean that the individual finds his way by religion alone or that he ends up any the less concerned for the "totality" of life. He must, however, become a perfected specialist, preferably in some professional field where his superior wisdom clearly distinguishes him as an authority in his field above common dispute. In general this is the ideal adjustment for the SEVEN destiny although many do not quite achieve this position of protected isolation.

First of all, the SEVEN destiny is encouraged to see things quite differently from others. It is the kind of difference to which something extra has been added. This extra can best be described as a depth of spiritual insight. Since the average man is more concerned with meeting the daily demands of physical and material concerns he is not very appreciative of spiritual implications except perhaps when he runs up against some terrible tragedy in his life which he is totally unable to handle. Sometimes in fear and superstition he frequently turns to religion.

True spirituality is a quality which generally goes unrecognized and unappreciated and by its very immateriality it seems very often to be of little help in coping with our currently overly material world.

SEVEN on the destiny tends to create of one's life the role of a catalyst which is to say that the individual life pattern becomes like an open switchboard through which others make contacts not otherwise possible, but the SEVEN destiny himself does not personally become an active part of these relationships.

The life path of SEVEN is also like setting out on a trip with a particular destination in mind, but the real value and purpose of the trip does not develop until later, after the trip is underway and comes about as an off-shoot, sideline or by-product from that originally intended. In the end it makes no real difference whether the original intention in taking the trip is accomplished or not. What does prove of lasting value, however, is something that may transpire along the way which never would have come about had the trip not been taken in the first place.

To believe in the validity of going through life with one's real concentration on the potential of these sidelines or by-products requires an abundance of faith. This faith is invariably based on a personal belief that there is a thread or pattern of destiny which runs through our lives whether we are immediately aware of it or not and that eventually everything will be revealed to us and then we will understand the real meaning of each part as it fits into this total pattern.

The SEVEN destiny seems peculiarly aware of the temporal value of our immediate objectives in contrast to the patterns that are always implied in even the little things we do. With this belief in mind they try to go through life watching for these subtle and mysterious signposts which prove for them again and again that these patterns of fate are working just as they knew they were.

SEVEN, naturally, is the most immaterial of all number vibration but that is not to say that material factors are entirely missing from their lives. Indeed SEVENS are quite shrewd and they see all material matters as merely reflections of the higher spiritual values on which they place such faith.

Since SEVEN is a lonely position, signs of SEVENNESS are usually associated with signs of antisocial behavior or lack of popularity or even social rejection. The SEVEN destiny has to cope with this type of situation early in life but this encourages him to develop in other ways which is what he is here for anyway. Since the cultural heritage which one civilization passes on to another is

115

sustained largely by SEVENS (because only things of the spirit survive the ravages of time and physical deterioration) the SEVENS, if they will, can sublimate their sense of immediate isolation by joining this ungoing cultural tradition which flows on and on irrespective of the more temporal conditions of life.

# NUMBER 8 FATE

Number EIGHT on the destiny pattern means that the general direction for the entire life is directed towards some active and conscious effort to restore some degree of radical balance which this individual feels is sadly lacking in some very important area of life. In order to accomplish this adjustment effectively it is generally mandatory to attack the elements with strong force and employ some form of "shock therapy" in order to catch the ingredients off guard. Simple tactics or mild persuasion will usually not work at all because the elements out of balance have so grouped themselves as to oppose any efforts short of dynamite to move them at all. Since these areas of life in need of such correction are deemed so important to the EIGHT destiny, there is usually a power struggle involved where those of weak heart are warned from the beginning that all the resources at their command must be summoned to support their judgment. They must expect some sort of counter attack from all sides, yet they must stand invincible in the rightness of their position. This power struggle can take place in any field of human endeavor which has reached such a stage of importance that such inbalance is worthy of their correction. Naturally the EIGHT destiny tends to take most easily to those fields with which he has some familiarity and obvious talents (usually from a former life). This talent is usually indicated by the index of his Character number. The challenge of the EIGHT destiny causes the individual to be regarded as an iconoclast or breaker of false images. And naturally when you step on someone's favorite cow the followers tend to rise up to smite you down. Then a real fight begins.

The perfect weapon, however, which the EIGHT destiny has on his side, if he will only believe in it enough to bring it out in the open, IS THE ABSOLUTE TRUTH. In the face of truth, clearly spoken, the elements which the EIGHT destiny is trying to forcibly bring into balance or perspective are strangely inoperative and eventually if the EIGHT destiny is tough enough and has at his command all the power tactics of EIGHTNESS he will win the battle, but the fight may be very bloody.

The roughness of the consequences together with the full use of power techniques is what the EIGHT destiny must be fully prepared for. Since this is the life pattern from the very beginning there are usually events in the childhood which specifically train him early in life for the intense battles to come. This may start with an early struggle with parents or with the material necessities of life which are somehow denied in early childhood. In any event the individual generally emerges a stronger and tougher person who can on occasion behave in an utterly ruthless fashion. But this is good because it takes this kind of training to contest the really big issues in life.

I should mention at this time, because the demands on the EIGHT destiny are so tough, that although there might be a wide variation in the degree of success which any of us achieve, that no one is totally unable to rise in some measure to the challenge of his destiny pattern whatever it may be. No matter how impossible someone else's destiny might seem to us, that individual has within himself the capacity to come to some sort of terms with his own destiny.

# NUMBER *9* FATE

Number NINE on the destiny pattern means that the general direction for the entire life is designed to detach that individual from the more personal and intimate commitments of life and send him forth on a path that it is hoped would ultimately enrich the "totality" of human experience. NINES are fated to wander the earth so that they may come in contact with the whole spectrum of human experience. In this way they can become a little something to all people. On lower levels of consciousness this may only represent a certain social detachment and clinical objectivism. On higher levels of application these NINE destiny people can become leaders of cults, powers of political persuasion, protagonists of social movements, pioneers in areas of human compassion and instruments of mob insurrection. The fanaticism of NINE runs deeps as they seem to gather all the primal instincts of mob psychology into their control. The NINE destiny can merely wander through life relatively untouched by passionate causes, or they can suddenly be thrust to the head of a movement which seems born by necessity out of time for just such an occasion. The course of history is littered with such uprisings and movements which suddenly flare up and then fade away. Their momentum is the strength of the passion and feeling they can capsulize from the moment. But no matter what his level of involvement, the NINE destiny will always respond with enthusiasm, interest and sometimes passionate devotion to large broad problems which touch the universality of life rather than be attracted in any way to the provincialism of petty affairs.

The special quality which the NINE destiny contributes to his purpose in life is the passion and intensity of his emotions which he tends to dramatize in such a way as to sweep the opposition aside.

119

His eventual influence, however, really comes from the larger assembly which gravitates behind him as he becomes their spokesman.

The interesting thing here is that these emotional uprisings exist whether there is merit or justice or even any real justification for their appearance. Such ground swells are like wars, pestilence and famine which suddenly flare up and consume whole bodies of people for apparently no justifyable reason at all.

Perhaps what is reflected here in this NINE type of expression is the dissolving of life preparatory to creating a new formation. NINENESS always implies dramatic endings which by contrast could suggest a passionately new beginning somewhere else.

When there are no individual letter symbols in the name to support the vibration quality called for in the destiny number, that individual suffers some difficulty in coping with the challenge of his fate. It is not easy for him to recognize the necessity of his following a certain pattern of behavior or developing the desired attitude of mind which is intended to profit him the most in life. Because it is his destiny, he will repeatedly be confronted both with the opportunity to participate in certain situations as well as to achieve some degree of success in this direction. But with a karma in this number it will take him some time to appreciate the real reason behind this. Somewhat instinctively he realizes that there is some significance for him in this direction, but he tends not to make the most of such opportunities that are given to him.

I have refrained in the book from too much reference to numbers by positive or negative characteristics because all aspects are involved with the full implication and expression of that number. Negative reactions seem more to relate to those who do not appreciate a certain type of expression rather than to relate to the one expressing that vibration.

In general, it might be said that when one is missing in their name the individual number of their destiny, others who experience his actions will tend to judge such efforts negatively and this undoubtedly makes it more difficult for that individual to feel right about pushing in this direction. He is less likely to see the significance of this continual drift in his affairs until he is fully into his mature years when he may also see that he has missed some or all of his best opportunities.

A karmic condition in the destiny vibration, therefore, suggests a lifetime of regret in opportunities not taken or programs not fully developed or diminishment of personal gratification of achievement because others were stirred up so negatively.

It isn't so much that one lacks any talent in the direction of his purpose (destiny) as much as one lacks the full implication of the total meaning of that expression on its highest level of achievement. In order words, this karmic situation accounts for fools vs. wise men and ordinary mortals vs. outstanding human beings.

# Chapter VI

# THE TIMING OF POINTS
# ALONG THE PATH OF FATE

While the challenge of the destiny (total of the birthdate) represents a life long effort in one direction of accomplishment, there are sub-cycles of time which have more immediate effect on the individual's daily behavior.

The logical way to explain the cycles (which are themselves cycles working within cycles) would be to start with the largest unit of timing in the pattern of destiny (which actually has already been done in Chapter V since this is the Fate Number) and work down to the next largest unit and so on down to the vibratory demands of a single day. But this method, however logical, is the most difficult and confusing for students to understand so I am going to start at the other end, which the DAILY VIBRATION, and work up.

## THE DAILY VIBRATION

What each day means to you personally is symbolized by the number which is derived by PERSONALIZING THAT DAY'S DATE. By various formulas (which I will explain in detail as we go along) we reduce any date to a number vibration which is PERSONALIZED TO OUR OWN DESTINY, What this number represents is THE DESIRED ATTITUDE OF MIND WHICH WE

SHOULD APPLY AGAINST ALL SIGNIFICANT MATTERS
WHICH CONFRONT US ON THAT DAY.

For example:

On a ONE day we should push to get things started.

On a TWO day we should hold back, wait, watch, observe and gather materials.

On a THREE day we should relax, use our imagination and express our views and opinions.

On a FOUR day we should hold fast, word hard, face facts and prepare a sound foundation.

On a FIVE day we should initiate changes, seek a new solution and prepare to compete or defend our position if necessary.

On a SIX day we should socialize, be friendly, accept responsibilities and fulfill our obligations.

On a SEVEN day we should get off by ourselves, take inventory, be philosophical and maintain our faith.

On a EIGHT day we should toughen up, restore balance whenever we sense it out of line, make decisions, recognize value and practice justice (which may mean jerking the rug out from under someone's unfounded position).

On a NINE day we should tie up loose ends, finish old jobs, let go, broaden out, forgive and forget.

To personalize any date we must first personalize the year itself. The personal year is what that particular year means to us in the sequence of each 9 years. TO PERSONALIZE YOUR YEAR ADD THE DIGIT OF YOUR MONTH AND DAY OF BIRTH TO THE YEAR IN QUESTION. For example, if you were born on 8-2 (August Second) you add this to 1973 and the total comes out a THREE. This means that for you, to every month and day in 1973 instead of using the TWO (which is the actual digit total of 1973) you would use your personalized number which is THREE. If the day in question is 11-22-1973, for you this reduces to 2-4-3 which reduces to NINE.

## THE MONTHLY VIBRATION

The days of the month all follow each other in the natural sequence of their number vibrations (whatever they may be for each of us). However the month itself may not begin on a ONE day or end on a NINE day.

The more immediate demands which confront us on a daily basis take their broader character from the personal vibration tone of the month. Again, to personalize each month to our own destiny we ADD THE DIGIT OF THE MONTH TO OUR PERSONALIZED YEAR (which in our example we already calculated that 1973 for us was a THREE year). So January is a FOUR month, February a FIVE month, and so on.

The challenge of each month is much the same as that for each day only on a broader scale, but also at this point the vibration of the month is qualifying the vibration of the day.

For example:

On a ONE DAY of a FOUR month we would start (1) to get organized (4).

On a TWO DAY of a FIVE MONTH we would patiently observe (2) the way in which we might take advantage of new methods (5) when the time was ripe (2).

On a THREE DAY of a SIX MONTH we would freely express our opinion (3) on group matters (6) or openly criticize (3) some domestic situation (6).

On a FOUR DAY of a SEVEN MONTH we would organize our facts (4) concerning our private reactions (7) or accept the truth (4) about some matter connected with our inner motivations (7).

On a FIVE DAY of a EIGHT MONTH we would initiate changes (5) in the area of some important judgment (8) which confronted us, or we might seek to gain some advantage (5) over factors which controlled our financial well-being (8).

On a SIX DAY of a NINE MONTH we would socialize (6) with others on some matter of broad interest (9), or we might get out and make contacts (6) in connection with some political movement (9).

On a SEVEN DAY of a ONE MONTH we would refine (7) our position with respect to some new project (1) we might be pushing, or we might carefully analyze (7) how we could become more self-reliant (1) on innovative matters (1).

On a EIGHT DAY of a TWO month we might take a more judicial attitude (8) towards our behavior in the direction of tactful diplomacy (2) or we might cash in (8) on some raw material we had been holding (2) but which we now judge (8) will not be needed.

On a NINE DAY of a THREE MONTH we might be philosophical (9) about some of our creative efforts (3) or we might finally give up or conclude (9) some form of relaxation (3) we had been enjoying.

When we examined the attitudes called for on a daily basis (independently on any larger cycle of time) we were not concerned with the exact sequence of happenings except to note that the days followed each other in their natural sequence and that months did not necessarily begin on ONE or end on NINE.

When we consider the next larger cycle above the individual day (namely the month) something else about TIMING begins to make its appearance.

First of all, the vibration quality of the months merge with each other. By this I mean that as June begins it is at first to some degree under the influence of May which went before. Since May is (let us assume here the actual vibration) a FIVE and June is a SIX the merged portion of June (which is that portion of June still effected by May) is the combination of both or FIVE PLUS SIX or a sub-tone of TWO. A certain portion of June, therefore, is not straight SIX but a quasi TWO.

Next there is an operational law about number vibrations when applied to cycles of time which states that the quality of a number to be expressed must wait until the sub-vibration is a ONE for beginnings or a FIVE for change (if someone failed to get effectively started in the right direction on the ONE time). Very often when there is no sufficient momentum for something to really get going when the sub-time is ONE it has to build up until the sub-time is FIVE to make the break and finally get moving. The vibration quality for the month should become more apparent when the day of the month is a ONE or a FIVE. Once however the quality has made its beginning, from then on it gathers momentum in the direction of the vibration, whatever it may be.

Referring back to this merging of the tone of one month with the tone of the next — the approximate timing on this is that the first two thirds of the month are under the sub-tone and only the last third is in the pure quality of the month itself. This is approximate depending on when the first ONE day comes up on or around the 20th of the month. This ONE day would be the significator for the beginning of the emergence of the pure vibration of the month.

In the examples I used FIVE for May and SIX for June with a sub-tone of TWO, but you should, of course, use your own personalized month vibrations when figuring out your own timing. If May in your case was a THREE month and June was a FOUR month, then the sub-tone would be SEVEN for approximately the first two thirds of June. With June as a FOUR month then the 15th of June would be a ONE day and start the emergence of the pure FOUR quality of June out from under the sub-tone of the SEVEN.

## THE PERSONAL YEAR

The challenge of the monthly vibrations (which are broader and qualifying to the daily vibrations) are themselves modified and controlled by the personal vibration of the year. As already explained, we personalize the yearly vibration by adding the digit of our month and day of birth to the digit of the year in question. Example, if you were born on 3-17 (March 17th) and the year you were interested in was 1938 for you 1938 would have been a 3-8-3 or a FIVE personal year.

Because September is the ninth month the essence of each year falls in approximately the last third of September. But in your affairs this may not necessarily be the most significant time of the year.

Referring to our LAW OF BEGINNIGS, where the quality has to BEGIN on ONE or sharply step up their tone on a FIVE . . .

ONE YEARS begin in September (the ONE month)
TWO YEARS begin in August (the ONE month)
THREE YEARS begin in July (the ONE month)
FOUR YEARS begin in June (the ONE month)
FIVE YEARS begin in May (the ONE month)
SIX YEARS begin in April (the ONE month)
SEVEN YEARS begin in March (the ONE month)
EIGHT YEARS begin in February (the ONE month)
NINE YEARS begin in January (the ONE month)

An interesting point is the pattern of November which in itself is an ELEVEN month. In numbers anything coupled to ELEVEN brings emotional tension and in this case a double accent on the vibration quality of the year. Example, if the year is for you a FIVE year, the month of November becomes an "11-5" pattern (which we write as 11-5/7). Many Number Analysts consider this period (of the FIVE year) even more significant than just the FIVE of September. Perhaps I should mention here, since other writers have attached too much importance to it, that in combining number vibrations and coupling numbers to TEN, ELEVEN or TWENTY TWO you can hold these numbers as accents against the number you are coupling with it and this, it is said, creates a valid sub-pattern. Example: the FIVE when so coupled would have patterns of 10-5/6, 11-5/7 or 22-5/9. (There is no TWENTY TWO month but you will be coupling numbers with TWENTY TWO when you get into the larger cycles of timing.) The rule here about these sub-patterns is NOT TO MELD THE NUMBER BUT HOLD IT "IN ACCENT WITH THE 10, 11 or 22.

Personally, although I myself made a big issue over this when I wrote my book NUMEROLOGY AND YOU (published in paperback 1961), I have since decided that it is more fruitful to reduce all numbers to their primary digits and then one is more likely to get to the heart of the matter. There is enough vital information in the basic numbers themselves without getting all tied up with the sub-qualities. But if it triggers some reaction in the reader which he doesn't get without it, then by all means USE IT. For most students, however, it is only confusing and particularly so in the beginning.

Somewhat in this same context, many people in number analysis place great importance on double numbers (before they are reduced to a single digit). For example, "C" is the 3rd letter of our alphabet, "L" is the 12th letter and "U" is the 21st letter. Some people find merit in thinking of "L" as "12" rather than reducing it to THREE and "U" as "21" rather than THREE. I, however, believe that these differences between the three different THREES is more adequately indicated as I outlined in Chapter I where I pointed out that letters "A" through "I" symbolize physical manifestations of that quality and letters "J" through "R" symbolize mental manifestations of that quality and letters "S" through "Z" symbolize spiritual manifestations of that quality.

\*      \*      \*

The vibration quality of individual years is influenced by the vibration quality of the previous year just as months are influenced, only not in the two thirds, one third ratio. As seen in the previous listing of the ONE month when each year starts, when the quality of the year gets started this varies from ONE years which start in September to NINE years which have a quasi start in January.

The early portion of the year (which varies from one month to as long as nine months) is under the sub-tone which is derived by adding the number vibration of the previous year to that of the current year. Example, if the vibration of the current year is SEVEN and the SEVEN quality starts to make its appearance in your affairs in the ONE month of March, the period of January through February would be under a sub-tone of the previous year (SIX plus the SEVEN of the current year or a tempo of FOUR).

The sub-tone of a ONE YEAR is a quasi ONE (9 + 1) which means the necessity for looking forward but still hampered by some conditions of the past which are still influential. Whatever was not effectively eliminated in the NINE year must really be thrown out in the first nine months of the ONE year. The sub-tone lasts from January through August (and even a little longer because of the merging of the months; it continues right up to September 18th which is the ONE day closest to the last third of the month).

The sub-tone of a TWO YEAR is a THREE (which amounts to a period of relaxation before the tensions and revelations of the TWO year get started). The sub-tone lasts from January through July (in fact up to August 18th).

The sub-tone of a THREE YEAR is a FIVE (which amounts to an apprehension of impending change before the freedom for the creativity of THREE is available). The sub-tone lasts from January through June (in fact up to July 18th).

The sub-tone of a FOUR YEAR is a SEVEN (which amounts to an introspective period prior to getting down to the real work effort of FOUR). The sub-tone lasts from January through May (in fact up to June 18th).

The sub-tone of a FIVE YEAR is a NINE (which amounts to a broadening of perspective with a view toward releasing certain elements of the immediate past which really aren't working out before the increase of tempo and opportunism of FIVE gets going). The sub-tone lasts from January through April (in fact up to May 18th).

The sub-tone of a SIX YEAR is a TWO (which is time out for observation of pertinent details and gathering nourishment for the social commitments and domestic responsibilities of the SIX year. The sub-tone lasts from January through March (in fact up to April 18th).

The sub-tone of a SEVEN YEAR is a FOUR (which is a period of discipline and facing facts before the personal inventory of SEVEN takes over). The sub-tone lasts from January through February (in fact up to March 18th).

The sub-tone of a EIGHT YEAR is a SIX (which is a period for discharging one's personal obligations before assuming the perogatives of judicial administration under the EIGHT). The sub-tone lasts during January and up to February 18th.

The sub-tone of a NINE YEAR is a EIGHT (which is a carry over of judgments made in the EIGHT year but which have to wait until the NINE year to finally be put into full effect. The actual execution of the important judgment resolved in the previous year sets off the endings which take place in the NINE year as an entire cycle of operations comes to a close. The sub-tone (while not following the same general pattern of the previous years) tends to hang over the NINE year from January through September (in fact right up to October 18th). The quality of the NINE year which starts to emerge in October (in a new way) tends to bring a more philosophical realization of the finality of the endings inherent in a long chain of experience.

\*     \*     \*

One final comment I would like to make about the number demands of timing (by personalizing the date to our own destiny) is the broader or NON-PERSONALIZED impact of this same timing. We call the actual number vibration of the date itself THE UNIVERSAL VIBRATION. In other words, the date of July 4th, 1776 (7-4-3) reduced has a total vibration of FIVE. We say that the world in general is responding to the demands of that day in a FIVE fashion. Your own vibration for the day may be the same or it may be some other number. If it is the same we say that YOU VIBRATE ON THE UNIVERSAL. Everyone whose month and day of birth add to NINE are on the universal. Example, January 8, 17 and 26.

February 7, 16 and 25. March 6, 15 and 24. April 5, 14 and 23. May 4, 13 and 22. June 3, 12, 21 and 30. July 2, 11, 20 and 29. August 1, 10, 19 and 28. September 9, 18 and 27. October 8, 17 and 26. November 7, 16 and 25. December 6, 15 and 24.

Those individuals whose personal vibrations are on the universal are more in tune with the broader trend of events going on around them than are those who are not on the universal. This may be said to have its advantages and its disadvantages. Anything that happens in the world around you (included distant and foreign affairs) in some way affects your life (although not necessarily directly, but perhaps your stream of consciousness). Others may appear to get more excited over certain events and even be themselves involved in them but these events will affect you in a deeper, more lasting way. When you feel out of sorts and it is a bad day in your affairs, one of the disadvantages of being on the universal is that it seems to multiply your troubles and resentments. Example, if the period is a FIVE for you someone during the day usually contests your position or gives you a fight or argument over some matter. If you are on the universal you are aware of other fights going on around you as though, sometimes it would seem everybody was fighting with one another on that day over something.

Referring again to the special qualities of November (with its vibration of ELEVEN) with application to the universal, many important events seem to happen in the world (and even in our own affairs — like personal tragedy) when the ELEVEN is somehow prominent. Many famous people seem to be born in November or on an ELEVEN day or in an ELEVEN year. Many famous (or infamous) dates in history also have ELEVEN pivotal in their vibration. The late President John F. Kennedy was assassinated on November 22nd, 1963 which was an 11-22-10 date or as you will note a combination of all three of the power accents of 10, 11 and 22. The date reduced to SEVEN (which was also President Kennedy's own Destiny number). In my mind the significance of that SEVEN indicates the widespread and irrevocable patterns of Fate itself; first where Kennedy himself with a destiny of SEVEN was called upon to act the role of Fate's agent or messenger and secondly, it points to the real significance of that day as a point of time from which many things will be dated as having started to come about because of his death which made them possible. Just how many changes in historical trends will date from that time has yet to be fully appreciated. As you see in this interesting and tragic date, sometimes you have to hold these accent patterns to clearly see the interesting phenomenon which is activated at these times, particularly with regard to the number ELEVEN.

## THE FOUR MAJOR PINNACLES OF TIMING

Perhaps I should reassure you at this point that for those who may feel that TIMING is getting too complicated to understand, although there are many more factors yet to consider, many of you can become quite psychic in forecasting with numbers by just using these three units of timing (personal days, months and years) and leave the rest for later.

Of far greater importance, but with less immediate effect on one's daily problems, are the four MAJOR PINNACLES OF TIMING, for these, when compared to the destiny number reveal at a glance the over-all course of one's life and particularly in what years the best part of one's life is likely to fall. This is covered in greater detail in Chapter IX.

First let me explain that each destiny pattern is set out in its entirety, which is not to assume that each pattern (or individual) lives out the completion of its program. People enter this life on the stroke of their destiny. It is this exact birthdate that identifies their fate. But physical death in the philosophy of number analysis (as it is in other occult structures of thought) is not an absolute termination but is regarded as a transition of the spirit. Therefore, an individual may die and pass out of the picture at any point of time (even immediately after birth) which breaks or ends that particular destiny pattern. This is a termination of life, but it is only the end of one experience and not the termination of the spirit which is considered to be eternal. Who knows in what shape or form this spirit lives on. And who knows — really — what life experience preceded this one and what life experiences will follow. Perhaps no person has such knowledge, but I, for one, sincerely believe that what is intended for us to follow (even on a day to day basis as I have already explained) is revealed to us through the mystic symbolism of the number vibrations in our date of birth. What we bring with us to handle this challenge is revealed to us in the mystic symbolism of our name label.

Assuming the theoretical life span of the individual (and this is just a round figure) to be about 90 years, we find that in terms of TIMING THE DESTINY there are THREE DOMINANT NUMBER PATTERNS controlling this timing and that each lasts approximately 30 years.

Before I get into a discussion of these three dominant number patterns which comprise more than just the DESIRED ATTITUDES OF MIND (that I have already been developing), I want to continue with these attitude patterns and advance them one more step in time above the cycles of one's personal years (which in themselves comprise cycles of a ONE year running through a NINE year followed by a new ONE year, etc.)

I will use the term PINNACLES here meaning the highest or culminating point to identify these dominant attitudes of mind which absolutely control and time all the sub-cycles of timing which are operating during their respective periods (namely: the personal years, their component months, the individual days and the various sub-tone relationships between them).

Let me first explain the time duration of these pinnacles.

The duration of the FIRST PINNACLE runs from the moment of birth to the birthday of the year when the individual has reached the age of 36 minus the destiny number. For example, for one whose destiny number is FOUR the time span on the first pinnacle is from zero to age 32. For one whose destiny number is EIGHT the time span on the first pinnacle is from zero to age 28(36 minus 8).

The duration of the SECOND PINNACLE is the 9 years immediately following.

The duration of the THIRD PINNACLE is the 9 years immediately following that.

The duration of the FOURTH PINNACLE is for the rest of the natural life span.

At first glance it would seem that I have departed from what I mentioned as the division of the destiny into three major cycles of approximately 30 years each, but this I will explain later after we introduce another factor into the TIMING PATTERN other than the one I have been detailing up to now, which was OUR DESIRED ATTITUDE OF MIND.

The numbers which symbolize each of the four pinnacles are derived from the date of birth as follows:

133

FIRST PINNACLE: Add the digit of the month to the digit of the day.

SECOND PINNACLE: Add the digit of the day to the digit of the year.

THIRD PINNACLE: Add the number of the first pinnacle to the number of the second pinnacle.

FOURTH PINNACLE: Add the digit of the month to the digit of the year.

Example: for a person born on April 14, 1916 (4-5-8) the destiny number is EIGHT.

The FIRST PINNACLE is NINE 9 (4 plus 5)

The SECOND PINNACLE is FOUR (5 plus 8)

The THIRD PINNACLE is also FOUR (9 plus 4)

The FOURTH PINNACLE is THREE (4 plus 8)

The pinnacles and their duration for the above example would be as follows:

Years 0 to 28 under pinnacle NINE

Years 29 to 37 under pinnacle FOUR

Yesrs 38 to 46 under pinnacle FOUR

Years 47 for rest of life under pinnacle THREE.

Always remember that as you reach your 28th birthday, starting on the day after is when you actually enter your 29th year. One is apt to overlook this when figuring the effective time of these pinnacles as some people confuse being a full 29 with being in their 29th year.

Whereas in explaining the refinements of timing in relation to the destiny (which is an over-all life time orientation) I began with the more immediate effect (that of the individual, personalized day) and worked up through the personal month vibration and the personal year cycles and now to pinnacles, in evaluating or judging the life-chart at a glance as I intimated earlier, one must essentially deal with only the largest patterns of time. The rest must fall into line according to the "total" pattern. The principles of evaluative judgment (which are the most important parts of number analysis) will have to be deferred until Part III which comes after we have set forth all the complexities of timing.

# THE THREE MAJOR CYCLES OF LIFE

The four major pinnacles (still denoting desired attitudes of mind) become the THREE MAJOR CYCLES OF LIFE by the introduction of another element in the timing pattern. This is the number which symbolizes THE TYPE OF MATERIAL against which these respective attitudes of mind are to be applied. Their derivation is quite simple. They are the three digit numbers of the month, day and year of the birthdate. Example, let us take the birthdate of September 16, 1934. Reduced this is 9-7-8 which is a SIX destiny. The four pinnacles are SEVEN (9 plus 7), SIX (7 plus 8), FOUR (7 plus 6) and EIGHT (9 plus 8). The duration of the pinnacles is 0-30, 31-39, 40-48, 49 to end of life.

The three major cycles of life derive from the month, day and year. These are developed as follows and again using the example above:

The duration of the FIRST CYCLE is always the same duration as the FIRST PINNACLE which in this case is 30 years. The pattern of the first cycle is then running from birth to age 30 and represents the application of a SEVEN attitude (the first pinnacle) to be applied against NINE type material (the number of the month of birth).

The duration of the SECOND CYCLE is always (for everyone regardless of their fate number) 36 years or three cycles of 9 years each, all of which attitudes will be applied against the material type of the day of birth. Using the above example this would mean that from age 31 to age 39 (the duration of the second pinnacle) the application is of a SIX attitude (the second pinnacle) against SEVEN type material (the number of the day of birth). This is followed by another 9 years from age 40 to age 48 with the application of a FOUR attitude (the third pinnacle) also against SEVEN type material and followed by another 9 years from age 49 to age 57 of a EIGHT attitude (the fourth and final pinnacle) also against SEVEN type material.

The duration of the THIRD CYCLE would in the above example run from age 58 for the rest of the life span and it would be a EIGHT attitude (again the final fourth pinnacle) against EIGHT type material (the number of the birth year).

The calculation of this could be shown graphically as follows: This is also the way a professional number analyst might quickly set up the whole time pattern of the destiny.

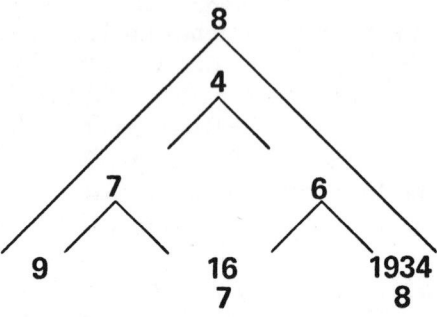

"Desired attitudes of mind" seems easier for people to grasp than the application of number qualities to "types of material". And applying the attitude to the material seems even more confusing. So if it bothers you, at first, then just forget about the type of material that fate provides and just stick to attitudes of mind and your environment (or fate) will automatically supply the type of material your destiny calls for. At least you won't have to worry about that. But if you would like to know in advance what type of material to expect and whether you are going to make it or not then you will have to let your mind play around with these combinations and number patterns.

ONE TYPE MATERIAL would be original, challenging, something lending itself or needing to be discovered, invented or liberated. It is likely to be spirited, unique, offer some resistance to easy domination, require a certain amount of courage and determination on the part of someone trying to handle or manipulate it. It is also likely to be composed largely (in terms of people) of men or highly masculinized types. It would not be material of complex composition but such as would lend itself to single units, easily identifiable as self-contained, simple, individual components which would also tend to stand out as something commanding or demanding attention or service. Initially it might appear as unmanageable or unlikely to be easily led, molded or adapted. In fact as material it may always maintain a certain independence which defies all attitudes of control which may be applied against it.

136

TWO TYPE MATERIAL would be inspirational, helpful, sympathetic, understanding, sensitive, diplomatic, tactful, rhythmic and timely. It would above all be sensitive to the needs of the immediate situation. As raw material it could, if properly handled, have all the ingredients of a profound REVELATION. Also its effect (when presented in just the right way at the right moment) could prove catastrophic to some persons, but a substantial boost to others. At first glance this TWO material could seem a harmless assemblage of infinite details and minute particles, but it could symbolize the heartbeat of reality and the potentiality of a SENSATION. As material it would not stand on its own or dictate its final format or eventual presentation. To get to the heart of the matter would take a sensitive probe from an inspired hand who "felt" an intuitive rapport; otherwise, the outcome would be likely to remain just an accumulation of fragmented parts.

THREE TYPE MATERIAL is likely to be colorful, decorative, artistic, spontaneous and capable of lifting the spirits to the point of enthusiasm and optimistic vision. Unlike TWO type material, which may seem totally unrelated, THREE type material on its own will seem to synthesize itself so as to suggest to the beholder a picture or pattern by which it may be further developed. In other words, part of the pattern process has already begun to take shape, which suggests any number of possibilities or directions for further development. As material it should not be demanding and insistent, but rather lying there available if and when the individual feels like experimenting with its development. There would be a marked absence of serious content or harsh facts, or practical demands for ulterior uses. The material should, on the whole, be just what it seems to be as of that moment — a window dressing or embellishment or artistic creation which gives pleasure without concern for what went before or what may come after. It should be something which can be enjoyed and in turn give pleasure and satisfaction by just being attractive. To be fully appreciated would suggest that it requires a certain freedom or leisure associated with relaxation or the frivolity of care free youth.

FOUR TYPE MATERIAL would be hard core reality in the full material sense. It should consist of facts, unvarnished elements of truth, pressing demands of priority, basic constituents of material necessity, appeal to common sense and cold, unsentimental logic.

137

The primary character should be essential foundations which make other things possible. The magnitude of the facts so assembled may by some standards seem overwhelming but not to those who have the capacity and strength to cope with the harsh conditions required to set the matter straight. Privation, duty, endurance, discipline and endless physical effort will seem obviously related in some way to handling this form of material.

FIVE TYPE MATERIAL would be fast moving, provocative, sensory oriented, flashy, exploitable, innovative, daring, unmoralistic, changeable, unconventionally new and probably overly exaggerated and even a little risque. This material would seem to have more to do with an ASPECT of life rather than to the SUBSTANCE. It might also represent what people would desire, if it were properly advertised and promoted, but it would have little connection with what they might really need. FIVE type material would suggest a game or competition for just the "spirit" of the thing rather than the importance or value of the undertaking. There could be a certain sexual suggestiveness or merely heightened physical participation. It is bound to keep people on the run or get them all stirred up or excited where they might puzzle later as to why they gave it such importance at the time. There is a definite potential for excitement or promotion of factors which create excitement. All FIVE type material suggests a lack of restraint, a breakdown of accumulated attitudes, a loosening of established standards and the possibility of setting up new goals which seem enticingly desirable at the time. The quality of FIVE is always pivotal, so exploitation of this type of material presents alternative choices where previously there may have been only one possibility. The endless variety which suddenly seems possible is likely to carry people away with the thrilling possibilities and excitement.

SIX TYPE MATERIAL would be material which strongly suggests the inter-relatedness of ties by which one factor is dependent upon another because of the "family" of relationships involved. There is an obvious lack of freedom to pursue matters on one's own for personal gratifications. It is the good of the whole or the abundance for the majority which has to be considered here. There is a grouping together of common demands in order to hold the fabric together. Morality and moral issues and particularly what we call middle-class virtues are all highly interwoven with any SIX type material. There is a social necessity which transcends personal preferences. Recognition of these responsible connections with viable group affiliations brings about a lessening of individuality in favor of "going along with the crowd". Protection and banding together to preserve the principles which are the contribution of many sources are mandatory to the requirements of the moment. The independence of any single position must give way to the pattern of group loyalities. Getting along as a team or community is the compelling factor in all SIX commitments.

SEVEN TYPE MATERIAL is something which is rare, specialized, highly refined, mysterious, mystical and hints of something spiritual or beyond the ordinary five physical senses. It's presence is suggested rather than real; it is felt emotionally rather than known rationally. The appeal here is to that which could be ideal rather than to what has to be put up with because of its expediency or practicality in the past. SEVEN material is never obvious and frequently comes to notice as a byproduct, side issue or offshoot from something else. It is also likely to be passed over by those more intent on direct practical objectives. In fact, those who find it seem to be led to its discovery by fortuitous circumstances rather than by direct design or planned purpose. Awareness of its real value or hidden potential is something which grows on the individual as he delves deeper and deeper into its hidden possibilities. To those not attuned to this wave length the material may even seem odd, peculiar and without popular appeal or merit. The public as a whole may take slowly to its acceptance, although they may be strangely aware of some significance which they are unable to explain or account for. Illusiveness and immateriality are part of its quality as well as cultured perfection and rare uniqueness. Such as it is, it is apt to be one of a kind rather than something which in any way can be easily duplicated or commonly found.

EIGHT TYPE MATERIAL suggests the character of big business, the politics of power manipulations, financial expansion, master plans conceived on a grand scale which affect many people on important matters. At the heart of this material there is apt to be a powerful grouping of strong elements which if not properly kept in perfect balance can blow up in such a fashion as to cause great public upheaval. The type of treatment demanded by this kind of material calls for superior talents above and beyond the requirements of ordinary leadership. Administrative control at its highest level of complex direction is mandatory in order to keep this vast mechanism operating efficiently without a catastrophic breakdown. In order to face this type of material at all one must be fully prepared emotionally and intellectually for all the resistance that will be met on every level to control and direct this gigantic complex. The higher one goes, or the more powerful example of EIGHT material that one encounters, the greater the demands for the cold blooded, ruthless projection of one's purpose. Inherent in facing this material is the function of judgment and in executing these judgments one is faced with the displeased wrath of those who are judged against; therefore, one must stick to their guns and weather the storm no matter what the emotional consequences may be.

NINE TYPE MATERIAL is the very substance of humanity and as such embraces all activity which mankind practices on a large scale. Universality is always a factor here as opposed to any form of narrow provincialism which fosters the needs of a specialized few at the expense of the masses. However, this universality need not be obviously on the surface, but must be inherent in the emotional pattern of the masses which need only the proper spokesman or saviour to bring it forth. Thus new and radical movements may spring up overnight, but only because a common spark has been touched off which lies dormant in the aspirations of many. NINE material is a mass movement, whatever the slogan or rally-point around which such movement takes off. The demand from the instigators is some degree of selfless service or humanitarian dedication, whether sincere or misguided. The appeal is to a primal instinct, which lies at the heart of all masses, even though their avowed goal is generally destructive or hopelessly idealistic. It is the feeling which each can share in common which must be exploited at the same time as the differences which separate its members must be put down. In order to handle or face up to NINE material a certain clinical objectivity and dispassionate vision is mandatory. As might be suspected, NINE type material is the stuff from which great art works may be produced.

## APPLYING ATTITUDES OF MIND
## AGAINST TYPES OF MATERIAL

THE ONE ATTITUDE would strive for leadership, direction and some form of original contribution. The position here is anything but that of just another follower; it is that of one who must provide spirit, push, pioneering effort, conviction, aggressive determination and who must be in some form of original contribution. The position here is anything but that of just another follower; it is that of one who must provide spirit, push, pioneering effort, conviction, aggressive determination and who must in some form be among the front runners and early champions of this matter.

THE TWO ATTITUDE represents one who stands back and provides nourishment and material for whatever is being fashioned. The function of tactful diplomacy, the instrumenting of delicate compromises, laying the groundwork for sensitive harmony, extolling the value of proper timing and the careful observance of relevant details, would all apply to the TWO attitude no matter against what application. Sometimes it may only require a gentle understanding, a helping hand or a simple sacrifice or possibly a more complex martyrdom so others may pass over a bridge of recognition thanks to you.

THE THREE ATTITUDE gives articulation and outspoken criticism to what may be involved. The purpose here is to synthesize matters in such a way that a "clear picture" is presented so others may "see" or get the message. There may be some embellishment, ornamentation, dressing up or artistic flourish necessary to enhance the "effect" or provide a "setting" or background for the action to take place. The need here is to communicate, broadcast or publish what is inherent in the material confronted. Advertising, promotion or describing in writing is needed to bring the matter to the attention of an audience that this material requires and deserves. The function of the applicator here is to express, proclaim or articulate something which is now become necessary in order to sell, distribute or display the material.

THE FOUR ATTITUDE lends physical effort and material support to dig up the facts and organize the basic truths necessary to build a foundation under the project. What is required here is a willing worker who will subject himself to discipline, privation (if necessary), routine and economy in order to PROVE what others may fail to acknowledge. The function of the applicator under FOUR is to build a solid foundation under the matter.

THE FIVE ATTITUDE is to improvise and seek a new, improved solution as to how to gain the ends one has in mind. The old established way will no longer work for what is needed now. There must be courage to break away and blaze a new path even though this may upset the more conventional or incur the resistance of the established groups in power. The old track record must be broken. One must outdo one's self in active competition or exploitative bally-hoo in order to outsell or outdistance the established market. One must speed things up, seek sudden advantages, be opportunistic, introduce sexuality into the campaign and beat your opponents at their own game. Take chances, play the long shoots and regard all things speculatively. If necessary tell yourself you are going along just for the adventure, excitement and thrills. The function of the applicator under FIVE is to make a break with the old pattern and try a new angle regardless of how this may upset some people.

THE SIX ATTITUDE is naturally a good deal more conventional as it endeavors to teach, instruct and educate rather than to take over (as in ONE), emotionalize (as in TWO), express creativity (as in THREE), organize (as in FOUR) , or effect changes (as in FIVE). The SIX attitude is to salvage and protect what the group wants rather than to foster individual viewpoints or considerations. There is also a desire to "spread" this formula around rather than to concentrate it in the hands of a few, no matter how well qualified. Expression of the SIX attitude calls for personal adjustment in the party expressing SIX in favor of influencing others over to your way of thinking because it tends to be morally right. Morality and group responsibility are always inherent in all SIX type matters and on the attitude requires moral rectitude of the person himself. The function of the SIX applicator is to moralize and codify the matter in such a way that it creates the most abundance for the family type relationships.

THE SEVEN ATTITUDE is again an individual position, only this time it is felt or considered to be aligned with forces outside and above the individual so that he feels a "spiritual" vindication behind him. He may even consider that fate or destiny itself supports him in this matter and very often he himself is only the agent for the

142

transmission of this program. To implement the SEVEN attitude effectively one should withdraw from the common scene so that he may develop and perfect some specialized viewpoint or technique. When needed he must be able to step forth as some form of authority where his word and experience will be beyond dispute. It may be contested or even ignored by those in control but there is some satisfaction in knowing that those who are indeed qualified to judge his position acknowledge him to be right. This may not result in enough popular support to change the tide but it may, in time, contribute substantially to a solution which would otherwise never have been possible. The SEVEN attitude is essentially shrewd and should be closely guarded. Under SEVEN one should never openly lay all their cards on the table. This would defeat the very advantage that SEVEN has by working from behind, pulling strings of influence which in turn control the more obvious factors. When in doubt silence would always be the best policy here. The function of the seven applicator is to exhibit that degree of faith and spiritual support necessary to bolster some situation which otherwise might be unsupportable.

THE EIGHT ATTITUDE is an all out fight with the forces in control so as to jerk them back into balance. Naturally this promises to meet with all kinds of opposition and resistance, because this realignment will probably cost the opposition a considerable investment in the position they now hold. Shock tactics are always a handy tool in these matters for they catch the opposition off guard and so gain an advantage which, however, must soon be followed up by even stronger tactics. One is seldom able to back down effectively, so it is best to be well grounded and thoroughly supported intellectually from the beginning. Sometimes, however, it may be necessary to admit a major error in judgment; but this must be followed through in the interest of justice no matter what it may cost the individual in loss of face. Very often, in the end, a stronger character emerges which others will recognize, but it takes a great deal of "guts" to admit these mistakes at the time. This is part of the price for playing with power politics for such high stakes. The function of the EIGHT applicator is to adjudicate and lower the boom on situations sadly in need of drastic correction.

THE NINE ATTITUDE is essentially dramatic as it appeals to the emotional substrata underlying the cause of movement which

143

captures the attention as the individual attempts in some way to develop as a spokesman or mouthpiece. There can also be a marked falling away of direct interest as the individual lets go from his more personal concerns and moves out in a wider circle of interest. Initially, perhaps, there is a tendency to drift with the tide until such moment as may arise when a more personal dedication is indicated. Sometimes this drifting, wandering and travel can extend indefinitely. But even so the individual gains a wide, broad perspective and sense of the "totality" of life which would never have been possible as long as he was tied to more personal issues. The actual propulsion to spokesman for the crowd (or cause) may come to only a few, but the individual always holds himself in possible readiness should such occasion arise. Actually he may tell himself he doesn't want it (which may be true), but he remains very much alive to all the natural drama inherent in all broad comprehensive issues. NINE has much to do with the "sweep of history" and the "tide of human events" in its widest perspective. The function of the NINE applicator is to lend depth, tolerance and compassionate understanding to this wider perspective.

# PART 3
## *JUDGMENT*
## *THE PERSPECTIVE OF THE WHOLE*

### *Chapter VII*
### *EVALUATING THE 81 CHARACTER PATTERNS WITH EXAMPLES OF FAMOUS PERSONALITIES*

First, in attempting to evaluate the chart as a whole one should study the number patterns which comprise the individual himself. The major indices of this, of course, are the Character, the Personality, and the Motivation.

The Character quality is dominant but substantially modified by the other two conscious points of interest, namely the Personality and the Motivation, so as you study each group, and particularly the example names of famous people in this pattern, always keep in mind that they are what the number of their character dictates, and the motivation and personality are qualifications.

While we work with only the 9 primary number vibrations which symbolize 9 Character types, there are 9 variations of each Character type as we consider each number vibration in turn on the Motivation and corresponding Personality. Thus we have altogether 81 Character patterns rather than just 9.

# THE 9 VARIATIONS OF THE ONE CHARACTER

ONE is the most individualized of all number vibrations. It is also the most self-centered, daring, original, spirited, determined, aggressive and dominating. Ego drive is its self-motivating force. To be themselves they must naturally consider what is best for them and let the rest of the picture fall in accordingly. Anything that detracts from this singleness of purpose lessens the ideal effectiveness of ONE.

Remember that all of these individual ONES may differ from the other ONES that follow by the qualification and modification of their respective motivation drive and personality image. Also, of course, each one may be challenged by a different fate pattern which we will take up in Chapter VIII.

# *1—9—1*

The 1-9-1 pattern has ONE on the motivation, NINE on the personality and ONE on the character. This is an exceptionally strong pattern. The inner motivation intensifies the character giving added range to the objectives to which the individual will dedicate himself with integrity, drive and spirit. The personality is not only comprehensive but tones down the harsher impact of the strong inner resolve which this individual has. Since all ONES are self-centered, egotistical (and therefore necessarily selfish), this pattern is even more so because it is the conscious motivation to constantly push in this same direction. Ego identity is the all driving force here. This is obviously a pattern more suitable for men than women. While current movements such as Women's Liberation groups are demanding that society equally accept women in all roles (patterns), which is a social ideal, highly commendable and one which I heartily endorse, it is nevertheless a biological fact of nature that men are so constituted as to be generally more suitable in this role than women. If individual women find that fate has thrust them in this traditionally masculine pattern, then we should acknowledge that individuals's right to be themselves as fate intended even though this may offend some people. The fact that it does offend some people is a social problem that is perhaps coming more to the foreground since a characteristic of our immediate times seems to be that fate is reversing these traditional roles for more and more people. However, to understand the function of these patterns (and particularly this one) it must be pointed out that men with this 1-9-1 pattern are masculine and women are masculinized to think and act in essentially male categories. Supreme ego identity is still the all driving force here. The NINE personality only disguises the full impact of this drive which is fortunate because NINE on the personality always accounts for considerable acceptance and broad popularity. This 1-9-1 combination may be considered as the most favored of all the 9 variations of the ONE character type. It preserves the integrity where it is needed most − that is − on the inside constantly controlling and reshaping the "intent". At the same time the NINE on the personality softens the exterior for greater cooperation from others but in such a way as to maintain a certain universality, charity, tolerance and compassion. Whatever compromises are made outwardly by the personality are done so with the broadest depth of vision to include the widest amount of dispassionate consideration. The ONE on the motivation intensifies the ONE character for constructive advancement while the NINE personality is a most congenial packaging of the product. While karmic conditions (missing individual numbers) in any of the pattern numbers must also be considered as important qualifications in the effective expression of these qualities, this pattern is so strong that karmas here are less likely to affect it adversely as they might with some other pattern.

Some famous people whose character is in the 1-9-1 pattern are:

| | |
|---|---|
| Marcel Duchamp | Tyrone Power |
| Leroi Jones | John L. Lewis |
| Theodore Freeman (astronaut) | Rose Kennedy |
| Pablo Casals | William F. Buckley Jr. |
| President Martin Van Buren | Alexander Graham Bell |
| Margaret Rutherford | Caryl Chessman |
| Mahalia Jackson | Martha Mitchell |

# 2—8—1

The 2-8-1 pattern has TWO on the motivation, EIGHT on the personality and ONE on the character. In some ways this is the least favorable of all the variations of the ONE character. Since ONE is already self-centered and hard driving this combines here with the harshest of all vibrations on the personality with the weakest of all numbers on the motivation. Here we have an individual whose motivation is diametrically opposed to his inevitable pattern of action (character) and at the same time even the best of his most considerate intentions are blurred by the super efficiency and materially hard-nosed qualities of his personality. A great deal of the driving force of the ONE character is lost by a sense of inner defeat through the sensitivities of the TWO motivation culminating in a stalemate. This might satisfy the compromise of the motivation but would defeat the pin-pointed direction of one's ultimate behavior. This individual desires to seek TWO (compromising) positions but can only do so in a ONE (individualistic) way. There is also a pronounced inner masculine/feminine struggle as the individual consciously tries to appease both the sensitivity of his feminine motivations and the ego focus of his masculine character. The end result is again likely to be a considerable departure from the best virtues of either vibration. The EIGHT personality does not help either side in this struggle (which to the individual is very personal), but instead lends a harshness in all material matters which indicates that where money or material advantages are concerned this individual will behave more like a ONE and far less like a TWO. There is also some tendency to add the materiality of EIGHT to the overly possessive quality of the TWO motivation. This is an unfortunate pattern for men. They are overly indulgent with women and all gentle, weaker types which defeats the integrity of their real position. It is somewhat more suitable for women (than the other variations of the ONE character pattern) as it signifies a desire to back down from an otherwise overbearing position. Their motivation is to strengthen feminine objectives even at the expense of their natural masculine, aggressive methods which may prove more rewarding in some way simply because they are, after all, women.

Karmic conditions in any of the numbers would considerably affect the polarity struggle of this pattern. A karma in TWO would considerably strengthen the character. A karma in ONE would considerably weaken the character. A karma in EIGHT would intensify the toughness of the personality.

Some famous people whose character is in the 2-8-1 pattern are:

| | |
|---|---|
| Margot Fonteyn | Florence Henderson |
| Eddie Fisher | Robert Kennedy |
| Van Cliburn | Cornelius Vanderbilt |
| James Baldwin | Robert S. McNamara |

# 3—7—1

The 3-7-1 pattern has THREE on the motivation, SEVEN on the personality and ONE on the character. This is a fairly well balanced pattern of forces which at the same time do not cancel or nullify the quality of each other. The THREE motivation wants to be happy and strives for self-expression. The SEVEN personality is discriminating and naturally aloof so a purity of purpose and originality of force is maintained to enhance the ONE character. While the SEVEN personality does not mix easily with all types, it is less likely to offend a number of people which would cut down on the effectiveness of the ONE leadership. Since the ONE character must develop originality (or they defeat their essential function) the SEVEN personality tends to encourage this through a separation from ordinary everyday matters. The THREE motivation meanwhile seeks an audience to register opinions and impressions so the ONE character is fairly assured of some kind of ego-identity. This pattern is equally favorable for men or women, remembering, of course, that the ONE character itself is generally more suitable for men. A karma in the THREE motivation does not serious hamper the balancing forces of this pattern. A karma in the SEVEN personality also does not seriously hamper the pattern either way. A karma in ONE, however, would considerably weaken the integrity of purpose and the strength of the overall outcome. Fortunately comparatively few people are completely missing a ONE in their name so this situation isn't often found.

Some famous people whose character is in the 3-7-1 pattern are:

| | |
|---|---|
| Elsa Maxwell | Orson Bean |
| Leontyne Price | Mayor John Lindsay |
| John Marin | Alexis Carrel |
| Andrew Wyeth | Justice William Rhenquist |
| Arthur Godfrey | Aimme Semple McPherson |
| Astronaut Donn Eisele | Mrs. Spiro Agnew |
| Rev. Harry E. Fosdick | Justice Benjamin Cardozo |
| Susan Strasberg | Joel Grey |

# 4—6—1

The 4-6-1 pattern has FOUR on the motivation, SIX on the personality and ONE on the character. This pattern is well balanced between material interests (FOUR) and social responsibilities (SIX) which tend to culminate in an original way (ONE). But the essential novelty and creative independence of the ONE is somewhat diminished by the consideration desired by the SIX which may not be altogether sympathetic with the direct simplicity necessary for the full development of the ego identity. The SIX personality will encourage the more responsible and therefore more constructive aspects of ONENESS and minimize the inherent tyranny and self-gratification which is also ONE. The FOUR motivation wants and seeks the truth about the matter which also strengthens the integrity of the ONE. A karma in the FOUR motivation tends to nullify the soundness of the pattern by exchanging hard headed prejudice for acceptance of truth. A karma in the SIX personality actually strengthens the pattern since it retains the apparent friendly sociality yet rejects the mediocrity of group restrictions which in this pattern would reduce the individuality of the ONE. A karma in the ONE reduces the effectiveness of the individuality but perhaps in this case enhances the workability of the practical awareness (FOUR) and the social alliances (SIX) which, however, reflects another type of person altogether but one which others may find more agreeable. This pattern is a bit more suitable for men than women because FOUR on the motivation is generally more natural and productive for men.

Some famous people whose character is in the 4-6-1 pattern are:

| | |
|---|---|
| Helen Keller | James A. Michener |
| Alicia Markova | Olivia DeHavilland |
| Jean-Claude Killy | Jack Webb |
| Alan Jay Lerner | Bernard Berenson |
| Grace Moore | Alistair Crowley |
| Edward Steichen | Huey Newton |
| Gunnar Myrdal | |

# 5—5—1

The 5-5-1 pattern has FIVE on the motivation, FIVE on the personality and ONE on the character. The pattern here is not balanced. In fact it contains a double portion of the quality which seeks so much uninhibited change as to lead the ONE integrity astray. FIVE is itself an unstable quality and here it is unfortunate that there are no counter balancing qualities to keep this restless action on a constructive basis. This individual is too apt to find any excuse or rationalization which suits his purpose at the moment. He is also prone to change direction at the very moment when he should be making an all out effort in some spearhead objective consistent with his ONE originality. In order to go as far, or fully develop all the possibilities of a single objective (ONE), an individual has to resist many of the exciting temptations offered or suggested by the curiosity of FIVE. While ONES struggle to establish a foothold, FIVES are bent on breaking away in some different and contrasting form of radical departure. The two qualifies could combine effectively but the natural tendency here is to bring out the least

151

desirable of both qualities rather than their best. The pattern is somewhat more suitable for men (Women's Liberation not with-standing). A karma in FIVE would probably lend more strength to the ONE character (which in this pattern would certainly be helpful). A karma in ONE would increase the difficulties already present with too much FIVE.

Some famous people whose character is in the 5-5-1 pattern are:

Henry R. Luce                       Douglas Fairbanks, Jr.
Alfred Hitchcock                    Marlon Brando
Della Reese                         Ernest Borgnine
Cab Calloway                        Cartoonist Frank Willard
Jim Bouton                          Senator George Murphy
President James Garfield

# 6—4—1

The 6-4-1 pattern has SIX on the motivation, FOUR on the personality and ONE on the character. This pattern is well balanced but perhaps not quite as favorably as its opposite pattern (4-6-1). The 4-6-1 pattern is more favorable because it places primary importance on factual reality combined with the social graces of the personality. In the 6-4-1 the conscious desire is on getting along in close cooperation with average situations, but hampered with a certain rigid reserve in the personality combined with a harsh proclivity for pointing out truthful facts which others may not want to hear. Both variations tend to water down the originality of the ego identity which for the ONE character should remain uppermost. The SIX motivation drives the individual away from the distinctive leadership demanded by ONE because the individual is more interested in his own social popularity and acceptance than he is in developing some original purpose of his own. The FOUR personality makes it equally difficult for him to move in any direction fast enough to project the uniqueness of his character. The discipline of FOUR should, however, contribute to the aggressive determination of the ONE. If a women has a ONE character pattern then this variation is slightly more variable than some of the others and by the same token is less favorable for men. A karma in the SIX or FOUR might strengthen the ONE. A karma in the ONE reflects a different type altogether where the ONENESS comes out as uncooperative rather than a valid position of independence.

Some famous people whose character is in the 6-4-1 pattern are:

| | |
|---|---|
| Rod McKuen | Robert Cummings |
| Sander Vanocur | Senator Ted Kennedy |
| Mortimer Adler | Harry K. Thaw |
| Pierre Van Paassen | George Hamilton |
| William Styron | Manly Hall |
| Max Eastman | Paul Foster Case |
| Beatrice Lillie | Jean Stapleton |
| Robert Mitchum | Nelson Rockefeller |

# 7—3—1

The 7-3-1 pattern has SEVEN on the motivation, THREE on the personality and ONE on the character. This is basically a strong pattern as both the inner and outer purpose contribute rather than detract from the best interests of the ONE. This pattern may be slightly more favored over its reverse 3-7-1 because with the SEVEN on the motivation the strength is within and the exterior impression (THREE personality) is more pleasing and creative. The preferred structure of number patterns should always be TO KEEP THE INNER PURPOSE STRONG AND AT THE SAME TIME SOFTEN THE PERSONALITY IMAGE so as to encourage social ease and effective outside cooperation. The SEVEN motivation has an even more highly refined sense of integrity than does the ONE itself and it also encourages the individual to develop resources on his own which might enhance his individuality once he sees a clear goal. The THREE Personality enables one to relax and save one's best strength for the push where it really counts. The pattern is equally favorable for men or women. A karma in the SEVEN or THREE does not impair the pattern significantly. A karma in the ONE changes the picture but still makes for a constructive and interesting individual in many fields.

Some famous people whose character is in the 7-3-1 pattern are:

| | |
|---|---|
| John Dewey | Ethel Kennedy |
| Bernard Baruch | Spiro Agnew |
| Prince Rainier III | Michael Arlen |
| Ethel Waters | Senator Carl Hayden |
| Rita Hayworth | Cherio |
| Kirk Douglas | |

# 8–2–1

The 8-2-1 pattern has EIGHT on the motivation, TWO on the personality and ONE on the character. This is a considerably stronger pattern than its reverse 2-8-1. The strength here is where it should be (on the inner motivation) and the spirit of cooperation is advantageously evident in the personality. However, the public is very prone to misjudge this individual, and as a consequence, be quite unprepared for his virtues as they ultimately function. This may or may not work to the individual's benefit. Certainly he will be given fewer opportunities than he is suited for as judged by his TWO personality which is a contradiction to his ONE character. Of all the variations of the ONE character this pattern is the most favorable for women and the least favorable for men. TWO on the personality makes anyone seem feminine, gentle and compromising. With a ONE character this can be an unfortunate contradiction but the contradiction (such as it is) is generally less fatal for women than men. With women it enables them to gain an advantageous position (supposedly suitable to them as women) which they can later manipulate for their own money-power (EIGHT) drive and domination (ONE) objectives. With most men circumstances would tend to work against them from the start because they would be judged on personality and relegated to positions usually unsuitable for men (that is any TWO type position) and only after much inner resistance and great courage can they make an effective break for themselves and do things their way (which would be the EIGHT drive combined with the ONE character). A karma in EIGHT weakens the pattern substantially by reducing the pattern function to a basic personal conflict between the masculinity of the ONE and the sensitive femininity of the TWO. A karma in TWO increases the pattern's strength. A karma in ONE confuses the direction and reflects an entirely different type of person altogether.

Some famous people whose character is in the 8-2-1 pattern are:

| | |
|---|---|
| Billy Rose | Joe Torre |
| Thomas Mann | Andrew Carnegie |
| Harper Lee | Fred Allen |
| Lorne Greene | James A. Ling |
| Peter Falk | Sen. Stuart Symington |
| Walter Jenkins | Angela Davis |
| William Boyle | |

# 9—1—1

The 9-1-1 pattern has NINE on the motivation, ONE on the personality and ONE on the character. This is a strong pattern and one well suited for leadership in a broad public capacity. The NINE motivation wants to serve the public and humanity in some manner and the ONE personality molds the individual for obvious leadership even to those who may not know him personally. This type would appear to be a born leader with a philanthropic purpose. The pattern is far more suitable for men as the personality here is totally masculinized. Even though some people may regard the ONE character as equally admirable in women, masculinization of the personality in women still remains awkward. A karma in NINE would not have a substantial negative effect. A karma in ONE would, however considerably alter the pattern as to reflect a totally different

155

type of person with admirable intention but lacking the strength or integrity to really put things across.

Some famous people whose character is in the 9-1-1 pattern are:

| | |
|---|---|
| James Hoffa | Hattie Carnegie |
| Pierre Curie | Waldo Frank |
| Floyd Patterson | Robert Young |
| Richard Daley | Charleton Heston |
| Dionne Warwick | Anthony Franciosa |
| President John Tyler | Representative Ogden Reid |
| Oscar Hammerstein | Annie Besant |
| Stephen Bechtel | |

## THE 9 VARIATIONS OF THE TWO CHARACTER

Number TWO is the most sensitive vibration symbolizing an individual who is soft, gentle, understanding, patient, sacrificing and helpful. Naturally it is an ideal vibration for the traditional concept of a woman's role in life. It is somewhat awkward for men as sensitivity and understanding have not been regarded as ideal masculine virtues.

Remember that all of these individual TWOS may differ from the other TWOS that follow by the qualification and modification of their respective motivation drive and personality image. Also, of course, each one may be challenged by a different fate pattern which we will take up in Chapter VIII.

# *1—1—2*

The 1-1-2 pattern has ONE on the motivation, ONE on the personality and TWO on the character. This is a very confusing pattern as are all number patterns which accent the basic polarity of the strong masculine (ONE) and receptive feminine (TWO) qualities in the same individual. The inner motivation here is strong and masculinized as is the personality but the final outcome is weak, vacillating, compromising, insecure and unstable in spite of intent or appearances to the contrary. The individual is alsc beset and troubled with a strong personal conflict between masculine and feminine qualities within himself. Much time and effort are spent in trying to resolve these differences which seriously detracts from and hampers the real issues at hand. The pattern is bound to generate in the motivation and exhibit through the personality a certain intense directness, but when it comes down to the line on constructive application in the character the results are generally too contradictory and diffused to be very effective. The pattern is not too favorable for women (as are any number patterns which masculinize the personality) but is considerably more fortunate than for men as women are traditionally forgiven for eventually acting as women even though they "come on" strong at first in a burst of masculinized aggression. In men the TWO on the character is more likely to be considered a character flaw. A karma in ONE strengthens the ideality of the TWO character which is needed. A karma in TWO probably improves the pattern function in another way but reflects an entirely different type of individual.

Some famous people whose character is in the 1-1-2 pattern are:

| | |
|---|---|
| Betrand Russell | Ida Lupino |
| Arthur Ashe | Ava Gardner |
| Jack Paar | Lenny Bruce |
| Indria Gandhi | Joseph Pulitzer |
| Mamie Eisenhower | Mary Frank Hague |
| Kate Smith | Margaret Truman |
| James M. Cain | Harry Houdini |

# 2—9—2

The 2-9-2 pattern has TWO on the motivation, NINE on the personality and TWO on the character. This is an excellent pattern of complimentary qualities which raises the personal sensitivity of TWO to a broader level of charitable understanding but still retains the warmth and immediacy of gifted insight. Any individual with this pattern is bound to be broadly responsive to life and well liked by his fellow men. There is a potentiality of the celebrity here or a person of wide public appeal. Because of its potentiality for wide universal acclaim and the absence of masculine/feminine polarity, this pattern could be equally suitable for men or women. A karma in NINE would probably not seriously lessen the patterns' advantages nor would a karma in TWO which would only increase the power of the NINE wavelength.

Some famous people whose character is in the 2-9-2 pattern are:

| | |
|---|---|
| David Merrick | Faye Emerson |
| Wilt Chamberlain | Senator Scoop Jackson |
| Kirsten Flagstad | Hugh Heffner |
| John Daly | Louis Wolfson |
| Bill Cullen | Caroline Kennedy |
| W. H. Auden | William Wirtz |
| Jane Wyman | Justice Louis Brandeis |
| Betty Hutton | Boris Spassky |

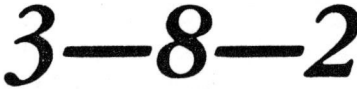

The 3-8-2 pattern has THREE on the motivation, EIGHT on the personality and TWO on the character. This is a strong and effective pattern which lends the creativity of THREE and the administrative thrust of EIGHT to the sensitive inspiration of TWO. This individual is also bound to be widely known in life. And again without the masculine/feminine polarity struggle this number pattern could prove effective for men or women. A karma in THREE would not be strongly detrimental and a karma in EIGHT might be a slight advantage as it lessens somewhat the harshness of EIGHT on the personality. However, a karma in TWO would be unfortunate as the eventual outcome would be so confused as to lessen the whole potential effect.

Some famous people whose character is in the 3-8-2 pattern are:

Johan Sibelius
Daniel Berrigan
Richard K. Mellon
George Meany
Glen Campbell
Robert Chaffee (astronaut)

President Rutherford Hayes
Carl Sandberg
Paul Muni
Carol Righter
Representative Carl Albert

# 4—7—2

The 4-7-2 pattern has FOUR on the motivation, SEVEN on the personality and TWO on the character. This is the pattern of a highly sensitized individual combining the ordinary insights of TWO with the more rarified and shrewd intuition of SEVEN yet balanced by the factual reality drive of FOUR. FOUR on the motivation always wants proof, facts and the unvarnished truth which here combine in an interesting fashion with the emotional vision of TWO and SEVEN. This individual may not become as widely known as other pattern variations of TWO because of the SEVEN of reticent withdrawal on the personality, but within his own circle of influence he may become quite distinguished. This pattern would be about equally favorable for men or women. A karma in FOUR would lessen the particular advantages of the practical vs. the theoretical balance in this pattern. A karma in SEVEN would not alter the effectiveness of the pattern substantially. A karma in TWO would increase the individual's inner conflicts as the basic polarity struggle of the material FOUR vs. the spiritual SEVEN took over without the mediating influence of the TWO which here is more ideal.

Some famous people whose character is in the 4-7-2 pattern are:

Joan Baez
Guy Lombardo
President Woodrow Wilson

Orville Prescott
Gwen Verdon
Godfrey Cambridge

Jean Stafford
Damon Runyon
Senator Margaret Chase Smith

James Earl Ray
Nikola Tesla
James Montgomery Flagg

# 5—6—2

The 5-6-2 pattern has FIVE on the motivation, SIX on the personality and TWO on the character. A basic contradiction is evident here with the unrestraint of FIVE contrasted with the moral protectiveness of SIX all of which is mediated through the TWO of constructive compromise and tactful diplomacy. The inner motivation tends to be constantly at cross purpose with all outward conventional appearances which can lead to a great deal of tension and apprehensive desires with inadequate direction or format. What the individual, by his ultimate character expression, tries to mediate in his motivation and character must of necessity remain diametrically opposed by the qualities of their nature. This individual is bound to become involved in any number of situations but his own contributions are apt to be of questionable importance. This is not a particularly fortunate pattern but it would be considered obviously more suitable for women. A karma in FIVE might be considered to improve the compatability of the pattern. A karma in SIX might also be somewhat helpful. A karma in TWO would not, however, improve the problems here but might result in a more committed person (for better or worse).

Some famous people whose character is in the 5-6-2 pattern are:

Norton Simon
Philip Johnson
Mohamad Ali
Adlai Stevenson
W. Averell Harriman
Walt Rostow
Pope John XXIII
Amy Vanderbilt
Joe Namath

Harry Cohn
Gary Player
Marian Anderson
Richard Dyer-Bennett
David Niven
Eric Sevareid
R. C. Firebrace
President James Monroe
President Warren Harding

160

# 6—5—2

The 6-5-2 pattern has SIX on the motivation, FIVE on the personality and TWO on the character. Although so similar to the reverse pattern above, the balance here is considerably more complimentary between the motivation and the character. The personality only "appears" out of line with what is finally resolved and put into action, therefore the promise of effective "influence" on others through the TWO character is definitely improved. This individual tends to be better at heart than they appear on the surface which is the opposite of the reverse 5-6-1 pattern where he tends to look better than he is. Also this 6-5-2 pattern is apt to be misjudged for the wrong reasons. What is intended generally finds a way to work things out constructively in spite of appearances. This pattern is slightly more suitable for women than men because of the domestic drive of SIX. A karma in SIX lessens the advantages gained from the reverse pattern above but in the case of a man might be an improvement where friendly social drives might be substituted for more domestic commitments. A karma in FIVE would tone down the disruptive and contradictory impressions of the personality hence some improvement. A karma in TWO could heighten the contradiction between FIVE and SIX hence be less favorable.

Some famous people whose character is in the 6-5-2 pattern are:

| | |
|---|---|
| General Douglas MacArthur | Gene Autry |
| Willie Mays | Robert Stanley Dollar |
| Roy Wilkins | F. W. Woolworth |
| Julie Harris | Yoko Ono |
| Claudette Colbert | |

# 7—4—2

The 7-4-2 pattern has SEVEN on the motivation, FOUR on the personality and TWO on the character. This is a well balanced pattern which combines insight with factual know-how culminating in some comprehensive and inspired form of effective cooperation. The inner motivations are highly selective and specialized but the outer personality is well grounded in practical issues. This pattern would be equally suitable for men or women (with the qualification that the TWO character is generally less suitable for men). A karma in SEVEN would not especially hurt the pattern. A karma in FOUR would, however, impair the balance between the two sensitivities of SEVEN and TWO. A karma in TWO might make the pattern somewhat more practical for men and correspondingly less effective for women.

Some famous people whose character is in the 7-4-2 pattern are:

| | |
|---|---|
| William S. Paley | Omar Sharif |
| Edward Durell Stone | Carroll O'Connor |
| Archbishop Ramsey | Charles Laughton |
| Rev. Paul Tillich | I. M. Pei |
| Rudolf Nureyev | Lou Costello |
| Earl Browder | Pat Nixon |
| Dizzy Gillespie | Senator Birch Bayh |
| Paul McCartney | Elmo Roper |
| President Zachary Taylor | |

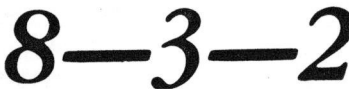

# 8—3—2

The 8-3-2 pattern has EIGHT on the motivation, THREE on the personality and TWO on the character. This is a deceptive pattern but strong and influencial. The outer personality is particularly low key and does not really convey the potential drive of the motivation or the inspiration of the possible outcome, but this individual is quite skillful at getting what he wants. The pattern is equally suitable for men or women with perhaps some advantages for women. A karma in EIGHT lessens the balance and heightens the polarity contradiction between the qualities of THREE and TWO. A karma in THREE heightens the driving force of EIGHT which perhaps raises the tone of the whole pattern. A karma in TWO would not especially defeat the pattern, in fact, it might prove some advantage by lessening the chances for over-compromise.

Some famous people whose character is in the 8-3-2 pattern are:

| | |
|---|---|
| F. Lee Bailey | Victor Borge |
| Justice Potter Stewart | Budd Schulberg |
| Rocky Marciano | Archibald MacLeish |
| Representative Joseph R. McCarthy | Jean Seberg |
| Sandy Koufax | Charles Chaplin |

# 9—2—2

The 9-2-2 pattern has NINE on the motivation, TWO on the personality and TWO on the character. This pattern leans toward a state of protracted suspense which tends to get nowhere or be so long in getting started that the individual is apt to miss his best opportunities. The TWO on the personality makes this person fussy over details somewhat in contrast to a broader and disspassionate motivation which he tries to maintain. In the end the result is apt to be a compromise which defeats the best qualities of either TWO or NINE. The pattern would be more effective in the arts where a natural inclination for depersonalization of material is combined with a touch of inspiration. The pattern is decidedly more suitable for women than for men although in the arts men might find this pattern workable and productive. A karma in NINE might help the effectiveness of the pattern (but not in the arts) as might also a karma in TWO which would broaden the field of application but lessen the degree of inspiration.

Some famous people whose character is in the 9-2-2 pattern are:

| | |
|---|---|
| Ted Shawn | Robert Benchley |
| Jim Thorpe | Margaret Leighton |
| Whitey Ford | David Janssen |
| Liberace | Charles Whitman (Texas mass murderer) |
| Eddy Duchin | Louis Diminguin (bull fighter) |

163

# THE 9 VARIATIONS OF THE THREE CHARACTER

THREE is the carefree, creative vibration which functions best when relatively free from serious responsibilities or overburdened with material considerations. They have the charm, naivety and spontaneous reactions of children which is part of the secret of their persuasive salesmanship. This is the vibration of individual creativity where the person himself becomes intricately involved with the creation. There is much natural enthusiasm, embellishment, decoration, imagination and ornamentation involved in everything they do. Duration is not a factor as these people look upon each moment as a separate and distinct stage setting or window dressing which momentarily captures their attention. All that is important to them is what is currently present or available and can be fitted into the general symthesis. There is a spontaneity and impetuosity that is charming, youthful, critical, inquiring, challenging and representational. Salesmanship is generally a talent with these people as well as an ability to entertain, captivate, provoke, instill, decorate and ornament. The number is equally favorable for either men or women.

Remember that all of these individual THREES may differ from the other THREES that follow by the qualification and modification of their respective motivation drive and personality image. Also, of course, each one may be challenged by a different fate pattern which we will take up in Chapter VIII.

# *1—2—3*

The 1-2-3 pattern has ONE on the motivation, TWO on the personality and THREE on the character. This pattern is almost one of those magical formulas which would be highly successful since it sticks to fundamentals with a minimum of complexity and has a healthy assurance of self-purpose which is hard to shake. They tend to know from the beginning what they want and how to get it. Their self-assurance gives them some measure of success even before they start. Their personality effectively disguises the self-gratification of their motivation yet manages to secure a general spirit of cooperative assistance. Their character may lack a certain depth or penetration, but they tend to go far in life and in fact outdistance a great many others. The pattern would be equally effective with both men and women because we are dealing here with creative types. The TWO personality for men, however, would give them an effeminate appearance which may or may not be important in their field of work. A karma in ONE would take away from the ideality of this pattern but might be some improvement for women. A karma in TWO would not be as negative as the karma in ONE but might be some improvement for men. A karma in THREE need not seriously impair the pattern, although the sense of personal gratification from one's accomplishments might be considerably reduced.

Some famous people whose character is in the 1-2-3 pattern are:

| | |
|---|---|
| Joseph Mankiewicz | Paul Newman |
| H. L. Hunt | Louis Jordan |
| Julian Bond | Senator Charles Percy |
| George Plimpton | Harold B. Stasson |
| Harold Laski | Carol Channing |
| Tallulah Bankhead | William Pahlmann |
| Mickey Rooney | Loren C. Eiseley |

# 2—1—3

The 2-1-3 pattern has TWO on the motivation, ONE on the personality and THREE on the character. This is generally not nearly as effective in operation as the reverse pattern above (1-2-3). In this pattern the motivation is weakened and the independence and self-assurance of the personality resists the helpful cooperation secured in the reverse pattern. The motivation under TWO is uncertain and vacillating and the personality under ONE is abrasive and definitely unsympathetic. This might prove effective in some fields of application but not nearly so generally sure of success as the 1-2-3. This pattern is slightly more preferred for men as the women will seem masculinized in the personality which is never particularly fortunate for women. A karma in TWO may strengthen the pattern as may a karma in ONE. A karma in THREE disturbs the creativity assurance and accents the polarity of the masculine/feminine polarity contradiction.

Some famous people whose character is in the 2-1-3 pattern are:

J. Edgar Hoover                    Melina Mercouri
Gloria Vanderbilt                  Karl Malden
J. P. Marquand                     Adam Clayton Powell

# 3—9—3

The 3-9-3 pattern has THREE On tne motivation, NINE on the personality and THREE on the character. This is an excellent pattern for broad creativity where the accent of the personality is less of a factor in the artistic creation. The NINE personality minimizes the "me" factor in the expression. There may seem to be some effort required to bring the universal down to the particular (which for all THREES is essential). The NINE on the personality may also waste time finding the right medium to project the personal ego or let many good opportunities slip away due to delay in sensing their "personal" value. The application between men and women would have no difference. A karma in NINE might slightly improve personalization of that which is expressed. A karma in THREE would change the picture so completely in favor of NINE (which is only the surface impression) as to reflect a different type of person completely.

Some famous people whose character is in the 3-9-3 pattern are:

Ella Fitzgerald                    Richard Speck
Mohandas Gandhi                    Eugene Grace
Alexander Woollcott                Ernest Hemingway

Axel Wenner-Gren
Yuri Gagarin
Gore Vidal
Jack Benny

Judith Anderson
Dr. Eric Berne
Ryan O'Neal

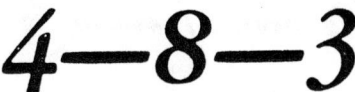

The 4-8-3 pattern has FOUR on the motivation, EIGHT on the personality and THREE on the character. This pattern makes for a very strong and hard nosed presentation of essentially a simple decorative thing. A relatively insignificant position is apt to be blown out of proportion and the effect may seem far less important after the smoke and fire has cleared away. The factual demands of the FOUR motivation coupled with the power manipulations of the EIGHT personality pave the way for a far more substantial and enduring result than the THREE product which finally emerges. Certainly the ingredients utilized will be on a grand and impressive scale but on careful examination the "pastiche" will be somewhat shallow by comparison. It is quite natural for some element of fraud to easily enter the picture. This is a better pattern for men than women. A karma in FOUR might further distort the proportion but a karma in EIGHT might lessen the pretentiousness. A karma in THREE might strengthen the pattern but reflect an entirely different type of person by minimizing the THREE as much as possible.

Some famous people whose character is in the 4-8-3 pattern are:

Arnold Palmer
Frankie Robinson
Al Hirt
Louis Armstrong
Vladimir Horowitz

Mary McCarthy
Ian Fleming
Joyce Cary
Helen Hayes
John Strachey

167

James McDivitt (astronaut)
President Andrew Jackson
Senator Frank Church

Pier Nervi
Theda Bara
Paul Lynde

# 5—7—3

The 5-7-3 pattern has FIVE on the motivation, SEVEN on the personality and THREE on the character. This is a lively combination of qualities that is bound to be inventive (FIVE) as well as different in most respects from any ordinary approach (SEVEN). The healthy curiosity is well balanced with a natural talent for perfection whose ultimate expression is bound to be imaginative and creative. A natural bouyancy keeps this pattern from getting too far removed or aloof from truly creative material. There would be no difference in application for either men or women. A karma in FIVE or SEVEN would not seriously hamper the effective combination here. A karma in THREE, however, might considerably lessen the final creative effect.

Some famous people whose character is in the 5-7-3 pattern are:

Norman Vincent Peale
Maria Tallchief
Jimmy Dean
Cyrus Eaton
Marconi
Edward Arnold
Prince Charles
William Anders (astronaut)
President Thomas Jefferson
Gertrude Atherton

Tammy Grimes
James Stewart
Raymond Massey
Alec Guinness
Pat Boone
Rossano Brazzi
James Earl Jones
Phyllis Diller
Karl Eichmann
Justice Oliver Wendell Holmes

# 6—6—3

The 6-6-3 pattern has SIX on the motivation, SIX on the personality and THREE on the character. This pattern makes for a very sociable and communicative talent which somewhat detracts from a more individual form of creative expression. The individual here gets wound up in teaching and explaining or in watering down his creation so that it has popular social acceptance which may have little to do with individual creative effort. This person is rather more concerned with his audience and what his audience may or may not accept than he is in producing "his thing" and letting it find its own audience which is what real creativity is all about. There is too much involvement here in what others are doing. or too much testing of one's personal ideas on others before getting down to real creativity. The best qualities are apt to be dissipated while trying to involve too many outside factors. This is, however, a socially pleasing pattern even if a great deal of individual creativity doesn't get accomplished. The pattern is slightly more suitable for women than men with the gossipy, domesticated SIX on the personality. A karma in SIX might help to individualize the effort. A karma in THREE would change the whole picture in favor of SIX to such an extent as to reflect a different type of person altogether.

Some famous people whose character is in the 6-6-3 pattern are:

Bette Davis
Richard Boone
James Garner
Johnathan Winters
Lynn Redgrave
Scott Carpenter (astronaut)

Representative John Tunney
Herman Wouk
Arthur Schlesinger
J. P. Morgan
Sir George Wilkins

# 7—5—3

The 7-5-3 pattern has SEVEN on the motivation, FIVE on the personality and THREE on the character. This lively pattern is slightly less favorable than its reverse (5-7-3) because here the motivation is unfocused and the personality turns too quickly from one situation to another, seeking novelty at the expense of something with greater depth. The SEVEN motivation is well aware of depth but is prone to be dissatisfied with most of the material which the five personality uncovers or drags forth. Although they are not contiguous vibrations, there is little in common between the qualities symbolized by the FIVE and the SEVEN. The SEVEN acts slowly on a purely non-material plane while the FIVE tends to upset or knock down with a material or sensory emphasis much that SEVEN is trying to establish. That is what is happening here but the balance is better functionally in the 5-7-3 pattern than the 7-5-3 pattern. The pattern is about the same for men or women. A karma in SEVEN or FIVE might improve the functional operation or lessen the incompatability. A karma in THREE might also improve the creativity angle.

Some famous people whose character is in the 7-5-3 pattern are:

| | |
|---|---|
| Barbra Streisand | Eric Hoffer |
| Harry Reasoner | Rod Steiger |
| George Santayana | Jack Lemmon |
| Margaret Sanger | Governor George Wallace |
| Marshall Field I | Herb Caen |
| President Chester Arthur | Henry Kissinger |
| Walter Lippmann | Janis Joplin |

# 8—4—3

The 8-4-3 pattern has EIGHT on the motivation, FOUR on the personality and THREE on the character. The pattern is strong because of the discipline and organization in the FOUR personality combined with the commanding material vision of EIGHT. Together they give a high powered material push to a persuasive and decorative creation (THREE). While the exploitation is top heavy (EIGHT and FOUR over only THREE) there is certainly a smooth compatability and consistency of material effort. The question here is what creative use can the simple THREE make of all this strong material (like fire and steam). While EIGHT uses the power of administrative control, THREE the capacity for creative symthesis, and FOUR shows the factual grasp and practical know-how, these qualities can merge in a combination which may be hard to beat. The danger is too much steam which has to condense into a relatively simple exposition. The pattern is rather more suitable for men than women. A karma in EIGHT might increase the creativity ratio and reduce the input of steam. A karma in FOUR might also magnify the creativity as it releases some of the necessity for sheer practicality. A karma in THREE reduces the creativity outlet for what is already too much material steam.

Some famous people whose character is in the 8-4-3 pattern are:

Elizabeth Taylor
Walt Disney
Rev. James Pike
Joe Frazier
Erroll Garner
Aretha Franklin
Mort Sahl
Howard K. Smith
Gloria Steinem
Graham Greene

Dale Carnegie
Simone Signoret
Sophia Loren
Senator Russell Long
Barry Fitzgerald
Frederick Wakeman
Percival Lowell
Elsie Janis
Dr. J. B. Rhine

# 9—3—3

The 9-3-3 pattern has NINE on the motivation, THREE on the personality and THREE on the character. This is a very favorable pattern for creative effort. The personal struggle to bring universals down to particulars is less troublesome here than with the pattern 3-9-3 where the individual is inclined to start some form of expression, then drift or edge away and finally rationalize the whole matter as not being too important anyway. But here in the 9-3-3 the individual is motivated to drift but invariably gets pinned down to specifics which tend to get whipped into some sort of effective shape, almost in spite of oneself. The tendency with the NINE motivation is not to start things, but once started by the personalization of the THREE personality, matters tend to work their way through to some sort of ornamental completion and much less material is lost or abandoned in this picture. The applicable difference is no different for men or women. A karma in NINE may cut down on some of the wandering. A karma in THREE, however, increases the depersonalization which is essential to THREE type expression.

Some famous people whose character is in the 9-3-3 pattern are:

| | |
|---|---|
| Johnny Mathis | President John Quincy Adams |
| Andre Previn | S. I. Hayakawa |
| Norman Rockwell | Angela Lansbury |
| Edwin Newman | Spencer Tracy |
| Neil Armstrong (astronaut) | Red Skelton |
| Sir William Crookes | Cyrus Vance |

## THE 9 VARIATIONS OF THE FOUR CHARACTER

FOUR is the most practical and realistic of all vibrations. It is also the most hard working, diligent and self-disciplined. The FOUR usually finds that sticking to one situation and seeing it through to the end can often prove more successful than trying to fit a more talented pattern into a more ideal situation. The mediocrity of simple but realistic efforts often achieve more than a superior but complex mechanism which is seldom (if ever) as advantageously situated. FOUR gains this advantage by determined, steady application which is sometimes mistaken for dull stupidity. FOURS can be stubborn and bury their heads in the sand, but if they consistently stick to the right thing it will usually work as beautifully as any number to be found. FOURS tend to be faced in the right direction from the beginning because of their accent on factual reality. It is undoubtedly a blessing that they don't see as many possibilities or yearn to take short cuts because this keeps them plugging away. In the end this is what proves materially gratifying which is exactly what they are best programmed for.

Remember that all of these individuals are FOURS and they differ from the other FOURS that follow by the qualification and modification of their respective motivation drive and personality image. Also, of course, each one may be challenged by a different fate pattern which we will take up in Chapter VIII.

# 1—3—4

The 1-3-4 pattern has ONE on the motivation, THREE on the personality and FOUR on the character. This is a very sound pattern combining inner determination with outward joviality culminating in a concerted and persistent practical application. This is an excellent pattern for the ambitious, hard working man but would require a women to turn her sights toward career rather than a home. May I say here that when I evaluate behavior patterns for men or women it is in reference to the traditional roles which each has been expected to accept. If society becomes so organized that the tradition in role playing is eliminated, then these comments would not be as pertinent. However, there still remains certain biological differences between men and women which created the tradition of roles in the first place. A karma in ONE would considerably weaken the ideality of the pattern. A karma in THREE would not be as serious. A karma in FOUR would also greatly reduce the ultimate applications which this pattern should be capable of.

Some famous people whose character is in the 1-3-4 pattern are:

Noel Coward

Agnes Moorehead

Dorothy Gish

Jackson Pollock

Duke of Windsor

Henri Desire Landru

Laurence Rockefeller

Thomas Hart Benton

Cyril Connolly

Marcel Breuer

William H. Vanderbilt

Jesse Jones

Dr. Rudolf Steiner

Howard Cosell

# 2—2—4

The 2-2-4 pattern has TWO on the motivation, TWO on the personality and FOUR on the character. The pattern here is somewhat confusing because of a natural diffusion of motivations combined with an over-willingness to accommodate or defer oneself for the sake of others all of which must somehow culminate in a solid core work effort which advances something useful and practical. This is an ideal pattern for a "helpmate type" with a more aggressive and dominating partner. This is more favorable for women than men because a man with this pattern would seldom get the meatier assignments and the eventual job to do would likely be what no one else wanted. Any pattern which feminizes the personality is generally unsuitable for men except, perhaps, in the arts. The motivation here is clearly to follow and perform the servile work which others are reluctant to do for themselves. A karma in TWO would lessen the unsatisfactory aspects of this pattern, and a karma in FOUR might also do this in another way.

Some famous people whose character is in the 2-2-4 pattern are:

Ronald Reagan

Floyd McKissick

President James Buchanan

Joseph P. Kennedy

Edward White (astronaut)          Jacqueline Kennedy Onassis
Jan Struther                      John Held Jr.
C. Day Lewis                      Lynda Bird Johnson
Lana Turner                       Eileen Garrett
Senator Hubert Humphrey

The 3-1-4 pattern has THREE on the motivation, ONE on the personality and FOUR on the character. This pattern is not nearly as ideal or fortunate as its reverse (1-3-4). The motivation leads the individual towards the very opposite pursuit of the down-to-earth application of his character. The independence of the ONE personality resists any good advice which may be offered as to how or why he tries to go in opposite directions at the same time. There is, however a compatability of self-interest in both the THREE and ONE which may help to keep the FOUR in his rut with his nose to the grindstone which he must do to accomplish his function. This could reflect a good solid business type who has the sense to relax and pace himself when necessary to avoid the strain of over-work. This is also the pattern of one who is hardly likely to continue pouring sand down a rat hole once the futility of the situation becomes obvious. The THREE motivation also suggests an imagination and vision that many ordinary business men do not have. The pattern, because of the masculinization of the personality, is preferred for men rather than women. A karma in THREE reduces what ideality the pattern may have but may increase the practical application of FOUR. A karma in ONE may increase the individual's resistance to cooperative efforts but he may lose some spirit of individuality in his work. A karma in FOUR changes the picture considerably but reflects an individual more suitable to one who oversees the labor of others rather than doing it all himself.

175

Some famous people whose character is in the 3-1-4 pattern are:

Charles Lindbergh
Lawrence Tibbett
Walter Gieseking
Ezio Pinza
Jascha Heifetz
Mary Quant
Betty Friedan

John Steinbeck
John Garfield
Marshal Tito
Robe Goldberg
Joyce Grenfield
David Packard
Representative Mendel Rivers

The 4-9-4 pattern has FOUR on the motivation, NINE on the personality and FOUR on the character. This is an excellent pattern for honest dedicated public service where the individual is more concerned with what he can contribute to a worthy situation than what he can get out of it for himself. The FOURS both act as a sound balance for keeping the NINE ideals and wishful thinking on a sound and practical basis. The NINE on the other hand, endears the individual to others so many opportunities may come his way through his broad contacts. This is the pattern of one who is always available when needed and invariably down-to-earth and constructive in the ways he tries to help. He is somewhat prone to be taken advantage of, up to a point, but with all his common sense this won't last for long. The pattern is about equally favorable for men or women. A karma in NINE would increase the work load. A karma in FOUR would dissipate the practicality of the efforts.

Some famous people whose character is in the 4-9-4 pattern are:

Justice Hugo Black
Leonard Bernstein
Oscar Levant
Robert Goulet
Yma Sumac

President Lyndon Johnson
Ginger Rogers
Julie Christie
Eddie Albert
Henri Cartier-Bresson

Renata Tebaldi
Gordon Cooper (astronaut)
Charles Conrad (astronaut)
Elliott See (astronaut)

Al Cap
Jean Paul Getty
H. L. Mencken
Justice Tom Clark

# 5—8—4

The 5-8-4 pattern has FIVE on the motivation, EIGHT on the personality and FOUR on the character. There is a cross current of interest here which may be profitable for the native but tend to be rather expensive or disastrous for the bystanders. This reflects an individual who profits from others through the advantages he seeks. He tends to receive more than he pays for although he pays the stated price. This is a type of individual who might be said to be looking for distressed merchandise or loop hole situations where he can make a quick killing. It is not so much that he is out to get something for nothing, but if people are going to be so foolish as to allow themselves to be so easily taken advantage of them he might as well gain some of the advantages for himself. This is the pattern of a person who is hard to fault because he plays his game carefully and generally aboveboard all the way. There are no particular problems when applied to either men or women. A karma in FIVE or EIGHT does not seriously impair the workability of the pattern although there may be some loss of personal ethics when dealing with others. A karma in FOUR would heighten the tendency to questionable practices because all FOUR karmas tend to expect something for nothing in this world.

Some famous people whose character is in the 5-8-4 pattern are:

William Randolph Hearst
Franco Ziffirelli
Tony Bennett
Maurice Chevalier

Vittorio Gassman
Glenn Martin
Lionel Barrymore
Fred Astaire

Woody Allen
Bob Hope
Mary Baker Eddy

David Brinkley
Lee Harvey Oswald
Jonas Salk

The 6-7-4 pattern has SIX on the motivation, SEVEN on the personality and FOUR on the character. This is a favorable pattern combining a sense of social obligation and group responsibility with specialized insight which can all be put to some practical and useful objective. There is much milk of human kindness and rare depth of understanding (especially for those who differ from the ordinary mold) in spite of the hard headed techniques or rigidity of attitude. This is the pattern of a person who is essentially good but a difficult individual to fully appreciate or understand. In the end his deeds will speak for themselves but in the meantime he may seem confusing or confused himself. There is no difference for men or women. A karma in SIX detracts from the advantage of the pattern. A karma in SEVEN might even increase some of the more obvious advantages and lessen some of the apparent confusion. A karma in FOUR would dissipate the outcome considerably so there would be less good deeds to prove one's worth.

Some famous people whose character is in the 6-7-4 pattern are:

Paul Mellon
Luchino Visconti
Harry Bridges
Ray Robinson
Fran Tarkenton
Judy Holliday

Ingrid Bergman
Ben Gazzara
Wally Cox
Justice Fred Vinson
Donald Rumsfeld
Clifford Irving

178

# 7—6—4

The 7-6-4 pattern has SEVEN on the motivation, SIX on the personality and FOUR on the character. This pattern has certain advantages over its reverse above (6-7-4). Here the individual is likely to have many more opportunities open to him through the friendly sociability of his SIX personality than with the reverse pattern with the superior aloofness of the SEVEN personality. People generally like to have this individual around since he is friendly, responsible and so square and reliable in making his contributions for the common good. He may tend to separate himself from the crowd as he seeks to pursue some special private interest, but he can be easily reunited with the social ties he acknowledges as binding him to his fellows. His private aspirations do not interfere with his work productivity and may enable him to turn out something quite unique which otherwise would not have been possible. The pattern is no different when applied to either men or women. A karma in SEVEN may in some ways improve the adaptability of the pattern. A karma in SIX would certainly increase the ways in which this individual preferred to be different. A karma in FOUR would reduce the practical achievements and place much of the effort on a purely theoretical rather than realistic basis.

Some famous people whose character is in the 7-6-4 pattern are:

Liza Minnelli
Groucho Marx
Henry Fonda
Adm. Richard E. Byrd
Justice Byron White
Benito Mussolini
Charles Bassett (astronaut)

Steve Smith
Robert Maynard Hutchins
John Updike
Bertolt Brecht
Virginia Graham
Henry Morgan
I. F. Stone

# 8—5—4

The 8-5-4 pattern has EIGHT on the motivation, FIVE on the personality and FOUR on the character. This is a very ambitious pattern and somewhat more constructive than its reverse (5-8-4) because the dynamic and relentless EIGHT blends well with the industrious expression of the FOUR. Here the FIVE changeable personality only stirs up fresh material instead of demoralizing the whole structure. The strength is here in the motivation (where it should be) and what is desired is not only dynamically ambitious but well matched with the material talents of the expression. The intemperate FIVE personality contributes a promotional touch rather than demoralizing motivation (as it does in the 5-8-4 pattern). This is the pattern of a real go-getter and one who not only tends to make the best out of what he has but is able to continually improvise new material as he seeks larger and larger programs to conquer. The pattern would be somewhat overly active and competitive for most women but should be ideal for men. A karma in EIGHT would weaken the pattern. A karma in FIVE might strengthen it just a little. A karma in FOUR would put the whole structure at cross purposes without a real practical down-to-earth application.

Some famous people whose character is in the 8-5-4 pattern are:

Mamie Eisenhower
John Lennon
President John Adams
President Ulysses Grant
Kim Hunter
Dick Powell
Richard Harris

Pablo Picasso
Gil Hodges
Art Carney
William Hickman
Justice Arthur Goldberg
Benson Ford

# 9—4—4

The 9-4-4 pattern has NINE on the motivation, FOUR on the personality and FOUR on the character. There is a decided conflict of interests here which tends to frustrate the native. The immateriality of the motivation does not blend well with the rigidity of the personality or the plodding regimentation of the expression format. The individual wants to do more than he can and on a level somewhat unsuited to his real talents. His contributions to the cause (such as they are) tend to get stuck on a very menial and laborious level. This pattern suggests a routine function in an idealistic project, such as a clerk in a politicians's office or an accountant in a charitable institution. The pattern is equally applicable for men or women. A karma in NINE might strengthen the workability. A karma in FOUR might also improve the pattern by releasing the individual from some of the more arduous tasks involved in causes or projects which capture his charitable interest.

Some famous people whose character is in the 9-4-4 pattern are:

Justice William Brennan
President James Polk
Louis Untermeyer
John Kenneth Galbraith
Catherine Drinker Bowen
Katherine Cornell

Polly Bergan
Robert Ryan
Alan Ladd
John Dos Passos
A. C. Gilbert (Gilbert Toys)

## THE 9 VARIATIONS OF THE FIVE CHARACTER

FIVE is the vibration of the innovator, the one who seeks to stir things up, upset the status quo, start a fight, undermine a position or open up a new approach. FIVE reflects a clever use of energy, a certain surprise advantage and a keen sense of competition. Their best techniques are speed, taking short cuts, seizing momentary opportunities, feeling out weak points for the sake of personal advantage, unconventional attitudes and a willingness to speculate and gamble when the individual feels he has sufficient control of the variables so as to offer more than a 50-50 chance of beating the odds. The path of opportunity for FIVE obviously lies in an opposite direction from that of FOUR and is somewhat different from any other Number vibration. Few of the rules which apply to others (particularly those concerned with balance or restraint) will work when applied to FIVE. The FIVE character is definitely out of step with most of the other numbers but this is what enables him to do with others cannot.

Remember that all of these individuals are FIVES and they differ from the other FIVES that follow by the qualification and modification of their respective motivation drive and personality image. Also, of course, each one may be challenged by a different fate pattern which we will take up in Chapter VIII.

# 1—4—5

The 1-4-5 pattern has ONE on the motivation, FOUR on the personality and FIVE on the character. This is a sound pattern although there is some contradiction between appearance on the personality and the final outcome as molded by the opportunism of the FIVE character. The real strength is on the inner motivation where it should be and this is conveniently coupled in the personality with a certain practical know-how and down-to-earth common sense, all of which the individual is able to put to some original purpose as he develops what ever opportunistic advantages there may be for him in each and every situation. This pattern should meet with a fair measure of success in most matters. Neither men or women are favored. A karma in ONE weakens the pattern. A karma in FOUR is some slight improvement because it releases the individual from certain dull routines which are really not quite his style. A karma in FIVE may considerably reduce one's ability to assume certain risks which are really to his advantage. The overall effect here of the FIVE karma would be to reflect a more conventional person less prone to FIVE type promotions.

Some famous people whose character is in the 1-4-5 pattern are:

J. William Fulbright           Fritz Kreisler
Representative Eugene McCarthy   William Faulkner
Johnny Unitas               Patricia Neal
Marie Curie                 Mary Tyler Moore
Justice John Marshall Harlan      Lauren Bacall
Gian-Carlo Menotti

# 2—3—5

The 2-3-5 pattern has TWO on the motivation, THREE on the personality and FIVE on the character. This pattern is considerably toned down from the usual FIVE character and is less favorable for circulating as widely or as freely as other FIVE types. The motivation is diffused and here somewhat overly senitized by intuitive implications. The personality is relaxed and carefree but inclined to let the best of the FIVE type opportunities slip by while he plays around. Since the motivation of TWO is keyed to watchful waiting and perfect timing, when combined with the gamble of FIVE this reduces the number of change opportunities the individual will be willing to take. The pattern is equally suitable for men or women. A karma in TWO enhances the restless competitive spirit of FIVE. A karma in THREE might be an overall improvement in effective performance under the circumstances. A karma in FIVE defeats the whole pattern and reflects quite a different type of person altogether.

Some famous people whose character is in the 2-3-5 pattern are:

Julie Andrews             Mary Margaret McBride
Grace Kelly              Marcello Mastroianni
Cyd Charisse            Charles Coburn
A. C. Neilsen (pollster)      Jack Ruby
Joe Walcott              Cardinal Terence Cooke

Harry Hopkins
Nat King Cole
Thelma Ritter
Willy Brandt

Pope Pius XII
Sydney Omarr
Edward Johndro

# *3—2—5*

The 3-2-5 pattern has three on the motivation, TWO on the personality and FIVE on the character. This pattern is even less favorable than the 2-3-5 for maximum utilization of the best advantages that FIVE has to offer. In both of these patterns there is too much inner conflict caused by the incompatability of the motivation and the personality. While the motivation seeks an audience for its views and opinions, the personality is overly concerned with how the individual can be of help or sympathy to other people's interests neither of which can provide chance opportunities for exploitation. The individual here is too busy showing off or blending in with more dominant figures to seize the best ways he might promote some significant and innovative changes in his life. This pattern is more suitable for women with its feminized personality. A karma in THREE or TWO might give more accent to the FIVE which is otherwise lacking. A karma in FIVE would also be some improvement but not for the pattern itself but because it would reflect a totally different type of person by taking the accent away from FIVE altogether.

Some famous people whose character is in the 3-2-5 pattern are:

Henry Wallace
Ravi Shankar
James Lovell (astronaut)
President Harry S Truman
Harold Pinter
Boris Pasternak
Charles Steinmetz

John Hay Whitney
William Manchester
Jane Wyatt
Laurence Olivier
Victor Mature
Ossie Davis
Richard Loeb (murderer)

184

# 4—1—5

The 4-1-5 pattern has FOUR on the motivation, ONE on the personality and FIVE on the character. This is a sound pattern which combines basic elements which can work together effectively. The motivation is well grounded in reality and practical know-how while the personality is enterprising and inventive. Both of these qualities can promote daring new departures on constructively pioneering projects. The pattern wih its ONE personality is more suitable for men. A karma in FOUR would not seriously impair the complimentary function of the pattern although the individual's talents would be far less effective in his personal affairs than when dealing with outside matters. A karma in ONE would be more serious in lessening the individual initiative. A karma in FIVE would greatly change the pattern but would still make a workable pattern but with more compliance between the ONE and FOUR.

Some famous people whose character is in the 4-1-5 pattern are:

Robert Mulliken  
Akira Kurosawa (director)  
Bobby Fisher  
Sarah Vaughan  
Isamu Noguchi  
Norman Mailer  
Somerset Maugham  
Earle Sanley Gardner  
Gertrude Lawrence  

Ethel Barrymore  
Don Ameche  
Taylor Caldwell  
Billy Graham  
Vincent Astor  
Henry Clay Frick  
Bernard Macfadden  
Brendan Behan  

# 5—9—5

The 5-9-5 pattern has FIVE on he motivation, NINE on the personality and FIVE on the character. This combination makes a lively interesting pattern which especially provides the free swinging FIVE with a wide range of worldly material in order to pursue his special talents. The result here is likely to accent all sensory freedoms combined with an unusual amount of tolerance, charity and compassion. There may be some inclination toward personal sexual indulgences since "anything goes" is the natural format, but the setting is right for making the most from what FIVE ideally has to offer. The pattern is equally suitable for men or women. A karma in NINE would increase the individual's license for purely personal gratifications. A karma in FIVE would increase the accent on dispassionate, clinical objectives.

Some famous people whose character is in the 5-9-5 pattern are:

| | |
|---|---|
| General George S. Patton | Lady Bird Johnson |
| George Gallup (pollster) | Clive Barnes |
| Justice Felix Frankfurter | Cornelia Otis Skinner |
| Woody Guthrie | Jean Arthur |
| Bernard Buffet | Sir Michael Redgrave |
| Julia Child | George Jessell |
| Frank McGee | Vincent Edwards |
| Ali Bhutto | Mrs. George McGovern |
| Martin Luther King | Mayor Robert Wagner |
| Eugene O'Neil | Beria (Russian Secret Police) |
| Russell Schweickart (astronaut) | Roman Polanski |
| Alan Bean (astronaut) | |

# 6—8—5

The 6-8-5 pattern has SIX on the motivation, EIGHT on the personality and FIVE on the character. In this pattern there may be considerable inner conflict between the individual's friendly social obligations and a sincere desire to just "fit in" and the upsetting innovations which he ends up promoting for his own advantages. The EIGHT personality considerably toughens the resistance to criticism and heightens the need for power manipulations to which social responsibilities must take second place. The end result is likely to produce a lively and interesting utilization of the type of thing FIVE can do best. Others who become involved may feel used and abused. The pattern would generally be more attractive for men although it certainly has the makings of a successful woman in a very worldly sense. A karma in SIX might improve the strength of the pattern since it would not take away the image of sociability but only its responsibilities. A karma in EIGHT would not seriously change the workability but would tone down the dynamics. A karma in FIVE would pack far less "punch" and therefore be less interesting and somewhat incomplete.

Some famous people whose character is in the 6-8-5 pattern are:

| | |
|---|---|
| Cecil B. DeMille | Alan Burke |
| Jack Nicklaus | Arthur Amory Houghton |
| Iris Murdoch | Gherman Titov (Soviet astronaut) |
| Doris Day | Senator Thomas Dodd |
| Robert Morse | |

# 7—7—5

The 7-7-5 pattern has SEVEN on the motivation, SEVEN on the personality and FIVE on the character. This is a difficult person to understand or work with. The pattern inclines to be overly shrewd and very clever in strange ways. The individual would tend to get what he wanted, but at other people's expense; however, the chain of events is so involved that people are not likely to be quite aware of exactly how this individual has used them to his advantage. There is a definite coldness in this pattern but certain invincible courage which will enable the person to accomplish unusual success as "one in a lifetime" opportunities. The individual is led to his best chances and seldom has to go out of his way to look for the opportunities that are ideal to him. There is also a very strong "luck" factor operating here which ordinary people would not have available. Never expect to duplicate what this person does because the combination of fortuitous circumstances would never be repeated. The pattern is suitable for either men or women. A karma in SEVEN or FIVE would still make the pattern workable although the individual's personal gratification for what he is able to do might be far less.

Some famous people whose character is in the 7-7-5 pattern are:

| | |
|---|---|
| Albert Schweitzer | John Young (astronaut) |
| Frank Lloyd Wright | Kim Stanley |
| John Foster Dulles | Mrs. Marjorie Merriweather Post |
| Shirley Chisholm | Mary Pickford |
| Beverly Sills | Eli Wallach |
| Eartha Kitt | William Powell |
| Harold Arlen | Senator Wayne Morse |
| George Braque | Justice Roger Taney |
| Jeane Dixon | Patrick Murphy (N.Y. Police) |
| Alan King | |

# *8—6—5*

The 8-6-5 pattern has EIGHT on the motivation, SIX on the personality and FIVE on the character. This is a similar but more effective pattern than its reverse (6-8-5) because here the driving power is on the motivation and the personality is conveniently cloaked in the social geniality of the friendly SIX. This undoubtedly gives the individual more freedom to pursue matters on his own without interference or social condemnation for many of the ruthless and upsetting things he is capable of. But in the interests of the fully expanded potentialities of FIVE this is a powerful and constructive pattern. The individual is sure to go far in most everything he tries to do. What debris he leaves in his wake he is likely to be forgiven for anyway. The pattern is equally favorable for men or women. A karma in EIGHT would considerably diminish the dynamics of the pattern. A karma in SIX would not have too much effect except to increase the potentiality of advantage for the individual himself. A karma in FIVE would be interesting but not as spectacular in the long run as the best opportunities might be passed up as being too risky for his taste.

Some famous people whose character is in the 8-6-5 pattern are:

Carl Gustav Jung
J. C. Penny
Gerard Swope
Kurt Weill
Abba Eban
Frank Borman (astronaut)
Justice John Marshall
Jack Anderson
Ruth Gordon

Miriam Hopkins
Leslie Caron
Anthony Quinn
Walter Pidgeon
Charles Boyer
Mrs. Marina (Lee Harvey) Oswald
President Theodore Roosevelt
Kenneth Fearing

# 9—5—5

The 9-5-5 pattern has NINE on the motivation, FIVE on the personality and FIVE on the character. This pattern is not as effective as its reverse (the 5-9-5). Here the motivation is diffused and generalized and the personality is more apt to offend the best opportunities. Certain people, of course, would be attracted to the more obvious aspects of sensory talents and proclivity for outright opportunism but this is less likely to provide the more constructive opportunities would combine the best of NINE and FIVE (as in the reverse pattern). Here the "eye" of motivation is somewhat in an opposite direction from the "here and now" techniques that must be utilized eventually to manipulate the FIVE into its best position. The motivation may be better intentioned than it would be under the FIVE in the reverse pattern, but the effectiveness just doesn't tie together in the best manner. The pattern is equally suitable for men or women. A karma in NINE might improve the pattern. A karma in FIVE would reflect an individual rather at hopeless odds with his best opportunities and would certainly lead to sexual indulgences of some kind.

Some famous people whose character is in the 9-5-5 pattern are:

| | |
|---|---|
| Henry Ford Sr. | Uta Hagen |
| Richard Tucker | Nanette Fabray |
| Merv Griffin | Princess Margaret Rose |
| Pierre Trudeau | Louis Pasteur |
| Daphine Du Maurier | Harriet Van Horne |
| Alan Watts | Jules Verne |
| Ezra Pound | |

## THE 9 VARIATIONS OF THE SIX CHARACTER

SIX is the vibration of the protector, the champion of group interests, genial sociability and symbolizes one who is always prepared to give and take in any get together relationship. There is a tendency to gravitate to average groups or situations which, while they may represent a cross section of the larger framework of society, are in themselves a closely knit composite of this averaging. The SIX is the mixer, the do-gooder, the joiner, the partner, the talker, the teacher, the instructor, the lecturer, the preacher, everybody's keeper and at times the busybody and the gossip. To fulfill his natural function the SIX should join with another or others and undertake matters in teamwork partnership.

Remember that all of these individual SIXS may differ from the other SIXES that follow by the qualification and modification of their respective motivation drive and personality image. Also, of course, each one may be challenged by a different fate pattern which we will take up in Chapter VIII.

# 1—5—6

The 1-5-6 pattern has ONE on the motivation, FIVE on the personality and SIX on the character. This is a confusing pattern where the individual's private motivation is to dominate rather than share ventures on a co-partnership basis and the personality impression is an opposite and contradictory quality of non-conformity rather than the ultimate group acceptance of the character determination. It is difficult to picture this pattern as being group active at all unless it be in the capacity of a leader or a strictly off-beat, nonconformist group. This individual is likely to lead whatever group he joins along paths that may be pioneering and adventuresome or he may advocate that social structures follow this approach. The pattern might be suitable for either men or women. A karma in ONE would give much less courage to pursue the policies he seems to advocate. A karma in FIVE would make him somewhat more group acceptable. A karma in SIX would make the group format more theoretical than actual.

Some famous people whose character is in the 1-5-6 pattern are:

| | |
|---|---|
| Lily Pons | Dustin Hoffman |
| Clifton Williams (astronaut) | Louis Calhern |
| Rex Stout | Warren Beatty |
| Gloria Swanson | President Herbert Hoover |
| Deborah Kerr | Peter Hurkos |
| Susan Hayward | |

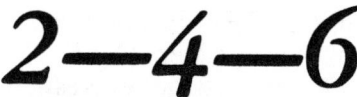

The 2-4-6 pattern has TWO on the motivation, FOUR on the personality and SIX on the character. This pattern is much more in keeping with the virtues of SIX by combining the desire to listen and follow with a certain practical, down-to-earth realism. The inclinations are sympathetic and motherly while the personality gives the assurance of one who is able to work hard to put over some common group purpose. This pattern would be ideal as a homemaker. The pattern is workable for both men or women. A karma in TWO would make the pattern somewhat stronger as a more individualized

191

member of the group. A karma in FOUR would lessen the soundness of practical contributions. A karma in SIX would impersonalize the group angle but increase the willingness to teach how one should act rather than the individual himself having to live up to the principles he advocates.

Some famous people whose character is in the 2-4-6 pattern are:

| | |
|---|---|
| Susan Sontag | Justice Warren Berger |
| Vance Packard | Senator James Buckley |
| Andre Malraux | Gary Moore |
| Hermione Gingold | President Franklin Pierce |
| Petula Clark | Stephen Spender |
| Laurence Harvey | Sacha Guitry |
| Charles Goren | Dr. Tom Dooley |
| J. Robert Oppenheimer | G. W. Vanderbilt |
| Justice Charles Evans Hughes | |

# 3—3—6

The 3-3-6 pattern has THREE on the motivation, THREE on the personality and SIX on the character. This is a happy pattern giving a more spontaneous vent to artistic expression and providing an entertaining and decorative style that generally finds a market of average community acceptance. The individual is outspoken and gives freely of his imagination when trying to develop a format which most people can easily understand. This is not a particularly ambitious pattern but the individual enjoys much personal gratification and social popularity from what he does. The pattern is equally good for men or women. A karma in THREE would add a more serious tone and encourage efforts towards self expression to prefer a medium such as writing rather than a face to face delivery. A karma in SIX would extend the boundries of what the individual feels comprise the audience who should appreciate what he has to offer.

Some famous people whose character is in the 3-3-6 pattern are:

| | |
|---|---|
| Federico Fellini | President Millard Fillmore |
| Richard Neutra | Lilli Palmer |
| David Dubinsky | Jennifer Jones |
| Jess Chandler | Lillian Gish |
| Rudolf Hess | Fay Dunaway |
| Eddie Arcaro | David Wayne |
| Bobby Darin | Sid Caesar |
| Carl Stokes | Vida Blue |
| Ronnie Cunningham (astronaut) | |
| Eugene Cernan (astronaut) | Barbara Hutton |
| John Glenn (astronaut) | Ariel Taylor |

# 4—2—6

The 4-2-6 pattern has FOUR on the motivation, TWO on the personality and SIX on the character. This is a sound pattern for ultimate SIX expression and has some advantages over its reverse (2-4-6) in that the personality is more gentle and sympathetic which insures more effective cooperation from others. The pattern, however, would be more suitable for women since it feminizes the personality image. The strength of the pattern is on the inner resolve (which is always preferable) and the outer image is soothing and inspirational. A karma in FOUR would not seriously upset the workability of the pattern but it would lessen the real value of the contribution. Truth and facts would become much more variable according to the allowances of the situation. A karma in TWO would strengthen the pattern by lessening the proclivity to knuckle under so easily. A karma in SIX depersonalizes the eventual format placing the group affiliations (such as they are), or the common interest which the individual attempts to serve, on a more theoretical basis.

Some famous people whose character is in the 4-2 6 pattern are:

| | |
|---|---|
| Frank Buck | Ethel Merman |

David Rockefeller
Howard Hughes
Walter Gropius
Leonard Woodcock
Harry Belafonte
Willem De Kooning
Moshe Dayan
Nguyen Cao Ky
Winston Churchill
Pres. James Madison

Joseph Cotten
Barbara Bel Geddes
Lord Snowden
Fanny Brice
Danny Kaye
Myra Kingsley
Justice Abe Fortas
Welton Beckett
Julius Rosenberg

# 5—1—6

The 5-1-6 pattern has FIVE on the motivation, ONE on the personality and SIX on the character. This pattern has a dynamic quality which is somewhat more workable than its reverse 1-5-6. The personality format here may be a good deal more acceptable for the individual which it reflects rather than the restless, investigative FIVE which is so contradictory to the ultimate function of the SIX. The FIVE here on the motivation seeks new ways to extend and improve the group while the ONE personality has the courage and self-reliance to put these matters across so they can be easily assimilated when directed or chaneled towards the SIX. The pattern is preferable for men since it masculinizes the personality. A karma in FIVE would tone down the dynamics. A karma in ONE would weaken the respect which the individual seeks. A karma in SIX would broaden the application by depersonalizing what constitutes the individual's group.

Some famous people whose character is in the 5-1-6 pattern are:

Perry Como
George Harrison
Henri Matisse
Walter Cronkite
David Frost

Richard Gordon (astronaut)
Joan Fontaine
Eleanor Roosevelt
Justice Stanley Reed
Alfred Sloan

# 6—9—6

The 6-9-6 pattern has SIX on the motivation, NINE on the personality and SIX on the character. This is a sound pattern for social communication on a broader and more universal level. Others should remember, however, that the individual himself is not as universally based as he would seem from his personality image. There are definite personal limits beyond which the individual will not commit himself, but he appears to think "big". This is a good pattern for politics, particularly on the local level. The pattern is equally suitable for men or women. A karma in NINE would personalize the action. A karma in SIX would correspondingly depersonalize the action and thereby broaden the base more in keeping with the broad universality which the NINE personality suggests.

Some famous people whose character is in the 6-9-6 pattern are:

| | |
|---|---|
| Jonathan Miller | Fidel Castro |
| Edward Everett Horton | Roy Innis |
| Montgomery Clift | William Waldorf Astor |
| Dirk Bogarde | Sen. John Sparkman |
| Max Ernst | Llewellyn George |

# 7—8—6

The 7-8-6 pattern has SEVEN on the motivation, EIGHT on the personality and SIX on the character. One can see that the pattern is a little top heavy in that there is more to the individual than he is actually able to produce. The motivation is select, shrewd and specialized, although it may not be easily communicated to others. The personality is hard, tough, driving, ambitious and bossy. The final application, however, must be tailored town to fit a formula designed for a more average type of client. WHENEVER A

PATTERN REFLECTS MORE IN THE MOTIVATION AND PER-
SONALITY THAN CAN BE UTILIZED IN THE EXPRESSION
FORMAT OF THE CHARACTER INDEX IT SUGGESTS A GREAT
DEAL OF AGITATION until the individual is mature enough to
realize the nature of his ultimate "market". The pattern is somewhat
more appropriate for men than for women because of the toughness
of the personality, that is, unless you happen to like ball-breaking
women. A karma in SEVEN is apt to throw the individual off his
course without his realizing how or why. It would considerably
lessen the unique qualities which this pattern represents. A karma in
EIGHT might make the pattern more workable because it would
tone down the abrasiveness of the personality. A karma in SIX would
be interesting but would reflect an entirely different type of person
by depersonalizing the closeness of the SIX application. In this
pattern this would be an improvement when trying to channel so
much inner steam through the lower SIX vibration.

Some famous people whose character is in the 7-8-6 pattern are:

| | |
|---|---|
| Gardner Murphy | Sen. Everett Dirksen |
| Lawrence Welk | Robert Taylor |
| Meredith Wilson | Sidney Poitier |
| Charles De Gaulle | Cardinal Mindszenty |
| Leslie Uggams | Fred MacMurray |
| Sen. Everett Dirksen | |

The 8-7-6 pattern has EIGHT on the motivation, SEVEN on the
personality and SIX on the character. This again is a pattern as
dynamic as its reverse 7-8-6. The advantages are about equal but the
tempo is quite different. The motivation here is stronger and the
personality, by its reticent aloofness, is somewhat less likely to set
off sparks of resentment. The essential difference between the two
would be the heavy accent on material drives and power manipulation in this pattern where in its reverse (7-8-6) the accent is really on

nonmaterial issues contrary to what the personality image suggests. The 8-7-6 pattern might have the edge in securing a larger slice in terms of money and material accomplishment but the 7-8-6 life style is likely to contain more depth and spiritual purpose. Both patterns, of course, generate considerably more pressure than they are generally able to effectively utilize under the SIX character and much depends on he opportunities which Fate would provide. The pattern is equally suitable for men or women. A karma in EIGHT harshens the material drive as it lessens the inherent sense of justice. A karma in SEVEN reduces the capacity for spiritual depth but might increase the exploitation for shrew manipulations. A karma in SIX widen the eventual field of application by depersonalizing the average SIX format.

Some famous people whose character is in the 8-7-6 pattern are:

| | |
|---|---|
| Pres. Franklin D. Roosevelt | Billie Jean King |
| Duchess of Windsor | Winthrop Aldrich |
| Alfred Kinsey | Pearl Buck |
| Karen Horney | Donald Douglas |
| S. H. Kress | W. K. Vanderbilt |

The 9-6-6 pattern has NINE on the motivation, SIX on the personality and SIX on the character. This is a very workable pattern for broader fields of application than the ordinary SIX format. The motivation is comprehensive and visionary and the application is always what can be brought home and used on an everyday personal basis. This is a happy pattern for the individual which gives respect, popularity, social graces and ease of understanding. The pattern is equally suitable for men or women. A karma in NINE lessens the scope of real social awareness and perhaps over personalizes the average quality of the SIX. A karma in SIX widens the scope as it depersonalizes the ultimate SIX program.

Some famous people whose character is in the 9-6-6 pattern are:

William Masters
Justice Harlan Stone
Norman Thomas
Gladys Swarthout
Grandma Moses
Dick Cavett
Charles Collingwood
Coretta King
Pres. Abraham Lincoln
Pres. William Howard Taft
Jan Valtin

Jane Fonda
Helen Gurley Brown
Charles Darwin
Jimmy Dorsey
C. S. Mott
George Baker
Maurice Utrillo
W. E. Boeing
Evangeline Adams
Adelle Davis

## THE 9 VARIATIONS OF THE SEVEN CHARACTER

SEVEN is the vibration of the specialist. It also reflects an individual who is complex and not easily understood or appreciated by others. In operation it symbolizes a departure from the main stream of life as though to suggest, or point out a factor, that is operative in our daily lives but not obviously apparent. The accent of SEVEN is to something which may exist behind what we see which implies that the surface realities of life, as we know them, are really a shadow of some enduring principle or "master plan". The material objectivists, of course, reject this subjective philosophy which in no way deters the SEVENS from their path, for they are guided by a spiritual faith and a mysterious mysticism. This dual perspective is inherent in all applications of SEVEN. It can represent the same thing in two different ways or two things in the same way. This duality also tends to isolate the SEVEN from other numbers because their position is different and there is also a lack of ready communication. It certainly presents problems to place such reliance on matters that others cannot themselves directly experience and this is made more difficult by the SEVEN preference to explore such matters on their own. If we consider the character as symbolizing the product which the individual contributes to the marketing complex of society, then the SEVEN product is undoubtedly a difficult item to sell in a generalized market. Certainly not everybody wants it and

198

a great many may even question that it has any real value at all. Especially is this true in our present day materially orientated and success-cult society. All these considerations contribute to the quality of loneliness and isolation associated with number SEVEN. Their best moments, however, are when they can stand alone yet fortified by their own faith. The SEVEN character always tends to be withdrawn, uncommunicative, cultered, refined, perfectionist, rich in wisdom, exclusive, authoritative, professional and esoteric. They can also be considered as odd balls, misfits, eccentrics, fools, saints, geniuses, prophets, charletans, ghosts, idealists, dreamers and practical failures.

Remember that all of these individual SEVENS may differ from the other SEVENS that follow by the qualification and modification of their respective motivation drives and personality image. Also, of course, each one may be challenged by a different fate pattern which we will take up in Chapter VIII.

# 1—6—7

The 1-6-7 pattern has ONE on the motivation, SIX on the personality and SEVEN on the character. This is a strong and well balanced pattern for the constructive application of the SEVEN expression. It has strength of character and integrity on the inner motivation combined with a congenial sociability on the personality which, although contradictory to the quality of SEVEN itself, helps to ease communication with others. Any vibration which pulls the SEVEN back into the social context in a congenial way is desirable in order that the SEVEN contribution not be lost or wasted. This is a good pattern for the professional specialist who can also communicate with forceful authority. The pattern is equally suitable for men or women. A karma in ONE weakens the pattern as it accents the polarity of the social responsibilites of SIX against the isolated specialization of SEVEN. A karma in SIX does not seriously disrupt the workability and may even help in some fields of application as it depersonalizes the SIX making it less contradictory to the SEVEN. A karma in SEVEN is still a workable pattern as it increases the effectiveness of the SIX audience and minimizes the pecularities of SEVEN.

Some famous people whose character is in the 1-6-7 pattern are:

| | |
|---|---|
| Jackie Gleason | Bob Consadine |
| Dean Rusk | Zoe Caldwell |
| George Shearing | Robert Redford |
| Pierre S. Du Pont | George Gobel |
| Irwin Shaw | Frank Parker |
| Tommy Dorsey | Sen. Jacob Javits |
| Henry Miller | John J. O'Neill |
| James T. Farrell | |

# 2—5—7

The 2-5-7 pattern has TWO on the motivation, FIVE on the personality and SEVEN on the character. This is an interesting pattern which combines the sensitivity of TWO with the depth of insight in SEVEN and packages this in the exploitative and promotional FIVE personality. The personality, being what the public sees on the surface, can be considered the packaging of the character product being sold. In this pattern the unconventional FIVE has created an expectation of excitement, change, variety, adventure and sensory gratification. While some of this is at variance with the quality which SEVEN symbolizes, at least it prepares the audience for the possibility of a pivotal change which is ideally timed by the rhythmic intuition of the motivation and so lays the ground beautifully for the spiritual suggestion the SEVEN may wish to leave. The pattern is equally suitable for men or women. A karma in TWO would impair the delicate timing for the proper introduction of the SEVEN message (or product). A karma in FIVE would not seriously effect the workability of the pattern because the audience is prepared by what it sees on the surface whether the individual is interested or not in the substance of the image he projects.

A karma in SEVEN would water down the product so the audience may not receive the full depth it anticipates or should have.

Some famous people whose character is in the 2-5-7 pattern are:

Leopold Stokowski
Stewart Udall
Thomas Stafford (astronaut)
Louis Bromfield
Oskar Werner
Louis Gray (F.B.I.)
Sen. George Smathers

Orson Welles
John Jacob Astor
Cliff Robertson
Charles MacArthur
Thomas Edison
Harry Warner

# 3—4—7

The 3-4-7 pattern has THREE on the motivation, FOUR on the personality and SEVEN on the character. This is a reasonably sound pattern for the application of SEVEN. It has the expressive THREE on the motivation to keep the individual actively in touch with an audience combined with the practical know-how and down-to-earth realism that packages the SEVEN product in a format that has practical everyday use value. Altogether this results in a considerable modification of the spirituality of SEVEN as it remolds this in entertaining (THREE) and practical (FOUR) ways. The pattern is equally suitable for men or women. A karma in THREE would add seriousness to the pattern, but it might prove considerably more difficult for others to accept. A karma in FOUR would lighten the pattern and might even make the SEVEN message much easier to take since there would be far less stress on everyday reality. A karma in SEVEN would be an interesting variation as the SEVEN message were made far more subtle and suggestive rather than authoritative and compelling. Not everyone is prepared for the SEVEN message (or product) which here in this pattern is presented with imaginative humor and hard core reality.

Some famous people whose character is in the 3-4-7 pattern are:

| | |
|---|---|
| Justice Earl Warren | Neil Simon |
| Eyde Gorme | Philip Roth |
| Marc Chagall | Edward G. Robinson |
| Dick Smothers | Leon Trotsky |
| Maxine Elliott | Anne Morgan |
| Kenneth Tynan | Nick Jagger |

# 4—3—7

The 4-3-7 pattern has FOUR on the motivation, THREE on the personality and SEVEN on the character. This pattern is very similar to the reverse above (3-4-7) but with definite advantages. Here the strength of reality is in the motivation and the packaging is done with imaginative humor and decorative flourish. It is always easier and consequently more gratifying in the long run to package a strong (or difficult) product in an attractive format that has obvious appeal to the waiting public or potential market. This pattern combines the facts of reality with the depth of spiritual implications and presents this in an entertaining engaging way. The pattern is equally suitable for men or women. A karma in FOUR would lighten the pattern considerably (there would be far less stress on reality and practical issues). A karma in THREE might limit the imagination but impersonalize the THREE type expression so as to cause the individual to turn to an intermediary medium in order to adequately express or packages what he has to offer. A karma in SEVEN would lessen the depth of the spiritual application or make it so subtle as to be missed by some people altogether. The buyer (or taker, or audience) might, however, be more pleased with his purchase in this pattern.

Some famous people whose character is in the 4-3-7 pattern are:

Margaret Mead
Fats Waller
Sammy Snead
Pres. Dwight Eisenhower
Thornton Wilder
Stewart Mott Jr.
Sir Ernest Oppenheimer

Vincent Sheean
Eva Le Gallienne
Peter Ustinov
George Peppard
Edgar Bergen
Shiran Shiran

# 5—2—7

The 5-2-7 pattern has FIVE on the motivation, TWO on the personality and SEVEN on the character. Compared to its reverse pattern (2-5-7) the chances for more gratifying success are better as the dynamics are now in the motivation and the personality here reflects a more sympathetic understanding which is more in keeping with the spirituality of the SEVEN message which must ultimately emerge. This is, of course, a more suitable pattern for women than men because of the feminization of the personality. A karma in FIVE would considerably weaken the inherent dynamics of the pattern and hence detract from its flavor. A karma in TWO might strengthen the pattern a little because the individual himself is less sensitive yet the public still sees him as an indulgent listener. A karma in SEVEN could confuse the real function here as it accents the contrast between the exploitative opportunism of FIVE and the motherly possessiveness of TWO.

Some famous people whose character is in the 5-2-7 pattern are:

Pres. George Washington
Pres. Grover Cleveland
James Reston
Adolphe Menjou
Johnny Carson
Lawrence O'Brien

Raoul Dufy
Haile Selassie
David Scott (astronaut)
Doris Duke
Ero Saarinen
Mario Lanza

# 6—1—7

The 6-1-7 pattern has SIX on the motivation, ONE on the personality and SEVEN on the character. The qualities symbolized do not compliment each other in this pattern. The motivation drive is in sharp contrast to the character format and the personality is self-centered, egotistical and hardly preparatory to the specialized wisdom one will eventually receive from this individual. This pattern is far less effective in operation than its reverse (1-6-7). In this pattern the motivation is weaker than the personality and accents within the individual the contradiction of seeking one thing yet being its opposite. ONE on the personality does nothing to mediate this contradiction and creates independent obstacles of its own to overcome. The pattern is more suitable for men because of the masculinization of the personality. A karma in SIX would depersonalize the motivation and lessen the inner conflict between SIX and SEVEN. A karma in ONE would soften the egotism of the personality. A karma in SEVEN would also make a more workable pattern but reflect a completely different person. The accent would then be on ONE and SIX. When the immaterial SEVEN is depersonalized by karma it may almost drop out of the picture completely.

Some famous people whose character is in the 6-1-7 pattern are:

| | |
|---|---|
| Burt Bacharach | Vivien Leigh |
| Nikita Khrushchev | Gregory Peck |
| James Farmer | Paul Henread |
| Walter Schirra (astronaut) | Sen. George McGovern |
| Pres. Calvin Collidge | Pope Paul VI |
| Sen. James Eastland | Enrico Fermi |
| Madame Blavatsky | Alfred G. Vanderbilt |
| Clare Boothe Luce | Peter Finch |

# 7—9—7

The 7-9-7 pattern has SEVEN on the motivation, NINE on the personality and SEVEN on the character. This is a sound pattern for the SEVEN character which assures not only a fair amount of success but also provides a fair measure of personal gratification to the individual himself. While the motivation is highly specialized, it matches the character, of course, and deepens the implication of the SEVEN message. The universal humanitarian on the personality immediately puts one on a path most likely to have need of this individual's contribution to the world since NINE reflects and attracts something of all mankind. The combination with SEVEN raises the compassion of NINE to a spiritual level which it by no means always has. Whatever set backs or dissapointments these individuals may undergo are not likely to give them much concern because they are so fortified by their personal faith and compassionate vision. The pattern is equally suitable for men or women. A karma in NINE would spoil the wonderful inner harmony of this pattern as the NINE removes the loneliness of SEVEN and supplies a never ending chain of contacts back into the family of human relationships. A karma in SEVEN would not be as unfortunate. It would merely mean that the spiritual implication could be taken or left alone as this individual dedicated himself to humanitarian service.

Some famous people whose character is in the 7-9-7 pattern are:

| | |
|---|---|
| Mies Van Der Rohe | Katherine Anne Porter |
| Ringo Starr | Ralph Nader |
| Duke Ellington | Marshall McLuhan |
| Roy Lichtenstein | Ann Landers |
| Milton Berle | Kingsley Amis |
| Virgil Grisson (astronaut) | Raquel Welch |
| Abigail Van Buren | Erich Von Stroheim |
| Arnold Toynbee | John D. Rockefeller |
| Orville Freeman | Joseph Stalin |
| Long John Nebel | |

# 8—8—7

The 8-8-7 pattern has EIGHT on the motivation, EIGHT on the personality and SEVEN on the character. This is a strong compulsive pattern which has a potential of great financial interest in the affairs of others. The powerful EIGHT on both the motivation and the personality is almost invicible even though the ultimate expression is in the contiguous vibration of SEVEN. The number vibrations of SEVEN, EIGHT, and NINE, although contiguous and therefore symbolizing somewhat contradictory qualities, are all vibrations of power and influence and consequently can function independently of these apparent contradictions. This is not true of vibrations ONE through SIX. In this pattern there is a remarkable concentration of talent for handling dynamic problems of balance, justice, administrative control, financial vision and power manipulation which are all themselves controlled and patterned by an amazing depth of spiritual understanding. The result is a very shrewd individual who is quite aware of much more in any situation than even all those material matters so obviously under his executive control. The individual is likely, however, to be under considerable strain from the constant awareness of the potential implications of the complex matters he is so sensitively keyed to. Unfortunately in this pattern there is no relief value to escape from this constant pressure. The pattern would be equally suitable for men or women but would inevitably pull women into the career field. A karma in EIGHT could lessen the ideality of the pattern but oddly enough might increase the probability for financial success since the EIGHT karma over values money, and invariably ends up with more of it than had they used better judgment. A karma in SEVEN would depersonalize the spiritual implications and probably increase the shrewdness thereby heightening the application to financial and material matters.

Some famous people whose character is in the 8-8-7 pattern are:

| | |
|---|---|
| Hugh Cullen | William Inge |
| Richard Helms | Ann Sothern |
| Ramsey Clark | Eve Arden |

Leo Durocher
Jacques Lipchitz
Drew Pearson
John O'Hara

Clark Gable
Jacques Piccard
Edward Weston
Bobby Clark

# 9—7—7

The 9-7-7 pattern has NINE on the motivation, SEVEN on the personality and SEVEN on the character. This is also a commanding pattern of importance but here the emphasis is on various applications of perceptive insight without particular concern for practical, material matters. This pattern has the advantage of providing alternate focal points for the individual's unique sense of perception so that he may either concentrate this on impersonal matters of broad social context (NINE), or he may turn this inward on more introspective concern for the illusive implications concerning one's spiritual challenge in life. The particular virtue of this pattern is the prospective utilization of the individual's personal revelations in a field of universal application which can correspondingly benefit all mankind as opposed to just satisfying one's individual answer. The pattern is equally suitable for men or women. A karma in NINE or SEVEN would not seriously impair the general workability of the pattern as it would only further depersonalize the individual's answers to himself.

Some famous people whose character is in the 9-7-7 pattern are:

Timothy Leary
Stavros Niarchos
Jack Dempsey
Thomas Huxley
Connie Mack
Buddy Hackett

Pres. Andrew Johnson
Robert Frost
Myrna Loy
Red Buttons
Sen. Ralph Yarborough

# THE 9 VARIATIONS OF THE EIGHT CHARACTER

EIGHT is the vibration of power, its source, its essence and its application. Ultimately there is also a balancing of material and ethical (or spiritual) considerations of which EIGHT is always acutely aware. This is what gives EIGHT the perogative to judge and to administer and, where necessary, to violently employ force to restore the delicate balance which we call justice. The demands of EIGHT are harsh and extreme because all personal consideration or sentiments must be put aside. All individuals who have a karma in EIGHT are initially loath to rise to this challenge in their personal lives. They do not wish to sit in judgment on others or on their own personal affairs. Nevertheless it is an imperative function that must be performed in life and is the job of EIGHT to carry it out, come hell or high water. The personal demand is toughness of attitude to the point of utter ruthlessness when necessary. It is obviously a powerful position and involves all the techniques of power manipulation. Its function is most often applied to the field of material and financial affairs but it can also apply to any area of human behavior where these delicate systems of balance and counterbalance assume some degree of importance in the individual's mind.

Remember that all of these individual EIGHTS may differ from the other EIGHTS that follow by the qualification and modification of their respective motivation drives and personality image. Also, of course, each one may be challenged by a different fate pattern which we will take up in Chapter VIII.

# 1-7-8

The 1-7-8 pattern has ONE on the motivation, SEVEN on the personality and EIGHT on the character. This is a sound, strong pattern although somewhat confusing to others as the personality does not prepare them for the possible shock of the EIGHT eventually. The motivation is strong, determined and self-centered for greater thrust. The personality is somewhat low key, aloof, refined and professionalized, both of which can contribute significantly to the EIGHT's administration of justice. In this pattern it will certainly be done with courage, integrity and an awareness of spiritual implications. The pattern is equally suitable for men or women. A karma in ONE might be some improvement as it would depersonalize the ego. A karma in SEVEN would harm the pattern somewhat as the SEVEN would not be as operative in balancing the drive of the ego with the EIGHT manipulation of power. A karma in EIGHT would reflect an interesting pattern as it depersonalized the requirements for power.

Some famous people whose character is in the 1-7-8 pattern are:

| | |
|---|---|
| Dinah Shore | Cesar Chavez |
| Claude Rains | Donald Slayton (astronaut) |
| Judy Garland | Dame Rebecca West |
| Raymond Burr | Lucy Baines Johnson |
| Sen. Edmund Muskie | Rep. Hale Boggs |

# 2—6—8

The 2-6-8 pattern has TWO on the motivation, SIX on the personality and EIGHT on the character. This is not a particularly strong or desirable pattern for the highest potential of EIGHT expression. The motivation is weak, overly sensitive and personalized to the point of motherly possessiveness. At best it is a sense of martyrdom, self sacrifice or idealism. The personality is too social and group evaluative to properly administer the EIGHT without the sentiment which it must eliminate. The pattern is well suited for some sort of group administrative work where on occasion a sympathetic indulgence is welcome. The pattern is equally suitable for men or women. A karma in TWO or SIX would help the pattern a little as it would throw more accent on the EIGHT which is needed here. A karma in EIGHT would reflect an entirely different kind of person entirely but one less likely to be torn between such conflicting goals.

Some famous people whose character is in the 2-6-8 pattern are:

Barbara Stanwyck
Ronald Colman
Margaret Sullivan
Thomas Watson Sr.
Francisco Franco
Kate Millett
Pres. William Harrison
Pres. John F. Kennedy
Majorie Main

Wendell Willkie
Allen Ginsberg
Van Wyck Brooks
Mack Sennett
John F. Kennedy Jr.
H. Ross Perot
Sen. John Tower
Louis De Wohl

# 3—5—8

The 3-5-8 pattern has THREE on the motivation, FIVE on the personality and EIGHT on the character. This is an interesting and clever pattern which on occasion can get a lot of serious work accomplished without upsetting others too profoundly. The motivation seeks an audience for personal gratification of ideas and opinions but the individual can also be quite amusing and witty which lightens the impact and possible devastation of his final impact. The personality is adaptable, adventuresome, eager and competitive, being constantly in search of interesting new situations. The final outcome is serious and profound and can be highly constructive. The pattern is equally suitable for men or women. A karma in THREE would not seriously impair the pattern. A karma in FIVE would however lessen the activity of a quality which helps considerably to make this pattern interesting. A karma in EIGHT would reduce the ultimate value or justice of the contribution.

Some famous people whose character is in the 3-5-8 pattern are:

Michelangelo Antonioni

Merle Oberon

Robert Young (railroad magnate)
Albert Shanker
Shirley Temple Black
Jesse Owens (track star)
Irving Berlin

Ina Claire
Van Heflin
Alan Bates
Germaine Greer
Marilyn Monroe

The 4-4-8 pattern has FOUR on the motivation, FOUR on the personality and EIGHT on the character. This is a sound pattern for material accomplishment but has perhaps an over-emphasis on just the material or financial side of life which may in the end severely limit the full potentiality of the EIGHT judgment. The application is ideal in the business world but is likely to reflect an individual who has little interest or purpose outside of this material routine. There is also some danger of the individual working himself to death as there are no mediating alternatives to this incassant challenge for more and more material accumulation and power. The accent here is double on the FOUR which symbolizes the worker himself while the real talent in the character is to be the boss and let competent underlings do most of the work so this individual is torn between an executive role which he should assume and actually doing most of the real work just because he likes to. The pattern is equally suitable for men or women. A karma in FOUR might be an improvement on the personal side as one would be more willing to delegate the work load. A karma in EIGHT would only increase the actual work load and lessen the individual's executive assignments.

Some famous people whose character is in the 4-4-8 pattern are:

Justice William O. Douglas
Representative Wilbur Mills
Joe Dimaggio
Elvis Presley
Tom Jones

Yevgeny Yevtushenko
Rex Reed
Marjorie Rawlings
Zero Mostel
Sydney Greenstreet

211

Cecil Beaton
Mike Wallace
President Benjamin Harrison

Glenn Ford
Governor John Connally
Bela Lugosi

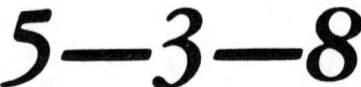

The 5-3-8 pattern has FIVE on the motivation, THREE on the personality and EIGHT on the character. This is more favorable than its reverse pattern (5-3-8) because here the motivation is more dynamic, competitive and less concerned with self-gratification or just pleasing one's self. The personality is more relaxed, casual and obviously decorative and amusing which is a mediating influence between the exploitive opportunism of the motivation and the hard driving finality of the character. The individual is better able to do what he wants here and get away with it because there is less incrimination or adverse reaction being fired directly at him. He is more likely to be forgiven for the shock intrusion which he is capable of. The pattern is equally suitable for men or women. A karma in FIVE would lessen the dynamics considerably. A karma in THREE might increase the power of the pattern yet not substantially lose much of the advantage of the THREE mask. A karma in EIGHT would considerably reduce the ultimate value of the end result because the individual would avoid the more demanding situations which would provide for a more significant expression of EIGHT power.

Some famous people whose character is in the 5-3-8 pattern are:

Ty Cobb
Dan Rowan
John Wanamaker
Alan Shepard (astronaut)
Tennessee Williams
George Bernard Shaw
W. M. Kiplinger

Shelley Winters
Debbie Reynolds
Phil Silvers
Boris Karloff
Bebe Rebozo
I. A. Richards

212

# 6—2—8

The 6-2-8 pattern has SIX on the motivation, TWO on the personality and EIGHT on the character. This is not a strong pattern for expressing the higher potential of EIGHT. The SIX motivation leads the individual into areas which are particularly resistant to corrective adjustment which would upset the status quo of organized groups. It is rather naive to expect that people, who are comfortable with the way things are, will welcome a violent rearrangement even if it provides more theoretical justice. Any emphasis on SIX connected with the application of EIGHT introduces the element of sentiment in regard to judgment, which is unfortunate. The TWO personality is confusing as it suggests a leniency, compromise or sell out, which may not ultimately be possible. This pattern is less workable in respect to the EIGHT than its reverse (2-6-8). The pattern would be more suitable for women as it feminizes the personality. On men the weakness would become almost intollerable by comparision to what the EIGHT ultimately demands. The pattern should not be judged on whether it reflects a likeable individual, by some people's standards, but whether the overall workability provides the best that the character has to offer. A karma in SIX or TWO would improve the pattern. A karma in EIGHT would seriously weaken the effectiveness altogether.

Some famous people whose character is in the 6-2-8 pattern are:

| | |
|---|---|
| Mike Todd | E. M. Forster |
| Alger Hiss | Alice Ghostley |
| Rev. Carl McIntire | T. S. Eliot |
| Bob Newhart | Laurence Housman |
| Justice Joseph Story | Kim Novak |
| Edwin Aldrin (astronaut) | Mia Farrow |
| Langston Hughes | Peter O'Toole |
| Colin Wilson | Richard Burton |
| Charles E. O. Carter | |

# 7—1—8

The 7-1-8 pattern has SEVEN on the motivation, ONE on the personality and EIGHT on the character. This is a sound pattern which reflects strength in the personality which is complimentary with the hard-boiled expression which ultimately follows. At the same time the motivation is "divinely" guided by the depth of its instinctive sense of values. The individual is more likely to make his main contribution in fields other than those of dominant or purely material values, although he may have to first secure his financial backing in such areas. The individual's ultimate purpose is on higher matters than just material control, which leads him into more complex situations of balance where the material factors are not so obvious. The pattern is more suited to men than women as it masculinizes the personality, but today many women working in special fields may find that this factor does not offer a serious handicap, if indeed any at all. This evaluation of masculinization or feminization of the personality has more direct bearing when the individual is limited to a social context which is restricted to more traditional views of how men or women are supposed to obviously behave. A karma in SEVEN might in some cases strengthen the pattern but would lose the ideality of the spiritual counterpoint against the super materiality of the EIGHT. A karma in ONE would improve the workable balance between SEVEN and EIGHT but would hold the individual back from the more daring challenges he may encounter. A karma in EIGHT would not be at all satisfactory. It might reflect a more rounded individual (by some people's standards) but the full implication of the EIGHT function or message would be missing.

Some famous people whose character is in the 7-1-8 pattern are:

| | |
|---|---|
| Otto Preminger | Clint Murcheson |
| Steve Lawrence | Calouste Gulbenkian |
| Hugh Downs | Rock Hudson |
| Jean Paul Sartre | Trevor Howard |
| Marianne Moore | Maggie Smith |

Lillian Hellman
John Wayne
Jerry Lewis

Grant Lewi
Vincent Lopez

# 8—9—8

The 8-9-8 pattern has EIGHT on the motivation, NINE on the personality and EIGHT on the character. This is an excellent pattern for EIGHT super efficiency. The motivation is strong and, of course, exactly matches the ultimate result. The personality reflects a broad, impersonal outlook which attracts a wide following. There is bound to be an above average degree of success in the world although the individual himself may not at times feel a complete sense of gratification with the way things turn out in the difficult tasks which he sets out for himself. There is apt to be a personal sense of loss in spite of outward achievement. This is fortified, however, by a worldly philosophy which eventually sees things as they should be. The pattern is equally suitable for men or women. A karma in EIGHT would broaden the objectives but lessen the impact and sometimes the inherent justice which in this situation is mandatory. A karma in NINE would intensify the toughness of the EIGHT qualities but still retain the compassionate mask the public sees.

Some famous people whose character is in the 8-9-8 pattern are:

Arturo Toscanini
Eric Segal
John Hersey
Ray Milland
William Holden
Billy Talbert

Mickey Mantle
Don Drysdale
Maxfield Parrish
Charles Kettering
George Jay Gould
Wallace Stevens

# 9—8—8

The 9-8-8 pattern has NINE on the motivation, EIGHT on the personality and EIGHT on the character. This pattern is not nearly as effective as its reverse (8-9-8). The motivation here is diffused and obviously out of step with the ultimate treatment to be administered. At the same time the personality image is tough and abrasive which unnecessarily warns people in advance of what they may expect in spite of this individual's sincere desire to regard them compassionately. It is the individual himself who suffers most from this disproportionate (or unfortunate) distribution of qualities in his make up. This may lead to some bitterness and harsh retaliation on his part. The pattern would be somewhat unsuitable for women because of the harsh exterior image reflected here but it is not a particularly fortunate pattern to begin with. A karma in NINE would heighten the efficiency of the EIGHT administration and reduce the individual's sense of personal disappointment. A karma in EIGHT would improve the balance and still might achieve some degree of judicial influence in broad, impersonal fields of application.

Some famous people whose character is in the 9-8-8 pattern are:

| | |
|---|---|
| Winthrop Rockefeller | Vanessa Redgrave |
| Dizzy Dean | Robert Montgomery |
| Pearl Bailey | John Cassavetes |
| Louise Nevelson | Eddie Cantor |
| Frank Gifford | John Warnecke |
| Golda Meir | W. T. Grant |
| Aleksei Kosygin | Andrew Mellon |
| F. Scott Fitzgerald | Clarence Dillon |
| Paddy Chayefsky | |

## THE 9 VARIATIONS OF THE NINE CHARACTER

NINE is the vibration of the healer, the saint, the pilgrim, the wanderer, the mendicant, the preacher and the politician. It symbolizes a state or plateau in human understanding where not only can one see the past in clear perspective, but also sense the pattern of the future. There is inherent in NINE a consciousness of endings together with some degree of preparation for what may be required in the future. The culmination of this awareness may invoke a certain sadness, but it also provides an instinct for whatever dramatic ingredients are present. NINE gives the individual a talent for projecting these dramatic ingredients in such a way as to symbolize for many people some instinctive emotional need. The question whether this emotional need should be brought to the surface or exploited in this way is somewhat beside the point as NINES unconsciously prepare for the future by contributing to the elimination of something in the past. The real good that NINES do, in many cases, may have to "live after them" because in the eyes of some, what they currently do may be considered more troublesome and disruptive than in any way desirable. Thus the NINE is literally caught between the "devil and the deep blue sea". While NINE broadens the compassion and understanding through a sense of "extended vision", it also cools the personal and intimate relationships to the point of clinical objectivity. This leads to the paradox that what sounds good in theory is not nearly as desirable when put into actual practice. NINES naturally stick to theory (like politicians which is a NINE vibration) and consistently avoid being tripped up by specific applications. The function of NINE, especially when strongly in accent, tends to diminish or eliminate the specific qualities of other numbers. This is less apparent, however, with SEVEN or EIGHT as these three vibrations symbolize qualities which are above the ordinary level of personal gratifications. In other words, these three qualities comprise a degree of power and influence which usually transcends the ordinary requirements of individuals.

Remember that all of these individual NINES may differ from the other NINES that follow by the qualification and modification of their respective motivation drive and personality image. Also, of course, each one may be challenged by a different fate pattern which we will take up in Chapter VIII.

# 1—8—9

The 1-8-9 pattern has ONE on the motivation, EIGHT on the personality and NINE on the character. This is an exceptionally strong and dominant pattern which invariably assures the individual of some degree of success and recognition. The motivation is determined, independent and courageous. The personality reflects an obvious talent for judgment, material vision and administrative control. The character determines that the ultimate format for this individual's programs will be broadly comprehensive, capable of universal application and at the same time be compassionately charitable. This is certainly a pattern for getting things done and a number of individuals are likely to get pushed around in the process. The pattern is equally suitable for men or women but requires the women to seek a career of their own. A karma in ONE weakens the pattern considerably. A karma in EIGHT would lessen the prospects in business. A karma in NINE would in some cases intensify the material business drives but weaken the ultimate integrity of the accomplishment as the individual turned to the gratification of more personal advantages.

Some famous people whose character is in the 1-8-9 pattern are:

| | |
|---|---|
| Le Corbusier | Bess Truman |
| Pierre Salinger | Al Jolson |
| Max Baer | Angus Wilson |
| Babe Ruth | Loretta Young |
| Ray Charles | George C. Scott |
| Queen Wilhelmina | Tony Perkins |
| Harold Wilson | Broderick Crawford |
| Bernadette Devlin | Marlene Dietrich |

# 2—7—9

The 2-7-9 pattern has TWO on the motivation, SEVEN on the

personality and NINE on the character. This is an influential pattern but the accent here is on the humanities and is not very concerned with the world of business affairs. While the motivation is highly sensitive, it is complimentary to both the personality index and the character for making a penetrating contribution to some matter of spiritual importance which influences many people. The personality reflects an even higher degree of intuition which is divinely guided to those situations for which it is ideally suited. The ultimate function of the character shows an individual of broad responsibilities and comprehensive awareness of the totality of life. This individual may seldom be found seeking the glare of publicity for the programs he selects, but his influence, particularly from behind the scenes, is likely to be instrumental and highly effective. The pattern is equally suitable for men or women. A karma in TWO would make the individual a little more ambitious. A karma in SEVEN would make the individual a little less spiritual. A karma in NINE would create a helpful individual but reduce the broadness of the application.

Some famous people whose character is in the 2-7-9 pattern are:

William Kunstler
Erich Fromm
Chet Huntley
Leonard Woolf
Harold Lloyd
Cary Grant
David Susskind

Sax Rohmer
Sir Bernard Lovell
Amory Houghton
Bud Fisher
Constantin Brancusi
W. L. McKnight

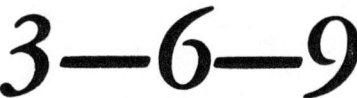

The 3-6-9 pattern has THREE on the motivation, SIX on the personality and NINE on the character. This is an ideal pattern for success in the creative arts. The motivation instills the imaginative desire for an audience. The personality lends ease of communication and popularity of response. The NINE insures a universal appeal where all can find something in common with the ultimate application. The individual is also likely to be a happy person who enjoys what he does and in turn shares his pleasure with others. The creativity here has a great sense of freedom and independence. The pattern is equally suitable for men or women. A karma in THREE would heighten the sense of social obligation and lessen the sense of independent freedom. A karma in SIX would heighten the independence of the creative urge yet not seriously impede the sociability when required. A karma in NINE would diminish the broad under base but reflect a more personalized artist or a more intimate rendition of the creativity.

Some famous people whose character is in the 3-6-9 pattern are:

| | |
|---|---|
| Katherine Hepburn | Mrs. Charles Payson |
| James Hilton | Juan Trippe |
| Karl Menninger | R. A. Hunt |
| Ingmar Bergman | William Rockefeller |
| Sosthenes Behn | Michael Collins (astronaut) |
| Roger Maris | Fritz Thyssen |
| Trini Lopez | Ruth Montgomery |
| Paul Anka | Michael Caine |
| Henry Moore | Bing Crosby |
| Steve Allen | Alan Arkin |
| Leonid Brezhnev | Senator Vance Hartke |
| Luther Burbank | Edgar Cayce |

# 4—5—9

The 4-5-9 pattern has FOUR on the motivation, FIVE on the personality and NINE on the character. This pattern introduces both a practical attitude and an adventuresome energy into the concept of depersonalized service. The motivation is strong, realistic and down-to-earth. The personality is versatile, competitive and eager for change. The ultimate format is still broad-minded and congenial, with the promise of "something for everyone." This individual is likely to seek his field of service (all NINES are committed to some sort of service) in more active fields where theory is not nearly as important as getting the facts properly organized to prove a point and at the same time generate enough new excitement which will change the map of things in a startling and innovative way. The pattern is suitable for either men or women. A karma in FOUR would lessen the practical sense of realism. A karma in FIVE would limit the individual's innovative efforts to break away from established molds. A karma in NINE would disturb the inherent balance in this pattern leaving a disturbing inner conflict between the contradiction in the qualities of FOUR and FIVE.

Some famous people whose character is in the 4-5-9 pattern are:

| | |
|---|---|
| Aristotle Onassis | Tom Smothers |
| Sargent Shriver | Sloan Wilson |
| Hazel Scott | Dorothy Kilgallen |
| Dame Myra Hess | Sandy Dennis |
| Jim Nabors | Elliott Gould |
| Whitney Young | Rev. Martin Niemoller |
| Harry Guggenheim | Alan Leo |

# 5—4—9

The 5-4-9 pattern has FIVE on the motivation, FOUR on the personality and NINE on the character. This pattern is not as lively or as promising as its reverse (4-5-9). The personality is considerably restricted and resistant to any easy adaptation to the opportunities which the restless but somewhat chaotic motivation pursues. The individual will start fewer projects but may work more consistently at seeing difficult situations brought to a conclusion. The broad application required by NINE is overshadowed by the practical demands of the personality and while the individual may desire more opportunities, fewer will be offered him because the personality image is contradictory to the ultimate talent. The pattern is equally suitable for men or women. A karma in FIVE would only aggravate the contradictory aims of FOUR and NINE. A karma in FOUR might loosen the pattern more in line with the motivation and the character. A karma in NINE would work at cross purpose to the best application of NINE.

Some famous people whose character is in the 5-4-9 pattern are:

| | |
|---|---|
| Truman Capote | Roy Chapman Andrews |
| Twiggy | Arthur Vining Davis |
| Sir Julian Huxley | Greta Garbo |
| Senator Mike Mansfield | James Mason |
| Gene Littler | Joe E. Brown |
| Roberta Peters | Dana Andrews |
| Eddy Arnold | Sen. Leverett Saltonstall |
| Edmund Wilson | Joe Pepitone |

# 6—3—9

The 6-3-9 pattern has SIX on the motivation, THREE on the personality and NINE on the character. This pattern is not as creative or as broadly comprehensive as its reverse pattern (3-6-9). Here the motivation is decidedly adverse to the ultimate NINE expression as it introduces the restrictive codes of localized groups as opposed to loosening the bounds which might unite all peoples regardless of local differences. The THREE personality, by its carefree indifference, instead of mediating the conflict somewhat contributes to it until there is a final and upsetting confrontation within the individual as to which goal he will seek. In the meantime much creative energy may be lost working on matters of little importance or failing to fully apply one's self to situations which really count. The pattern is equally suitable for men or women. A karma in SIX would improve the creative expression of the NINE purpose. A karma in THREE would heighten the contradiction between SIX and NINE. A karma in NINE might relax the pattern so a happier compromise was achieved but the real intent of the pattern would be minimized.

Some famous people whose character is in the 6-3-9 pattern are:

Ed Sullivan
Pres. William McKinley
Conrad Aiken
Lee Remick
Rosalind Russell
Shirley Booth
Mary Astor
Rev. Oral Roberts

Lee Trevino
Georgia O'Keefe
Larry Rivers
A. P. Giannini
Henry J. Kaiser
H. F. Sinclair
Senator Strom Thurmond

# 7–2–9

The 7-2-9 pattern has SEVEN on the motivation, TWO on the personality and NINE on the character. This, like its reverse combination (2-7-9), has more spiritual than practical application of the humanitarian interests. The individual here is more intense and somewhat more gifted in intuitive matters. The motivation is deeper and more specialized while the personality is a good deal more approachable and obviously sympathetic. Any pattern where complimentary qualities are so arranged as to place the strength in the motivation and to make the personality seem more pliable assures one of greater success in achieving the ultimate purpose of the pattern (namely expression of the character vibration). While, generally speaking, it is more suitable for men to be masculinized on the personality and women to be feminized, when expressing the humanitarian function of NINE it is perhaps less important. A karma in SEVEN would personalize the achievements. A karma in TWO would decidedly depersonalize the individual. A karma in NINE would reduce the broadness of the ultimate application.

Some famous people whose character is in the 7-2-9 pattern are:

Albert Einstein
Joan Sutherland

Robert Vaughn
Rudy Vallee

Joey Bishop
Ralph Abernathy
James Thurber
Raymond Chandler
Martha Raye
Shirley Maclaine

Tony Curtiss
Sen. Tom Eagleton
Stokely Carmichael
Edwin Land
Joan Crawford

# 8—1—9

The 8-1-9 pattern has EIGHT on the motivation, ONE on the personality and NINE on the character. This, like its reverse pattern (1-8-9) is ideal for application in the world of business. In fact it exactly matches the number pattern of the word BUSINESS itself. This pattern has a slight edge on its reverse pattern because the ONE on the personality is a bit easier for others to take. Here the personality reflects an obvious talent for courage, leadership, independence and pioneering spirit rather than a personality which reflects a typical high pressure "boss" attitude. Both patterns, however, are assured of above average success in whatever they undertake. The direction here is more money/power wise and correspondingly less on individual daring and progressive leadership. The pattern is more suitable for men because of the masculinization of the personality. This is somewhat contradictory to the statement above about either sex working in the humanities but this pattern is definitely more slanted towards the broader aspect of the business world. A karma in EIGHT would lessen the interest in business. A karma in ONE would weaken the personal integrity. A karma in NINE would increase the business and material emphasis but lessen the best chances for broad application or universal appeal.

Some famous people whose character is in the 8-1-9 pattern are:

Linus Pauling
Buckminster Fuller
Barry Goldwater

Tricia Nixon
Sir Francis Chichester
Carol Reed

Kaye Ballard
Salvador Dali
Jesse Jackson
Niels Bohr

Babe Didrikson Zaharias
Anne Bancroft
Dean Martin
Burt Lancaster

# 9—9—9

The 9-9-9 pattern has NINE on motivation, personality and character. This is, of course, an unusual pattern but may not prove to be especially effective. The individual is prone to drift with the tide until such time (if it ever arises) when he may be called upon or pressed into, some sort of service commitment. Usually the application here is in a supportive and dedicated role which calls for much forebearance and personal philosophizing on the individual's part. The life pattern is apt to be sad in some respects unless the individual is thoroughly aware of the depersonalization of his own make up and how this is likely to affect others. Much would depend on the tempo of the destiny which is coupled with this particular pattern. While NINE symbolizes an impersonal form of brotherly love it can also provoke a consuming hatred which can flare up and become quite destructive. This is especially true in this pattern of NINE. There is a lack of balance here and too much of just the single vibration in this pattern. The pattern is equally suitable for men or women. A karma in NINE would actually improve the situation somewhat. The individual would be less likely to drift quite as much but would still lack a proper focus.

Some famous people whose character is in the 9-9-9 pattern are:

Dr. Benjamin Spock
Moira Shearer
Sen. William Proxmire
Jerry Herman
Queen Elizabeth II
Malvina Hoffman

Rachel Carson
Maxwell Anderson
Robert Millikan
Carl Payne Tobey
J. Gaither Pratt

# Chapter VIII

# EVALUATING THE 81 PATTERNS OF CHARACTER IN RELATION TO THEIR DESTINY WITH EXAMPLES OF FAMOUS PERSONALITIES

All this while under judgment and evaluation on the 81 variations of the character pattern, we have been discussing the potentialities of the individual himself. But it must be remembered that NO ONE FUNCTIONS INDEPENDENTLY OF HIS ENVIRONMENT, or as we prefer to state in number philosophy, independently of the specific opportunities which are provided by the pattern of one's fate or destiny.

The individual is considerably influenced and molded by the pattern of his destiny. This should be obvious when one considers that the pattern of the destiny symbolizes the quality of the experience and the opportunities that the individual will encounter on his path through life.

Before proceeding to list the general effect of each destiny vibration on the character, let me repeat the general comments on the destiny itself.

The vibration of the destiny is a life long challenge. As a challenge, no matter how well this matches the individual's own pattern, there are still obstacles to be overcome in pursuing this particular path in life and there is always some degree of reluctance to constantly face this particular challenge and thereby achieve one's spiritual purpose. In the context of reincarnation it might be stated that no matter how many times in former lives the individual had faced this particular challenge before, there are still lessons to be learned in this life in facing this same challenge again. So, as one might well ask, why must I go through this whole thing again? The answer is that you have to do it because you still have something to learn in this matter. This may not be much of an answer to most people, but it is the obvious answer which couples human life with a spiritual purpose.

In matching the individual to his destiny the more significant correspondence is when the destiny vibration matches the character. This does not necessarily make the challenge easier, but it does mean that the individual HAS THE IDEAL TALENTS FOR MEETING THAT CHALLENGE.

When the destiny vibration matches the personality the individual, in the eyes of others, SEEMS TO HAVE an obvious talent for the pursuit of this objective. This is partially true, but since the match here is to the personality, not the character, the individual's ultimate approach and treatment of the problem (challenge, confrontation, opportunity, etc.) will be in some combination of his CHARACTER IN RELATION TO HIS DESTINY. The individual will, however, find it easier to meet the challenge of his destiny because the quality of the personality functions instinctively without conscious effort on his part.

When the destiny vibration matches the motivation the individual is particularly grateful for any opportunity which fate provides for him to reach in this direction. It is not as easy here for him as when the match is on the personality, but HE GETS MORE PERSONAL SATISFACTION from it.

If the match of the destiny to either the character, personality or motivation is to a vibration in which the individual has a karma, there is some loss of perspective on the matter and the individual will accept the challenge with some reluctance or misgivings. He does not immediately throw himself wholeheartedly into the situation. The interesting point here is, however, that since life offers us a great number of chances to rise to the occasion indicated by the karmic vibration, the individual with a karma in his destiny number actually encounters MORE OPPORTUNITIES IN THIS DIRECTION than the individual without a karmic destiny. Example, an individual with a karmic EIGHT destiny has more opportunity to make money and utilize power than the one without a karmic EIGHT.

228

# THE 9 VARIATIONS OF DESTINY TO THE ONE CHARACTER

## THE *1* CHARACTER IN RELATION TO THE *1* DESTINY

Naturally this intensifies the ego drive but offers a spendid opportunity to make a significant mark in life. Matching the character, the individual has a real talent for seizing the unique opportunities which life will offer. Although the entire life span is an uphill struggle and the individual will seldom be completely satisfied with what he does, he is the type of person who has the capacity to always outdo himself. A karma in ONE will simply make life in all respects more painful and difficult to understand or accept.

Some famous people whose ONE character confronts a ONE destiny are:

Edward Steichen
Andrew Wyeth
Della Reese
Grace Moore
Jean-Claude Killy

Anthony Franciosa
Rita Hayworth
Beatrice Lillie
Aimee Semple McPherson

Remember that all of these individuals are ONES who confront a ONE destiny but they may not all be the same type of ONE as modified by their respective motivation drive and personality image.

# THE *1* CHARACTER IN RELATION TO THE *2* DESTINY

The polarity contradiction here between the qualities of ONE and TWO is bound to create intense emotional stress in the individual's life. Each time he feels he has landed right on target and has all the factors substantially under his control is the very time he will become acutely aware of an alternative approach that may be equally valid. The indecision of the multiple choice, where before he considered he had the only possible solution, will tend to tear him apart. As a masculine type he will find that feminized people in some way hold an important key in the development of his fate. A karma in ONE minimizes the requirements of the individual in favor of his fate pattern. A karma in TWO indicates a reluctance to follow the direction of his life as layed out for him by fate with a consequent loss of opportunities he may have taken.

Some famous people whose ONE character confronts a TWO destiny are:

| | |
|---|---|
| Sander Vanocur | Rose Kennedy |
| Dionne Warwick | Spencer T. Olin |
| Eddie Fisher | Representative Ogden Reid |
| Kirk Douglas | |

# THE *1* CHARACTER IN RELATION TO THE *3* DESTINY

This is very favorable for an individualistic contribution in the arts or some outstanding form of creative self expression, but in terms of the other destiny combinations to the ONE character it is a bit of a step down. The individual is prepared to assume a more dominating position in life than he will be given opportunity for. The THREE destiny assures him of general conditions of ease in life while his ONE character is prone to take a more independent and self-reliant stand. A karma in ONE increases the ease with which the individual will accept his fate. A karma in THREE would increase his independence and encourage the individual to turn down some of his best opportunities because they did not live up to the outstanding specifications he usually demands.

Some famous people whose ONE character confronts a THREE destiny are:

Bobby Kennedy
Teddy Kennedy
Mahalia Jackson
Joe Torre
James Hoffa
James Ling
Alfred Hitchcock
Charleton Hester

Lorne Greene
Gracie Allen
Susan Strasberg
Spiro Agnew
John Lindsay
Martha Mitchell
Joel Gray

# THE *1* CHARACTER IN RELATION TO THE *4* DESTINY

This is a good sound combination where the determination of the character is able to consistently build and accumulate a sound material foundation for itself. It would be one of the patterns for continual effort, work and discipline. A karma in ONE relegates the individual to more supression by his fate than a ONE would normally accept. A karma in FOUR would increase the leadership qualities as the individual secured others to perform the more menial drudge work in his life.

Some famous people whose ONE character confronts a FOUR destiny are:

Fred Allen
Hattie Carnegie
Rod McKuen

Douglas Fairbanks Jr.
Orson Bean
Harry K. Thaw

Alan Jay Lerner
Leontyne Price
John L. Lewis
Elsa Maxwell

James Michener
President John Tyler
Annie Besant

# THE *1* CHARACTER IN RELATION TO THE *5* DESTINY

This is a dynamic pattern which provides the inventive thrust of the character with many interesting, exciting and adventuresome changes in life. The accent here would be on aiming for spectacular achievement rather than for something more basic or durable. A karma in ONE severely limits the courage to undertake the adventure and risks demanded by the fate. A karma in FIVE of the destiny vibration would encourage the individual to believe that he himself was creating or selecting his best opportunities (as opposed to the chance occurrences of fate) so in order to maintain this false assumption he would be likely to miss a number of good "boats" he might have taken.

Some famous people whose ONE character confronts a FIVE destiny are:

Marcel Duchamp
Michael Arlen
Floyd Patterson
Helen Keller
Robert Young (actor)
Robert Mitchum
Marlon Brando

Waldo Frank
Harper Lee
Pierre Van Paassen
Mayor Richard Daley
Senator George Murphy
Robert S. MacNamara
Manly Hall

232

# THE *1* CHARACTER IN RELATION TO THE *6* DESTINY

This pattern magnifies a very divergent point of view where the character is keyed to place his own self interest above all other considerations yet the demand opportunities of the destiny require that the individual give up some of his independence and ADJUST SOMETHING ABOUT HIMSELF in order to effect closer group cooperation. A karma in ONE would lessen the contradiction. A karma in SIX would confuse the very context through which the purpose in life must be developed.

Some famous people whose ONE character confronts a SIX destiny are:

| | |
|---|---|
| Thomas Mann | Billy Rose |
| Oscar Hammerstein | Ethel Waters |
| Donn Eisele (astronaut) | Florence Henderson |
| Charles Merrill | Alicia Markova |
| Cordy Freeman (astronaut) | William Styron |
| Prince Rainer | George Hamilton |
| Jim Bouton | Cherio |
| John Marin | Nelson Rockefeller |
| Henry R. Luce | |

# THE *1* CHARACTER IN RELATION TO THE *7* DESTINY

This pattern is sound and complimentary as there is no basic incompatability between the independent, self sufficient position of the ONE and the lonely, isolated, introspective direction in life this individual is forced to take. In fact, ONE on the character rather fortifies the individual with unusual courage and determination to make the most of his oddly twisting life style. All those with the SEVEN destiny are called upon at one time or another to act as fate's messenger in the lives of others and in this pattern such acts could be uniquely inspiring in the quality of their leadership. A karma in ONE would greatly lessen the individuality of the life style. A karma in SEVEN would still push the individual into unusual situations but he would be less likely to personally understand their full significance at the time.

Some famous people whose ONE character confronts a SEVEN destiny are:

| | |
|---|---|
| Bernard Berenson | Margot Fonteyn |
| Stephen Bechtel | Max Eastman |
| Pierre Curie | Mortimer Adler |
| Leroi Jones | William F. Buckley |
| Arthur Godfrey | President James Garfield |
| Bernard Baruch | Sen. Stuart Symington |
| Ernest Borgnine | Alistair Crowley |
| Tyrone Power | Paul Foster Case |
| Olivia de Havilland | |

# THE *1* CHARACTER IN RELATION TO THE *8* DESTINY

This pattern is very strong and indicates an individual who is well fortified to meet the tough demands of the EIGHT destiny. This person is bound to leave his mark on the world although it may be a a life froth with difficult situations and tremendous pressures. A karma in ONE would cause the individual to suffer acute misgivings from the horrendous decisions he must make in life. He will often not feel up to what is expected of him. A karma in EIGHT heightens the egotism of the ONE domination without being fortified with the delicate sense of material justice implied in the important opportunities in his life.

Some famous people whose ONE character confronts a EIGHT destiny are:

Andrew Carnegie
Alexander Graham Bell
Alexis Carrel
Ethel Kennedy
Gunnar Myrdal
John Dewey
Peter Falk
Robert Cummings

Brendan Behan
James Baldwin
Pres. Martin Van Buren
Harry E. Fosdick
Senator Carl Hayden
Jean Stapleton
Huey Newton

# THE *1* CHARACTER IN RELATION TO THE *9* DESTINY

This is a promising pattern which takes a strong individual into many different and distant areas of life (or the world) so that he may broaden his scope of influence and enhance his contributions to some cause far beyond the limitations of his own ego. A karma in ONE would lessen the force of the ego and increase the broad sense of humanity. A karma in NINE would dramatize the leadership potential when speaking for large groups (or mobs) of excitable people.

Some famous people whose ONE character confronts a NINE destiny are:

Justice William Rehnquist
Cab Calloway
Van Cliburn
Pablo Casals
William Boyle
Jack Webb

Margaret Rutherford
Cornelius Vanderbilt
Caryl Chessman
Walter Jenkins
Justice Benjamin Cardozo
Angela Davis

235

# THE 9 VARIATIONS OF DESTINY TO THE TWO CHARACTER

## THE *2* CHARACTER IN RELATION TO THE *1* DESTINY

This is a difficult pattern for the individual to handle or come to terms with. The individual himself is highly sensitive, yet must somehow reverse the very essence of his nature in order to favor the opposite of his own position. There is a strong polarity struggle here between the masculine and feminine qualities within the individual himself. This individual is apt to spend much of his time trying to resolve impossible personal conflicts rather than to develop consistently in a generally constructive direction. A karma in TWO or ONE helps somewhat in that it throws an advantage to just one side of the personal struggle. This, at lease, offers some relief in terms of possible compromise.

Some famous people whose TWO character confronts a ONE destiny are:

| | |
|---|---|
| Joseph Pulitzer | Charlie Chaplin |
| Nikola Tesla | Claudette Colbert |
| John Daly | James M. Cain |
| Guy Lombardo | Pres. Zachary Taylor |
| George Meany | Pres. Rutherford Hayes |

Remember that all of these individuals are TWOS who confront a ONE destiny but they may not all be the same type of TWO as modified by their respective motivation drive and personality image.

# THE *2* CHARACTER IN RELATION TO THE *2* DESTINY

The character vibration here is exactly matched to the destiny which should make for complete harmony between what one has to sell and the demands of his best customers. A karma in TWO would be confusing and heighten the emotional tensions involved in this tempestuous life pattern as the life style rises and falls like waves in a storm.

Some famous people whose TWO character confronts a TWO destiny are:

James Montgomery Flagg          Jane Wyman
Valentina Tereshkova (cosmonaut) Ida Lupino
Gene Autry                      Amy Vanderbilt
Glen Campbell                   Harry Houdini
Omar Sharif


# THE *2* CHARACTER IN RELATION TO THE *3* DESTINY

This is a sound combination for a sensitive, artistic contribution in the creative area. The individual is challenged to put his personal wishes aside and express what flows "freely" rather than to control or restrict what he is inspired to produce. A karma in TWO might increase the workability or acceptance of the destiny over the character. A karma in THREE would make the life style more sensational but less relaxed and spontaneous.

Some famous people whose TWO character confronts a THREE destiny are:

Indria Gandhi           Gary Player
Richard Dyer-Bennet     William S. Paley
Louis Dominguin (bullfighter)  Archbishop Ramsey

Robert Stanley Dollar          Elmo Roper
Wilt Chamberlain               William Wirtz

## THE *2* CHARACTER IN RELATION TO THE *4* DESTINY

This is a good combination where a sensitive individual is given an opportunity to prove his inspiration in practical common sense ways. The individual is fortunate in being able to feel what is best for himself and at the same time is given ample encouragement to build a firm foundation under his most cherished ideals. A karma in TWO would increase the material accent in the pattern. A karma in FOUR would depersonalize the idealism of TWO and provide far less adjustment to practical realities.

Some famous people whose TWO character confronts a FOUR destiny are:

Mayor Frank Hague          Hugh Hefner
Johan Sibelius             Julie Harris
Harry Cohn                 Gwen Verdon
Philip Johnson             Carl Sandberg
Justice Potter Stewart     W. H. Auden
Roy Wilkins                Mamie Eisenhower
Paul McCartney             Sen. "Scoop" Jackson
Dizzy Gillespie            Carol Righter
Jim Thorpe

## THE *2* CHARACTER IN RELATION TO THE *5* DESTINY

This is an upsetting combination where the natural timing of the individual is continually thrown off balance by the sudden intrusion

238

of surprising elements which alter the outcome so drastically as to unnerve the self assurance. What the TWO tries to hold onto with possessive fixation, the FIVE manipulates in such a way that the individual wonders what his real purpose can be. A karma in TWO or FIVE restores more balance by throwing supporting weight to the contradictory opposition.

Some famous people whose TWO character confronts a FIVE destiny are:

| | |
|---|---|
| Liberace | Ava Gardner |
| Bill Cullen | Rudolf Nureyev |
| Eric Sevareid | Ted Shawn |
| Victor Borge | Robert Benchley |
| Bertrand Russell | Archibald Macliesh |
| F. Lee Bailey | Pat Nixon |
| John Dorrance | R. C. Firebrace |
| Betty Hutton | |

# THE *2* CHARACTER IN RELATION TO THE *6* DESTINY

This is a compatable combination because the individual is willing to step aside from his own position while the destiny increases the advantages of joint partnership activity. The success of the group commitment is increased because the individual is always prepared to sacrifice his own position to make it work. A karma in TWO would obsecure the realization of exactly how a compromise would help matters. A karma in SIX would limit the individual because of the disappointment encountered with those partnerships he tries to join.

Some famous people whose TWO character confronts a SIX destiny are:

| | |
|---|---|
| Louis Wolfson | Margaret Leighton |
| F. W. Woolworth | Faye Emerson |
| Edward Durell Stone | James Earl Ray |

Eddy Duchin
Kirsten Flagstad
Sandy Koufax
Whitey Ford
Norton Simon
David Merrick
David Niven
Sen. Margaret Chase Smith

Orville Prescott
Jean Stafford
Pres. Warren Harding
Pres. Woodrow Wilson
Rev. Paul Tillich
Rep. Carl Albert
Caroline Kennedy
Boris Spassky

# THE *2* CHARACTER IN RELATION TO THE *7* DESTINY

This is a compatable combination where sensitivity on two levels combines to fortify the insight which each can contribute (from the personal viewpoint and from the more abstract, complex level). The life style is apt, however, to be over emotionalized or too responsive to unrealistic programs. A karma in TWO would stabilize the pattern in favor of a deeper and more comprehensive understanding of life. A karma in SEVEN would weaken the range of effective influence which this individual might otherwise have.

Some famous people whose TWO character confronts a SEVEN destiny are:

Jack Paar
Joan Baez
Kate Smith
Arthur Ashe
Willie Mays

Richard Mellon
David Janssen
Walt Rostow
Senator Birch Bayh

# THE *2* CHARACTER IN RELATION TO THE *8* DESTINY

There is an ultimate conflict of interests here where the quality of the character is to soften the distinctions and compromise for sake of harmony while the fate demands a harsher attitude in favor of tough decisions which promote a specific justice. The individual is really not constituted in the talents demanded by the opportunities he must face in life. A karma in TWO increases the chances of a more effective EIGHT accomplishment. A karma in EIGHT weakens the dynamics of the pattern even though it might promote a little more personal harmony.

Some famous people whose TWO character confronts a EIGHT destiny are:

| | |
|---|---|
| Roger Chaffee (astronaut) | Damon Runyon |
| Mohamad Ali | President James Monroe |
| Joe Namath | Senator Joseph McCarthy |
| Rocky Marciano | Earl Browder |
| Douglas MacArthur | Adlai Stevenson |
| Charles Laughton | Godfrey Lowell Cabot |
| Carroll O'Connor | Justice Louis Brandeis |
| Godfrey Cambridge | Margaret Truman |

# THE *2* CHARACTER IN RELATION TO THE *9* DESTINY

There is some slight contradiction as the TWO reaches for some possessive personal satisfaction while the NINE requires a lessening of all ties in favor of a complete depersonalization in the life pattern. The individual is apt to be saddened by what he faces in life because what he personally cherishes most tends to continually slip away. Eventually he must reach a stage of maturity where he will understand the value and reason for this broader perspective. A karma in TWO makes this broader view more possible. A karma in NINE makes the separations in life, which the individual must accept, somewhat more difficult.

Some famous people whose TWO character confronts a NINE destiny are:

| | |
|---|---|
| Lou Costello | Budd Schulberg |
| Marian Anderson | Daniel Berrigan |
| Paul Muni | W. Averell Harriman |
| Jean Seberg | Pope John XXIII |
| Charles Whitman | Yoko Ono |

## THE 9 VARIATIONS OF DESTINY TO THE THREE CHARACTER

*THE* **3** *CHARACTER IN RELATION TO THE* **1** *DESTINY*

This is a good pattern for individuality of creative effort. The individual will be constantly challenged in life not to stand on his laurels or achievements but to keep pressing on to more enterprising forms of creative expression. The life style is apt to prove quite unique, original and pioneering. A karma in THREE would make the creative medium harder to come by but the demands of fate will keep pushing the individual forward. A karma in ONE would cause the individual to resent the incessant demands made on him to keep topping his best efforts.

Some famous people whose THREE character confronts a ONE destiny are:

| | |
|---|---|
| Ernest Hemingway | George Santayana |
| Pier Nervi | Spencer Tracy |
| Sir William Crookes | Louis Jourdan |
| James McDivitt (astronaut) | Sophia Loren |
| Adolf Eichmann | Lynn Redgrave |
| Edwin Newman | Janis Joplin |
| Walt Disney | Paul Lynde |

Remember that all of these individuals are THREES who confront a ONE destiny but they may not all be the same type of THREE as modified by their respective motivation drive and personality image.

# THE *3* CHARACTER IN RELATION TO THE *2* DESTINY

This combination has much promise of a spectacular effect in artistic matters. All persons with a TWO destiny are exposed to the limelight and the possibility of becoming a celebrity in some field. A karma in THREE causes some confusion as to the validity of the individual's artistic efforts. A karma in TWO pushes the individual in a direction he may not understand or appreciate.

Some famous people whose THREE character confronts a TWO destiny are:

Edward Arnold
Yuri Gagarin (cosmonaut)
Julian Bond
Prince Charles
Gloria Vanderbilt
Jimmy Dean
Axel Wenner-Gren

Barry Fitzgerald
Jack Benny
Judith Anderson
Henry Kissinger
Senator Charles Percy
Loren Eiseley

# THE *3* CHARACTER IN RELATION TO THE *3* DESTINY

This is obviously a happy combination but may not spur the individual on to outstanding accomplishment. The inclination as well as the opportunity to just relax and enjoy what life has to offer may prove singularly unproductive in most matters. There may be too much of a good thing here. A karma in THREE might snap up the action and lead the individual to develop a more colorful and distinctive life style.

Some famous people whose THREE character confronts a THREE destiny are:

Eugene Grace
Sir George Wilkins
Johnny Mathis
Louis Armstrong
Ella Fitzgerald
Frank Robinson
Red Skelton
Jonathan Winters
Alec Guiness
Tammy Grimes
Helen Hayes
Frederick Wakeman

Eric Hoffer
Herman Wouk
Gore Vidal
Harold Laski
Pres. John Quincy Adams
Pres. Thomas Jefferson
Pres. Andrew Jackson
Rev. James Pike
Senator Frank Church
Cyrus Vance
Ryan O'Neal

## THE *3* CHARACTER IN RELATION TO THE *4* DESTINY

There is a polar contradiction here where the creative talents must be made to conform to some type of practical and realistic application. The individual will have to work hard to develop his particular style and get it just right before it will fit into a pattern which has "use value". A karma in THREE will increase the practical angle. A karma in FOUR will lessen the chances for a truly realistic adjustment. The individual is encouraged to leave the more basic adaptations to realism for others.

Some famous people whose THREE character confronts a FOUR destiny are:

J. P. Morgan
Marconi
Andre Previn

Walter Lippmann
Mary McCarthy
George Plimpton

244

Arnold Palmer  
James Garner  
Karl Malden  

Adam Clayton Powell  
Rep. John Tunney  

## THE *3* CHARACTER IN RELATION TO THE *5* DESTINY

This is a dynamic and impulsive pattern where the individual's creative efforts are continually pushed in a new direction which in turn provides a new source of creative inspiration. The individual on his own would be far less likely to undertake all the activities which fate will stir up for him. In the end it will be to his advantage to follow these impulsive leads for only in that way will he be able to avoid the stagnation that would surely have developed in his life. A karma in THREE would increase the individual's aptitude for opportunistic speculation. A karma in FIVE will stir up the life style but with less constructive purpose because the resistance and lack of understanding of the advantages involved would tend to defeat the pattern itself.

Some famous people whose THREE character confronts a FIVE destiny are:

Scott Carpenter (astronaut)  
Howard K. Smith  
Al Hirt  
Cyrus Eaton  

Joseph Mankiewicz  
James Earl Jones  
Simone Signoret  
S. I. Hayakawa  

## THE *3* CHARACTER IN RELATION TO THE *6* DESTINY

This is a combination of complimentary qualities which tend to be more instructive than purely creative for its own sake. Each expression is ladened with a message or some form of social awareness. Creativity is not so much the object as putting things across in an expressive manner. A karma in THREE would add seriousness to the outcome and lessen the individual's joy or enthusiasm in the matter. A karma in SIX would place a barrier between the individual and his ultimate audience because of personal difference on matters not of direct concern but still a problem for the individual to accept.

Some famous people whose THREE character confronts a SIX destiny are:

| | |
|---|---|
| Marshall Field I | Maria Tallchief |
| Dale Carnegie | Herb Caen |
| Richard Boone | John Strachey |
| Pat Boone | Ian Fleming |
| Phyllis Diller | J. P. Marquand |
| Richard Speck | Sen. Russell Long |

## THE *3* CHARACTER IN RELATION TO THE *7* DESTINY

This combination offers interesting and unusual possibilities where the individual creative effort is best transmitted in an indirect manner or by use of highly stylized forms which may also be overly cultural for ordinary people. The challenge here is to create for a specialized and refined audience and to forget about mass acceptance or common place popularity. A karma in THREE would encourage the individual to substitute someone else to produce the medium while he concentrated on its more effective distribution. A karma in SEVEN would draw the individual into more personal contact with what is expressed and what it idealizes.

Some famous people whose THREE character confronts a SEVEN destiny are:

| | |
|---|---|
| William Anders (astronaut) | Arthur Schlesinger |
| Margaret Sanger | Gertrude Atherton |
| Valdimir Horowitz | J. Edgar Hoover |
| Bill Pahlmann | Harold Stassen |
| James Stewart | Justice Oliver Wendell Holmes |
| Angela Lansbury | Dr. J. B. Rhine |

# THE *3* CHARACTER IN RELATION TO THE *8* DESTINY

This is a powerful combination involving the utilization of spontaneous opinions to maniupulate important situations by some form of shock therapy. The method is light and persuasive while the intent is harsh and compelling. A karma in THREE would magnetize the power manipulations and commercial possibilities. A karma in EIGHT would obscure the real intent and therefore lessen the consistent drive for effective control of the powerful material potential in the life pattern.

Some famous people whose THREE character confronts a EIGHT destiny are:

Percival Lowell
Neil Armstrong
Mort Sahl
Aretha Franklin
Barbra Streisand
Rod Steiger
Rossano Brazzi
Raymond Massey
Paul Newman

Mickey Rooney
Elizabeth Taylor
Graham Greene
Joyce Cary
Alexander Woollcott
Norman Vincent Peale
Gov. George Wallace
Dr. Eric Berne

# THE *3* CHARACTER IN RELATION TO THE *9* DESTINY

This is a happy combination of factors where the individuality of expression is further enhanced in some broad field of general application which was probably not envisioned when the inspiration started to take shape. All combinations of THREE and NINE are much more sympathetic than where SIX is coupled with either number because THREE and NINE both function with the same sense of individual freedom which SIX specifically denies. The pattern here is of an individual who is beguiled into a life style which is far more expansive than he would assume for himself on his own, but the individual may be initially confused as everything he creates on a personal level tends to merge into larger and larger perspectives.

A karma in THREE would make the acceptance of this larger perspective easier. A karma in NINE would sadden the individual as he continually confronts his loss of individuality as circumstances force him into a larger perspective than he is used to. (or in some sense, talented for).

Some famous people whose THREE character confronts a NINE destiny are:

| | |
|---|---|
| Elsie Janis | Jack Lemmon |
| Mohandas Gandhi | Bette Davis |
| Harry Reasoner | Melina Mercouri |
| Norman Rockwell | Carol Channing |
| Joe Frazier | Tallulah Bankhead |
| H. L. Hunt | Pres. Chester Arthur |

## THE 9 VARIATIONS OF DESTINY TO THE FOUR CHARACTER

### THE *4* CHARACTER IN RELATION TO THE *1* DESTINY

This is a potentially constructive pattern in spite of the resistance of the character to forgo many of his regular (but limiting) personal routines in favor of continually pushing in a new direction. The FOUR is more at home when left to work and rework a fixed pattern or situation and is not inclined to continually seek new goals. In this pattern he may have to be forced to accept such new beginnings. A karma in FOUR would make the person less stubborn and more agreeable to new directions. A karma in ONE would considerably reduce the courage to strike out in new fields.

Some famous people whose FOUR character confronts a ONE destiny are:

| | |
|---|---|
| Gordon Cooper (astronaut) | Harry Bridges |
| Betty Friedan | Bob Hope |
| Maurice Chevalier | Ingrid Bergman |
| Oscar Levant | Noel Coward |
| Fran Tarkenton | John Held |

Remember that all of these individuals are FOUR who confront a ONE destiny but they may not all be the same type of FOUR as modified by their respective motivation drive and personality image.

# THE 4 CHARACTER IN RELATION TO THE 2 DESTINY

This is a rather difficult combination to work with because what the rigid practicality of the FOUR character is required to relinquish in this pattern is not as obviously advantageous as it is in favor of some type of martyrdom or self-sacrifice. Most people would consider this less of an incentive to stop being what one is and face in a different direction, which is what is required here. What FOUR builds up with diligent labor may have to be put aside for some sympathetic ideal which may require some maturity before the individual can appreciate the wisdom of this choice in his life pattern. A karma in FOUR would make this sacrifice somewhat easier. A karma in TWO would make the necessary acceptance of this compromise somewhat tragic.

Some famous people whose FOUR character confronts a TWO destiny are:

Charles Bassett (astronaut)
Edward White (astronaut)
Benito Mussolini
David Brinkley
Al Capp
Tony Bennett
Yma Sumac
Luchino Visconti
Lionel Barrymore
Kim Hunter
Jacqueline Kennedy Onassis

John Mitchell
Ronald Reagan
Jean Paul Getty
Jesse Jones
H. L. Mencken
Bertolt Brecht
Benson Ford
A. C. Gilbert
David Packard
Clifford Irving

# THE *4* CHARACTER IN RELATION TO THE *3* DESTINY

This pattern presents a polarity of interests in opposite directions where the character is firm and diligent but the best opportunities in life come from a joy of living through creative self expression. The eventual outcome is likely to be a compromise of practical hard core facts which somehow have decorative value. The step down here from the comfortable security of material reality to the imagined delights of a more attractive life style may be undertaken with some obvious resistance. A karma in FOUR would ease this shift of accent. A karma in THREE would only make it harder and the individual may miss the point entirely as to why he should make this shift at all.

Some famous people whose FOUR character confronts a THREE destiny are:

| | |
|---|---|
| Henri Cartier-Bresson | Dick Powell |
| Charles Conrad (astronaut) | John Garfield |
| Mary Quant | William Hickman |
| Walter Gieseking | John Dos Passos |
| Ray Robinson | James Watson (Nobel biologist) |
| Franco Zeffirelli | |

# THE *4* CHARACTER IN RELATION TO THE *4* DESTINY

This is obviously a suitable match but can be too much of the same thing which is this case is apt to be heavy and depressing like biscuits without baking powder. There is little to relieve the monotony of hard core realism but there is certainly plenty of opportunity for building a constructive future providing the individual kepps constantly plugging away and sees each situation through to its bitter end. A karma in FOUR might somewhat relieve the over-emphasis of FOUR by encouraging the individual to leave the more menial chores for others.

Some famous people whose FOUR character confronts a FOUR destiny are:

Rube Goldberg
Ben Gazzara
Lana Turner
Elliott See (astronaut)
Dorothy Gish
Henri Landru

Woody Allen
Joseph P. Kennedy
Lynda Bird Johnson
Donald Rumsfeld
Howard Cosell

# THE 4 CHARACTER IN RELATION TO THE 5 DESTINY

The combination of qualities in this pattern is apt to be confusing to the individual as he is continually called upon to stop working on his best projects and take off in an opposite direction which may come just when his accomplishments seem to be amounting to something. The challenge here is to make a break from established molds yet be consistently realistic and practical. A karma in FOUR would encourage the willingness to take speculative chances. A karma in FIVE would make it somewhat impossible for the individual to see the necessity for many of the important changes which intrude on his life.

Some famous people whose FOUR character confronts a FIVE destiny are:

John Steinbeck
Jan Struther
Cyril Connolly
Justice Tom Blark
Justice Fred Vinson
Justice Byron White
John Olin

Henry Morgan
Marshal Tito
Robert Ryan
Judy Holliday
Lee Harvey Oswald
Eileen Garrett
Joyce Grenfell

# THE *4* CHARACTER IN RELATION TO THE *6* DESTINY

This is a solid pattern of compatable qualities which should insure an above average of success through hard work in socially responsive fields. The pattern here is lacking a little in color, dash and imagination, but is amply rewarded for the sound manner in which most team work activities are handled. A karma in FOUR would raise the work effort to a more administrative level. A karma in SIX would indicate that the individual is likely to suffer some disappointment with his best efforts because of a real lack of group appreciation.

Some famous people whose FOUR character confronts a SIX destiny are:

William Randolph Hearst          Laurence Rockefeller
Duke of Windsor                  Richard E. Byrd
Jackson Pollock                  Fred Astaire
John Lennon                      Vittorio Gassman
Jascha Heifetz                   Julie Christie
Lawrence Tibbett                 Louis Untermeyer
Gil Hodges

# THE *4* CHARACTER IN RELATION TO THE *7* DESTINY

This combination indicates an unusual life style for someone who is inherently quite traditional, disciplined and routine. The opportunities provided by fate will take this person along many unaccustomed paths where his ultimate purpose may turn out to be the unique way in which he introduces a fatalistic reality into other people's lives. This result may be entirely unintentioned on his part. A karma in FOUR would make the individual more adaptable to his life style. A karma in SEVEN would make this person's life more mysterious and puzzling even to himself.

Some famous people whose FOUR character confronts a SEVEN destiny are:

| | |
|---|---|
| William H. Vanderbilt | Polly Bergen |
| Virginia Graham | Agnes Moorehead |
| Leonard Bernstein | John Kenneth Galbraith |
| Elio Pinza | Justice Arthur Goldberg |
| Paul Mellon | Justice Hugo Black |
| Art Carney | Rep. Mendel Rivers |
| Wally Cox | |

## THE 4 CHARACTER IN RELATION TO THE 8 DESTINY

This combination reflects a very ambitious and practical minded individual who is likely to achieve a position of some importance and power in life. He is well equipped to make the most of any important job assignments which may come his way since he is not looking for an easy way out, but welcomes any tough situation which will test and prove his talents. A karma in FOUR increases the adaptability to more administrative opportunities. A karma in EIGHT causes this person to misjudge and mismanage many important situation in life which may cause others to suffer more than he. This individual is more likely to accumulate more money and influence with an EIGHT karma than if he has an EIGHT because EIGHT karma always brings out the burden of money along with its possession.

Some famous people whose FOUR character confronts a EIGHT destiny are:

| | |
|---|---|
| Floyd McKissick | Ginger Rogers |
| Pablo Picasso | Alan Ladd |
| Renata Rebaldi | Pres. James Polk |
| Robert Goulet | Pres. Grant |
| Dr. Jonas Salk | Pres. Lyndon Johnson |
| Groucho Marx | Sen. Hubert Humphrey |
| Eddie Albert | Mary Banker Eddy |
| Katharine Cornell | I. F. Stone |
| Liza Minnelli | |

# THE *4* CHARACTER IN RELATION TO THE *9* DESTINY

This combination combines qualities of behavior which are normally quite unrelated and generally unsympathetic. The character here is rigid, unflexible, stubborn and unimaginative, while the challenge of the destiny is to value emotional understanding over practical issues and increase one's charitable compassion for even the most lazy and unrealistic of mankind. The combination should indicate an exacting but subordinate role in an organization or movement based on worldly ideals. Examples, an orderly in a hospital, an accountant in a religious foundation, a porter who carries the gear on an exploratory mission, etc., but of course some famous people have this combination as well which indicates they have been able to function as "master engineers" (TWENTY TWO vibration) in world affairs. A karma in FOUR would raise the level of application since the individual would be less willing to do all the dirty work himself. A karma in NINE would narrow the fields of compassionate interest to those which could be directly applied to his familiarity with certain practical values.

Some famous people whose FOUR character confronts a NINE destiny:

Thomas Hart Benson
Robert Maynard Hutchins
Charles Lindbergh
Richard Harris
Henry Fonda
Catherine Drinker Bowen

John Updike
Pres. John Adams
Pres. James Buchanan
Justice William Brennan
Dr. Rudolf Steiner

# THE 9 VARIATIONS OF DESTINY TO THE FIVE CHARACTER

## THE *5* CHARACTER IN RELATION TO THE *1* DESTINY

This is a good combination where the adaptability of the character is encouraged to greater feats of individual accomplishment. The same qualities in nature tend to support both the aggressive demands of the fate as well as the sense of advantageous competition in the character. This is not a person to stand in one spot for long or loose out on the best opportunities that fate pushes him against in life. A karma in FIVE would make the individual less adventuresome and more likely to see more situations further along before he dared to take off on something new for speculative gain. A karma in ONE would remove the yardstick of personal integrity as the character proceeded to take outrageous advantage wherever it could.

Some famous people whose FIVE character confronts a ONE destiny are:

| | |
|---|---|
| Frank Borman (astronaut) | William Powell |
| John Young (astronaut) | Ruth Gordon |
| Martin Luther King | Cornelia Otis Skinner |
| Georges Braque | Somerset Maughan |
| Bernard Buffet | William Manchester |
| Sarah Buffet | Clive Barnes |
| Johnny Unitas | Billy Graham |
| J. C. Penny | Sen. William Fulbright |
| Akira Kurosawa | Robert Mulliken |
| Robert Morse | Sen. Thomas Dodd |

Remember that all of these individuals are FIVES who confront a ONE destiny but they may not all be the same type of FIVE as modified by their respective motivation drive and personality image.

# THE 5 CHARACTER IN RELATION TO THE 2 DESTINY

This is a combination likely to reflect a hazardous up and down life without too much to show for it at any one point of time. The spirit of adventure, or the idealism of making a spectacular example of one's self alternates between periods of pulling one's self together for the next banana peel escapade. This pattern reflects anything but a stable person so he might as well fling discretion to the winds and make the most out of whatever comes along. A karma in FIVE would help to keep the sense of adventure from getting completely out of hand. A karma in TWO would minimize the individual's ability to understand why and how his escapades didn't add up to more than they do.

Some famous people whose FIVE characters confronts a TWO destiny are:

| | |
|---|---|
| Bernard MacFadden | Henry Ford I |
| Cecil B. Demille | Victure Mature |
| Kenneth Fearing | Uta Hagen |
| Gherman Titov (cosmonaut) | Julie Andrews |
| Abba Evan | Jack Ruby |
| Alan Burke | Norman Mailer |
| Eartha Kitt | Lady Bird Johnson |
| Joe Walcott | Frank Lloyd Wright |
| Bobby Fischer | Jules Verne |

# THE *5* CHARACTER IN RELATION TO THE *3* DESTINY

This is a happy combination of freedom demanding qualities which go hand in hand towards finding and enjoying a full, exciting, colorful and happy life. The individual generally lands on his feet even when he might have been recklessly foolish. This is a good pattern for some types of sport where the risk is high and an above share of fool's luck is helpful. The pattern is obviously not indicative of heavy responsibilities or weighty problems, but there is much promise of an unconventional good time. A karma in FIVE would reflect a person who was not nearly so unconventional as his actions would indicate. A karma in THREE would lessen the individual's ability to see the humor or ridiculousness of some of the situations he gets into. To let go and laugh is sometimes the most effective relief valve for what could otherwise be an utterly impossible situation.

Some famous people whose FIVE character confronts a THREE destiny are:

John Hay Whitney
James Lovell (astronaut)
Alan King
Merv Griffin
Mrs. Lee Harvey (Marina) Oswald
A. C. Nielsen (pollster)
Shirley Chisholm

Charles Coburn
Ossie Davis
Kim Stanley
Ethel Barrymore
Patricia Neal
Boris Pasternak

# THE *5* CHARACTER IN RELATION TO THE *4* DESTINY

This combination is more fortunate than its reverse pattern (the FOUR character with a FIVE destiny) because here the native's adaptability is continually brought into realistic focus instead of having sudden, drastic intrusions into situations which are working well. The best of the innovative talents are here given a chance to prove themselves in profitable ways, if and when the individual allows himself to be disciplined along lines of close regimentation. A karma in FIVE would lubricate the transition from restless change to productive routine. A karma in FOUR confuses the individual as to just why his best efforts may miss the point by inches. While there might be an acceptance of realistic standards for others, this person fails to see where they apply to him.

Some famous people whose FIVE character confronts a FOUR destiny are:

| | |
|---|---|
| Arthur Amory Houghton | Thelma Ritter |
| Gerard Swope | Sen. Eugene McCarthy |
| Pierre Trudeau | Mrs. Eleanor McGovern |
| Nat. King Cole | Marie Curie |
| George Gallup | Sen. Wayne Morse |
| Walter Pidgeon | Sydney Omarr |
| Leslie Caron | Miriam Hopkins |
| Gertrude Lawrence | |

# THE *5* CHARACTER IN RELATION TO THE *5* DESTINY

This is certainly a dynamic pattern which promises an exciting life style if the individual can hold together in one piece. Some sort of exploitation of sex is involved here which has direct bearing on this person's best opportunities. What comes after may provide the real merit in the situation but you may be sure that most contacts in life start with the suggestion or promise of some sort of sexuality. This is the pattern of one who can get away in life with many things that would trip most people up. A karma in FIVE would depersonalize the individual's sense of responsibility towards that part of any situation which he himself triggered. This could lead to a lack of moral integrity which relieves the individual from responsibility towards his own actions.

Some famous people whose FIVE character confronts a FIVE destiny are:

Harold Arlen
Richard Tucker
Ravi Shankar
Sir Michael Redgrave
Doris Day
Lauren Bacall
Richard Loeb

Alan Watts
Earle Stanley Gardner
William Faulkner
Pres. Theodore Roosevelt
Beria (Russian secret police)
L. Edward Johndro
Patrick Murphy (N.Y. Police)

# THE *5* CHARACTER IN RELATION TO THE *6* DESTINY

This pattern is more constructive than its reverse (SIX character to FIVE destiny) because here the virtues of the FIVE nature, which are innovative for pushing change, are channeled towards areas of social responsibility and matters that promote group values. It is hoped the best of the FIVE qualities can be retained but utilized in a different (SIX) way. A karma in FIVE increases the individual's acceptance of group limitations. A karma in SIX reflects a confusing condition where the individual is unable to understand why he can't operate as he is but must answer to values quite foreign to his basic nature.

Some famous people whose FIVE character confront a SIX destiny are:

Eugene O'Neill
Mrs. Marjorie Merriweather Post
Alan Bean (astronaut)
Princes Margaret Rose
Noguchi
Kurt Weill
Beverly Sills
Roman Polanski
Anthony Quinn

George Jessel
Nanette Fabray
Mary Pickford
Jane Wyatt
Iris Murdoch
Harold Pinter
Henry Wallace
Charles Steinmetz
Justice John Marshall

259

# THE *5* CHARACTER IN RELATION TO THE *7* DESTINY

This is a favorable combination for providing an aggressive and competitive fighter for unpopular causes or individuals who are not really understood or appreciated by average people. The SEVEN destiny here will lead the adventuresome FIVE in and out of many situations where, without realizing it fully at the time, this individual will trigger results which would otherwise never have happened. In one sense this person is a volatile catalyst who makes things happen without himself becoming an integral part of the ingredients. A karma in FIVE will cause this person to carry on his function in life on a more subtle level. A karma in SEVEN will also increase the subtly of the interplay but cloud the individual's own recognition of the significance of the roles he plays.

Some famous people whose FIVE character confronts a SEVEN destiny are:

| | |
|---|---|
| Frank McGee | Pres. Harry Truman |
| Fritz Kreisler | John Foster Dulles |
| Woody Guthrie | Harry Hopkins |
| Vincent Edwards | Louis Pasteur |
| Flora Robson | Justice John Harlan |
| Mary Tyler Moore | Harriet Van Horne |

# THE *5* CHARACTER IN RELATION TO THE *8* DESTINY

This is a dynamic pattern where two power forces or techniques combine so as to throw the opposition off guard. The leverage advantage here is definitely constructive if the individual will allow himself to ruthlessly investigate all the possible exploitable value in each situation, yet hold himself ready to pursue anything more promising that happens to come along. A karma in FIVE would increase the accent on material matters at the expense of investigative change. A karma in EIGHT would depersonalize the sense of justice so the individual is likely to have little moral concern for some of the rough, tough schemes he rips off.

Some famous people whose FIVE character confronts an EIGHT destiny are:

Henry Clay Frick
Robert Woodruff
Russell Schweickart (astronaut)
Ali Bhutto
Willy Brandt
Gian-Carlo Menotti
Gen. George S. Patton
Eli Wallach
Marcello Mastroianni

Laurence Olivier
Cyd Charisse
Grace Kelly
Ezra Pound
Daphine De Maurier
Taylor Caldwell
Cardinal Terence Cooke
Mayor Robert Wagner
Brendan Behan

# THE 5 CHARACTER IN RELATION TO THE 9 DESTINY

The accent in this pattern is away from practical everyday matters and towards the high road of broad adventure. The restless, freedom loving FIVE spirit is well suited to the wanderlust and clinical detachment implied in the NINE destiny which also functions best when relieved of ordinary responsibilites and personal ties. This pattern provides a good chance for the best of FIVE and NINE to combine in a constructive, helpful manner where many people can benefit. A karma in FIVE increases the responsiveness to the selfless tolerance of NINE. The sexual energy of FIVE is sublimated to an impersonal brotherly compassion for all people. A karma in NINE would reduce the humanizing results of the final outcome. In the meantime the sensuality of the personal life style is apt not to be as healthy or as compassionate as it might be.

Some famous people whose FIVE character confronts a NINE destiny are:

Vincent Astor
Mary Margaret McBride
Julia Child
Jack Nicklaus
Carl Gustav Jung
Don Ameche

Charles Boyer
Jean Arthur
Albert Schweitzer
Justice Felix Frankfurter
Pope Pius XII

## THE 9 VARIATIONS OF DESTINY TO THE SIX CHARACTER

## THE *6* CHARACTER IN RELATION TO THE *1* DESTINY

This is a sound, constructive pattern but there is a subtle contradiction here where the character, which is prone to personal adjustments or allowances in favor of group commitments, is pushed by fate to take a more decisive and independent stand irrespective of the provincialism of the group. To smoothly integrate this apparent contradiction (inclination in two directions) requires a maturity of the individual sufficient to understand the facts and develop an equitable solution. A karma in SIX would increase the acceptance for independent action. A karma in ONE would minimize the individuality of the final outcome.

Some famous people whose SIX character confronts a ONE destiny are:

William Waldorf Astor
William K. Vanderbilt
Dr. Tom Dooley
Jeff Chandler
Carl Stokes
Charles Collingwood
Perry Como
William Masters

David Wayne
Barbara Bel Geddes
Herione Gingold
Welton Beckett
Justice Stanley Reed
Mary Jo Kopechne
Ariel Taylor

Remember that all of these individual are SIXS who confront a ONE destiny but they may not all be the same type of SIX as modified by their respective motivation drive and personality image.

# THE *6* CHARACTER IN RELATION TO THE *2* DESTINY

This pattern has more obvious points of compatability as both the talent and the destiny demand are in tune with a certain sacrifice or adjustment on the indivudual's part in consideration for others. This pattern reflects the possibility of sacrifices assuming such magnitude as to make the individual quite well known or highly celebrated. The reference here for which the individual achieves fame or notoriety is based on a successful expression of SIX which is itself limited in that it reflects an average, normal composite of valuations. The expression of some number other than SIX might reflect something more universal, uniquely individual or spiritually penetrating. A karma in SIX would idealize the pattern as the individual resisted the personal implication and prejudices of his own case. A karma in TWO would (strange as it may seem) heighten the potentiality of limelight attention. This is because karmic conditions INCREASE rather than decrease the number of opportunities provided by the destiny pattern. A lack of personalized sensitivity, with a TWO karma, would make the individual less hesitant to bask in such glare of publicity.

Some famous people whose SIX character confronts a TWO destiny are:

| | |
|---|---|
| Barbara Hutton | Leonard Woodcock |
| Sen. Everett Dirksen | Gardner Murphy |
| Charles Stewart Mott | Karen Horney |
| William Boeing | Fred MacMurray |
| John Glenn (astronaut) | Sidney Poitier |
| Roy Innis | Susan Hayward |
| Bobby Darin | Leslie Uggams |
| Peter Hurkos | Pres. Herbert Hoover |
| Eddie Arcaro | Llewellyn George |

# THE 6 CHARACTER IN RELATION TO THE 3 DESTINY

This is a happy combination of qualities which pairs the sociability and friendly orientation of the character with a comparatively easy life of freedom to develop as creatively as possible. There is probably a good deal more social commitment and group relatedness within the individual than he will be able to express creatively but the final medium he develops should strike a responsive note. A karma in SIX would promote the more individual side of creativity as the individual himself would be more resistant to group values. A karma in THREE would lessen the sense of freedom from the responsibility entanglements which the individual chooses for himself.

Some famous people whose SIX character confronts the THREE destiny are:

| | |
|---|---|
| Donald Douglas | Gloria Swanson |
| S. H. Kress | Faye Dunaway |
| Nguyen Cao Ky | Lillian Gish |
| Garry Moore | Justice Harlan Stone |
| Lily Pons | Evangeline Adams |
| Montgomery Clift | |

# THE *6* CHARACTER IN RELATION TO THE *4* DESTINY

This is a sound, contructive combination where the moral consciousness and common communication patterns of the character are easily focused on matters of practical importance by the opportunities provided by fate. The life pattern requires constant work and effort but the individual is rather more prepared than most to accept his share of responsibility, especially when he can relate to common personal interests immediately surrounding him. A karma in SIX would increase the acceptance of hard core reality without some of the sentimental hang-backs of SIX. A karma in FOUR somewhat defeats the more constructive potential that this pattern might achieve since there would be a natural reluctance to face facts as opposed to sentimentalizing over the way one prefers things to be.

Some famous people whose SIX character confronts a FOUR destiny are:

| | |
|---|---|
| Pres. Franklin Pierce | Grandma Moses |
| Maurice Utrillo | Harry Belafonte |
| Charles Luckman | Vida Blue |
| Alfred P. Sloan | Sid Caesar |
| Henri Matisse | Laurence Harvey |
| Fidel Castro | Fanny Brice |
| Duchess of Windsor | Stephen Spender |
| Dick Cavett | J. Robert Oppenheimer |

# THE *6* CHARACTER IN RELATION TO THE *5* DESTINY

This combination reflects a tempestuous life where the individual is forced to change his position many times before he finally comes to understand exactly wherein his own moral contribution may fall. The morality of the character is considerably at variance with the exploitative demands of the destiny. In this pattern it is the individual himself who must adjust his moral values (whatever they may be) in order to allow for a free interpretation of life consistent with the infinite variety which composes it, rather than in any way to impose his morality on so-called non-members. A karma in SIX would lubricate the ultimate adjustment. A karma in FIVE would prevent the individual from seeing exactly wherein he must change, rather than others having to change to conform to his views.

Some famous people whose SIX character confronts a FIVE destiny are:

| | |
|---|---|
| Clifton Williams (astronaut) | Pres. Abraham Lincoln |
| Coretta King | Pres. Franklin Roosevelt |
| Moshe Dyan | Charles Darwin |
| Anthony Armstrong Jones | Richard Neutra |
| Walter Cronkite | Pres. James Madison |
| Billie Jean King | Sen. John Sparkman |
| Frank Buck | Justice Charles Evans Hughes |
| Joan Fontaine | Adelle Davis |

# THE *6* CHARACTER IN RELATION TO THE *6* DESTINY

Like all patterns which constitute an exact match in the same vibration, there can be too much of one quality without a corresponding balance wheel to give spark, vitality, tone and dynamics to the life style. Here the over-emphasis is on fitting into average situations with ordinary people. The pattern reflects, however, the potential for a contented life without too many out of the ordinary interferences to upset the natural sequence of "give and take." There will be a number of lessons in "give and take" to contend with. A karma in SIX would elevate the consciousness to a more theoretical level which may at times be quite inconsistent with other people's position on the "give and take". This is likely to bring about bitter feelings on the domestic level as well as with other social commitments in life.

Some famous people whose SIX character confronts a SIX destiny are:

George W. Vanderbilt
Charles De Gaulle
David Frost
Willem De Kooning
Gladys Swarthout
Howard Hughes

Federico Fellini
Alfred Kinsey
Danny Kaye
Vance Packard
Sen. James Buckley

## THE *6* CHARACTER IN RELATION TO THE *7* DESTINY

This combination presents certain problems where the moral loyalty to the group is often at variance with the more subtle influences which the individual is aware of but dares not openly champion or endorse. The function of SIX normally operates on an open friendly basis while the demands of SEVEN call for certain undercover secretiveness because this is the best way to protect oneself from those who do not understand and therefore tend to destroy what they cannot appreciate. This pattern reflects an awareness of this conflict leaning toward a solution which will inevitably isolate the individual from the morality he originally projected. The pattern also suggests that the spirit of cooperation that emanates from the SIX consciousness is itself refined and merged with even more idealistic or spiritual values which transcend the provincialism of groups. It is the destiny challenge in this life pattern for the individual to spiritually expand in this subtle and complex direction. A karma in SIX lubricates an expansion in this

267

desired direction. A karma in SEVEN reduces the individual consciousness of the spiritual significance of the changes taking place in his life but it may increase his role as fate's messenger as he unconsciously triggers events in other people's lives.

Some famous people whose SIX character confronts a SEVEN destiny are:

| | |
|---|---|
| Eugene Cernan (astronaut) | Jennifer Jones |
| Ronnie Cunningham (astronaut) | Helen Gurley Brown |
| Rudolf Hess | Pearl Buck |
| Winston Churchill | Andred Malraux |
| Max Ernst | Eleanor Roosevelt |
| Petula Clark | Norman Thomas |
| David Rockefeller | Walter Gropius |
| Robert Taylor | Justice Warren Burger |
| Deborah Kerr | Cardinal Mindszenty |

## THE *6* CHARACTER IN RELATION TO THE *8* DESTINY

This is a potentially dynamic combination of qualities where the communicative talents of the individual, as he easily relates to others in most situations, is challenged to take sides in judgment on some important issue. An advanced degree of maturity is required of this individual in order for him to be less insistent about the sentimental aspects of his personal morality and exercise the force necessary to realign the balance in some unjust situation which demands his attention. A karma in SIX eases this adjustment. A karma in EIGHT makes it more difficult as the individual is loath to develop an attitude "gutsy" enough to correct the injustice.

Some famous people whose SIX character confronts a EIGHT destiny are:

| | |
|---|---|
| Meredith Wilson | Joseph Cotton |
| George Harrison | Louis Calhern |
| David Dubinsky | Warren Beatty |

Winthrop Aldrich
Tony Randall
Dirk Bogarde

Jane Fonda
Lilli Palmer
Jan Valtin

# THE *6* CHARACTER IN RELATION TO THE *9* DESTINY

There is an ease of adjustment possible in this pattern where the moral consciousness of the individual is easily led to larger and larger groups so eventually he comes to view the whole world in one totality. The adjustment he is accustomed to making on a personal level becomes comparatively easy on a broader scale once he has acquired a sense of universal tolerance as opposed to the narrow provincialism which for him is more natural. This individual is used to evaluating matters in their direct and personal context. He must ultimately, however, learn to see them in an impersonal, objective application which may take some time. A karma in SIX would make this transition less difficult. A karma in NINE would cloud the issue entirely where the individual would not be able to see why his personal situations all tend to disintegrate while the broader field of application seems to lack any appeal at all.

Some famous people whose SIX character confronts a NINE destiny are:

Jimmy Dorsey
Sacha Guitry
Julius Rosenberg
Richard Gordon (astronaut)
Lawrence Welk
Charles Goren
Jonathan Miller
Edward Everett Horton

Dustin Hoffman
Ethel Merman
Rex Stout
Susan Sontag
Pres. William Taft
Justice Abe Fortas
Myra Kingsley

269

# THE *7* CHARACTER IN RELATION TO THE *1* DESTINY

This is a strong pattern which gives the perfected wisdom in the character an opportunity to pioneer in some new field which calls for marked individuality of effort. The quality of both number SEVEN and ONE call for individual isolation in most respects which working together here in this life pattern make it somewhat easier for the individual to discover for himself exactly where his true spiritual strength resides. It is exactly this type of strength that must be utilized in providing the leadership called for in this pattern. A karma in SEVEN would limit the depth of understanding on which this individual must ultimately place his reliance. A karma in ONE would increase the purely theoretical and "other worldly" application of this pioneering effort which would obviously avoid a more direct, obvious thrust towards a single goal.

Some famous people whose SEVEN character confronts a ONE destiny are:

| | |
|---|---|
| Doris Duke | Raquel Welch |
| Hugh Roy Cullen | Ralph Nader |
| Milton Berle | Thornton Wilder |
| Buddy Hackett | Robert Redford |
| Ringo Starr | Sen. Jacob Javits |
| George Gobel | |

Remember that all of these individuals are SEVENS who confront a ONE destiny but they may not all be the same type of SEVEN as modified by their respective motivation drive and personality image.

# THE 7 CHARACTER IN RELATION TO THE 2 DESTINY

This is a combination of compatible qualities where the almost mystical insight of the character is challenged to provide some form of personalized inspiration as guidance to others. The two types of sensitivity are here combined in such a way that the individual is given a series of rare opportunities to become a celebrity. This may not be a position in which this individual feels the most comfortable, but it does promise a degree of influence that SEVENS would not normally provide on their own. A karma in SEVEN would magnify the individual's unique talents in some strange way which even he would be unable to account for with normal explantations. A karma in TWO would direct the life style into unusual situations but increase the nerve strain as the individual is less prepared to accept the personal sacrifices he is called upon to make.

Some famous people whose SEVEN character confronts a TWO destiny are:

| | |
|---|---|
| Burt Bacharach | Katherine Anne Porter |
| Stavros Niarchos | Philip Roth |
| Oskar Werner | Pres. Calvin Coolidge |
| March Chagall | Richard Helms |
| Bobby Clark | John Jacob Astor |
| Adolph Menjou | Charles MacArthur |
| Paul Henreid | Walter Schirra (astronaut) |
| Eve Arden | Thomas Stafford (astronaut) |
| John O'Hara | Long John Nebel |

# THE 7 CHARACTER IN RELATION TO THE 3 DESTINY

This pattern reflects something of a step down in life in terms of the individual's potential talents (which are highly specialized) and the opportunity which fate provides for their use. This need not, however, particularly disturb him as he is generally content with the depth and comprehension of his own intuitive philosophy even though he is only encouraged by fate to apply this special awareness of life towards embellishment of some decorative (as opposed to substantive or structural) purpose. The challenge in life (as always under the THREE) is to relax and offer one's highly imaginative suggestions spontaneously and without restraint as the occasion arises. The SEVENS on their own would not be as free to share their insights and certainly not without being filtered through some sort of subtle restraint. These opportunities may not arise in areas other than the arts and general creativity, but the individual usually accepts this with complete understanding, if not to say relief. A karma in SEVEN would push the individual into a more active participation in creative media because he is less likely to dwell on introspective attitudes. A karma in THREE would turn the individual towards the creativity of others as he attempted to depersonalize the creative urge within himself.

Some famous people whose SEVEN character confronts a THREE destiny are:

| | |
|---|---|
| Eydie Gorme | Abigail Van Buren |
| Margaret Mead | Neil Simon |
| Vivien Leigh | Henry Miller |
| Eva Le Gallienne | Dean Rusk |
| Zoe Caldwell | Ero Saarinen |
| Ann Landers | Sen. George Smathers |

## THE 7 CHARACTER IN RELATION TO THE 4 DESTINY

This is a difficult life pattern to adjust to because the sensitivity of the SEVEN is somewhat out of place in a world where material objectives and practical principles are the sole criteria of value. The SEVEN character on its own would prefer an atmosphere more suitable for subjective theorizing or mystical contemplation rather than to be constantly required to prove one's principles in common-sense, everyday realities. The over-all life style is apt to be

272

difficult and strenous and not too rewarding in terms of inner accomplishments. A karma in SEVEN would improve the compromise by accenting the adaptability to work on purely practical matters. A karma in FOUR would release the individual from the more arduous and menial labors (which he would turn over to others) and he would therefore be able to concentrate more on the refinement of his subjective vision.

Some famous people whose SEVEN character confronts a FOUR destiny are:

John D. Rockfeller Jr.
Joseph Stalin
Jacques Lipchitz
Fats Waller
Frank Parker
Edgar Bergen
Shiran Shiran
Drew Pearson

Marshall McLuhan
Bob Considine
Pres. Andrew Johnson
Ramsey Clark
Sen. George McGovern
Jacques Piccard
Enrico Fermi

## THE 7 CHARACTER IN RELATION TO THE 5 DESTINY

This is a dynamic combination where the rare insight of the character is provided with an exciting and adventuresome series of experimental situations to apply his professional wisdom. The individual on his own might prefer a more background position in life but the pattern of his fate pushes him into active and unusual situations which require an impromptu adaptation to rapidly moving factors. A karma in SEVEN would make this adaptation somewhat easier. A karma in FIVE would reduce the effectiveness with which the individual tried to cope with his demanding opportunities.

Some famous people whose SEVEN character confronts a FIVE destiny are:

Edward Weston
Pierre S. Du Pont
Johnny Carson

Leo Durocher
Clark Gable
Robert Frost

273

Raoul Dufy
Leopold Stokowski
George Shearing

Lawrence O'Brien
Justice Earl Warren
Madame Blavatsky

# *THE* 7 *CHARACTER IN RELATION TO THE* 6 *DESTINY*

Because of the contradiction of contiguous number qualities, the individual is confronted here with a trying choice in life in which he must relinquish or diminish the essence of his own character traits and special talents in favor of a compromise with group values. These collective ideals may be at considerable variance with his own subjective appraisal of life. On his own, he would prefer to leave matters alone and pursue his own private interests, but the demands of his fate will insist on him sharing a good deal of his life with others. A karma in SEVEN would make the acceptance of group values a good deal more agreeable since the individual here would be considerably less aware of his own. A karma in SIX would confuse the issue as to why he must turn away from his own natural preferences and cast in his lot with others on a collective basis. Invariably, each time he tries to make this adjustment he is met with disappointment from the collective values which he resists.

Some famous people whose SEVEN character confronts a SIX destiny are:

Harry Warner
Leo Corrigan
Duke Wellington
James Reston
Pres. Eisenhower
Peter Ustinov

Orville Fredman
Pope Paul VI
Thomas Edison
L. Patrick Gray (F.B.I.
Anne Morgan
Mick Jagger

274

THE *7* CHARACTER IN RELATION TO THE *7* DESTINY

This combination insures an unusual life style where the individual, who is naturally possessed of exceptional talents, is ideally led to just the right situation at just the right time enabling him to generally appear in the most advantageous position possible. These unusual breaks are always better than he might have been able to manipulate for himself even though he will envision himself in such ideal situations long before they came about. He must therefore always bide his time and let fate provide the exact time, place and circumstances. A karma in SEVEN would make the individual's life style more of a mystery to him than he would openly acknowledge even though he was well aware of the unusual combination of fatalistic factors invariably interacting in his behalf. The individual here would be more susceptible to acting as fate's messenger in other people's lives without any prior motivation of his own.

Some famous people whose SEVEN character confronts a SEVEN destiny are:

Virgil Grissom (astronaut)          Kenneth Tynan
James Farmer                        James T. Farrell
Haile Selassie                      Irwin Shaw
Nikita Krushchev                    Maurice Medcalfe
Roy Lichtenstein                    Thomas Huxley
Myrna Loy                           Peter Finch
Kingsley Amis

THE *7* CHARACTER IN RELATION TO THE *8* DESTINY

Although this pattern involves the basic contradiction of contiguous number qualities, those qualities symbolized by the numbers above SIX (namely SEVEN, EIGHT & NINE) are able to confront each other with more independent consideration without nullifying the effects of the other. In this combination the qualities of the character, while formulated on a highly subjective and somewhat esoteric basis, are challenged to project themselves into the arena of material power situations. The individual is called upon in life to fulfill a mission of judicial correction wherein he takes upon himself the necessity to forcibly correct certain conditions which he considers to be out of balance and in need of realignment, restatement or reappraisal. He does this in the name of justice. His awareness of such necessity is intuitive rather than factual and because he comes to this position from other than have physically grown up in the actual situation, his right to pass judgment may be severly challenged by the very factors he is trying to correct. However, those who are also primarily guided in life by their intuition will automatically sense the correctness of his position which fate will ultimately make evident to everyone. In the meantime there is little gratitude for the contribution this individual struggles to make. A karma in SEVEN would make the over-all situation somewhat easier for the individual as he might appear to be more factual than intuitive in his judgements. A karma in EIGHT would limit the individual's sphere of application and thereby reduce the opposition from larger more powerful groups.

Some famous people whose SEVEN character confronts a EIGHT destiny are:

| | |
|---|---|
| Sir Ernest Oppenheimer | Arnold Toynbee |
| Alfred G. Vanderbilt | Vincent Sheean |
| Erich Von Stoheim | Cliff Robertson |
| Dick Smothers | Mies Van Der Rohe |
| Jack Dempsey | Stewart Udall |
| Timothy Leary | Pres. George Washington |
| Gregory Peck | Sen. James Eastland |
| Maxine Elliott | John J. O'Neill |

# THE 7 CHARACTER IN RELATION TO THE 9 DESTINY

This pattern combination is considerably easier to operate than the SEVEN to EIGHT challenge. The individual here is less pressured to force his personal awareness of life's value structures on volatile situations of apparent unbalance (or injustice). Instead he is able to detach himself from most everyday matters and wander about until he chances on some situation which obviously acknowledges the need of the very insight he is prepared to offer. This makes for much greater rapport, understanding and acceptance between what the individual has to give, the conditions under which it is offered and the utilization by those who are helped in a humanitarian, charitable way. These individuals not only have much to contribute in life, but their influence is likely to be felt on a wide, universal basis. A karma in SEVEN would tend to depersonalize the spiritual depth of what the individual has to contribute. He himself is less conscious and articulate about what it may be. A karma in NINE would hold the individual back from the wider fields of application because he would initially resist the compassionate appeals which really require his attention and devotion.

Some famous people whose SEVEN character confronts a NINE destiny are:

| | |
|---|---|
| Mario Lanza | Red Buttons |
| John D. Rockefeller I | Ann Sothern |
| Tommy Dorsey | Clare Boothe Luce |
| David Scott (astronaut) | Louis Bromfield |
| Jackie Gleason | Edward G. Robinson |
| Sammy Snead | Stewart Rawlings Mott III |
| Orson Welles | Sen. Ralph Yarborough |
| George Peppard | |

# THE 9 VARIATIONS OF DESTINY TO THE EIGHT CHARACTER

*THE* **8** *CHARACTER IN RELATION TO THE* **1** *DESTINY*

This is an excellent combination which promises considerable success in the material world. The toughness in the character is most likely to respond constructively to the challenge of the fate pattern for continual self-betterment. Fortunately this individual is better prepared than most (and also eager) to keep pushing towards new goals which offer him an advantage of both leadership and power control. A karma in EIGHT would discredit the judgment and reflect someone who was not nearly as tough in his own affairs as he should be. A karma in ONE would limit the fields of application to such an extent that he is likely to resist his best opportunities.

Some famous people whose EIGHT character confronts a ONE destiny are:

| | |
|---|---|
| Trevor Howard | Sen. Edmund Muskie |
| Jerry Lewis | W. T. Grant |
| Sydney Greenstreet | John Warnecke |
| Zero Mostel | H. Ross Perot |
| Colin Wilson | Sen. John Tower |
| W. M. Kiplinger | Alice Ghostley |
| Winthrop Rockefeller | |

Remember that all of these individuals are EIGHTS who confront a ONE destiny but they may not all be the same type of EIGHT as modified by their respective motivation drive and personality image.

*THE* **8** *CHARACTER IN RELATION TO THE* **2** *DESTINY*

This is not a particularly fortunate combination because the ultimate demand of the destiny tends to defeat or undermine the effectiveness of the individual's real talents. If there is anything EIGHT must do to fulfill its natural function, it is to stand firm in the face of opposition or conflict UNTIL FACTS AND FACTS ALONE MAY HAVE NECESSITATED A REVISION OF POLICY OR JUDGMENT. Hypothetical "ifs", "ands" or "buts" cannot be tolerated. The result of the TWO destiny leads the individual to some sort of compromise which may support some particular position nicely, but is essentially bound to negate the judicial integrity in the spirit of absolute justice. A karma in EIGHT would considerably lubricate the acceptance of such compromises as became necessary. In this pattern compelling compromises certainly will become necessary. A karma in TWO would depersonalize the necessity for sacrifice so something other than the individual himself may become the sacrifice.

Some famous people whose EIGHT character confronts a TWO destiny are:

Andrew Mellon
John Wanamaker
Donald Slayton (astronaut)
Hugh Downs
Cecil Beaton
Dizzy Dean
Mike Todd
Joseph Dunninger
Richard Burton
Phil Silvers

Claude Rains
Debbie Reynolds
John Hersey
Pres. Benjamin Harrison
John Connally
Shirley Temple Black
Rev. Carl McIntire
Louis De Wohl
Vincent Lopez

# THE *8* CHARACTER IN RELATION TO THE *3* DESTINY

This can be a powerful and effective combination where the instinctive sense of balance with factors of significant importance are brought to bear in a creative field and the individual is challenged to express something with decorative and artistic flourish. There is a good deal of potential power and steam here which must eventually find its way into some form of creative self expression. A karma in EIGHT would disguise the talent for getting at the heart of volatile matters of commanding importance. It would however somewhat ease the transition into self expression. A karma in THREE would limit and diminish the individual's facility for freely expressing, capsulizing or synthesizing the powerful ingredients which he has at his finger tips.

Some famous people whose EIGHT character confronts a THREE destiny are:

| | |
|---|---|
| Clarence Dillon | Maggie Smith |
| Mack Sennett | Ina Claire |
| Maxfield Parrish | Judy Garland |
| Thomas Watson Sr. | F. Scott Fitzgerald |
| Ray Milland | Rebecca West |
| John Wayne | Rep. Wilbur Mills |
| Ronald Colman | Lucy Baines Johnson |

# THE *8* CHARACTER IN RELATION TO THE *4* DESTINY

This is a sound combination for material achievement and success which should ultimately build something of lasting value. The individual has rather more talent for executive and administrative roles than for the down-to-basics, shirt sleeve opportunities that his fate provides. His challenge in life is to forgo or put aside his distant material vision in favor of pitching in and laying the required ground work himself. A karma in EIGHT would ease the individual's acceptance of lesser roles and a more active participation in the hard, menial labor demanded in his life. A karma in FOUR would enable the individual to escape some of the more menial tasks so he could devote more of his time and energy to the development of his administrative talents.

Some famous people whose EIGHT character confronts a FOUR destiny are:

| | |
|---|---|
| Kate Millett | Dinah Shore |
| Don Drysdale | Kim Novak |
| Robert Montgomery | Barbara Stanwyck |
| William Holden | Marjorie Rawlings |
| Boris Karloff | Wendell Willkie |
| Mia Farrow | I. A. Richards |

## THE *8* CHARACTER IN RELATION TO THE *5* DESTINY

This combination may seem unsettling to the individual as the firm position which his character naturally assumes is frequently thrown off balance by intrusions into his life of matters never originally envisioned or allowed for. Frequently there may be a compelling necessity to drop one assignment to start another rather than a disparagement of his original formula on how that particular job should be executed. Anyone with a FIVE destiny must face many sudden and unexpected changes in life, but it is only by capitalizing on these interruptions, which the FIVE fate pattern provides, that the individual will ultimately profit. In this case the individual when forced to move or change, faces a comparatively larger investment than most (because of the EIGHT level) in the situation which must be dropped or drastically revised. A karma in EIGHT prepares the individual for the speculative risks which his fate demands. A karma in FIVE would indicate a loss of opportunity through a reluctance to change over when such is clearly indicated to be for his best interests.

Some famous people whose EIGHT character confronts a FIVE destiny are:

Charles Kettering
Jacob Blaustein
Robert Young
Dan Rowan
Pearl Bailey
Arturo Toscanini
Irving Berlin
Rep. Hale Boggs
Billy Talbert

Glenn Ford
Shelly Winters
Lillian Hellman
Marianne Moore
Tennessee Williams
Yevtushenko
Van Wyck Brooks
Bebe Rebozo

## THE *8* CHARACTER IN RELATION TO THE *6* DESTINY

This is a sound combination where the executive talents of the individual are encouraged to find some form of collective purpose through which he can function in a manner which will benefit others besides himself. Such significant character traits as he has for sensing balance and inbalance is given a group orientation which insures both acceptance and appreciation for the contributions which the individual makes. While the SIX tends to water down the intensity of other qualities connected with it, it insures cooperation and ease of personal relationships (including satisfaction for the individual himself). A karma in EIGHT would lessen the friction between the individual's sense of what should be theoretically and what the group will actually accept. A karma in SIX would depersonalize the group demands so much less of the individual himself need be toned down or compromised from the theoretical ideal his character imposes.

Some famous people whose EIGHT character confronts a SIX destiny are:

Mike Wallace
Louise Nevelson
Steve Lawrence

Merle Oberon
Margaret Sullivan
Erich Segal

Joe Dimaggio
Michelangelo Antonioni
Otto Preminger
John Cassavetes
Vanessa Redgrave

Jean-Paul Sartre
T. S. Eliot
Langston Hughes
Calouste Gulbenkian

# THE 8 CHARACTER IN RELATION TO THE 7 DESTINY

This is a powerful combination of independent forces which indicate that the individual, who is indeed a strong character of tough, uncomprising qualities, will eventually be led along paths of application which implement the hand of fate in some mysterious manner. The professional techniques for management in which this individual is obviously talented are here encouraged to practice in specialized fields, somewhat off the beaten path or in ways which plumb new depths, or expose heretofore unknown elements which were not previously common knowledge. A karma in EIGHT minimizes the individual's insistence on certain perogative rights and maximizes his ease to follow unknown or uncertain directions. A karma in SEVEN clouds the individual's awareness of the real direction in which his best contribution may lie. He is more likely to take false turns or resist taking the obvious turn just because it does not follow his original plans which are very firmly structured in his character.

Some famous people whose EIGHT character confronts a SEVEN destiny are:

Germaine Greer
Golda Meir
Albert Shanker
Eddie Cantor
Marilyn Monroe

Pres. John F. Kennedy
John F. Kennedy Jr.
Pres. Benjamin Harrison
Justice William O. Douglas
Edwin Aldrin (astronaut)

# THE 8 CHARACTER IN RELATION TO THE 8 DESTINY

The life style in this combination is apt to be ruthlessly tough on the individual leaving him little or no choice to do anything except live up to the hard material demands that fate constantly imposes upon him. The double accent on EIGHT can prove to be too much of one thing, which in this instance can be considerably exhausting and nerve shattering by the violence involved and the constant demand from life to be tougher and tougher. A karma in EIGHT would reduce the reaction level to where the individual's nerves could probably accept the demands because he was actually not fully aware of just how intense the pressure against him was.

Some famous people whose EIGHT character confronts a EIGHT destiny are:

Bob Newhart                    Raymond Burr
Jesse Owens (track star)       Marjorie Main
Alan Shepard (astronaut)       George Bernard Shaw
Ty Cobb                        Rex Reed
Mickey Mantle                  Minoru Yamasaki
Cesar Chavez                   Grant Lewi
Peter O'Toole

# THE 8 CHARACTER IN RELATION TO THE 9 DESTINY

While the individual has talents for performing a tough job with efficient dispatch, in this combination his fate dictates a certain lessening of personal control and the necessity for objective detachment in order that he may circle around in search of broader fields of application where ultimately the humanitarian touch is more important than the inherent justice of each individual case load. What is given up here, in terms of balance and efficiency consciousness, is strengthened by a more compassionate attitude towards life and individuals. Universal goodwill through selfless service become the final answer for this individual rather than pressing for absolute conformance to a theoretical pattern of ideal efficiency. A karma in EIGHT eases the transition to this broader and more charitable viewpoint. A karma in NINE depersonalizes the individual's field of application where he feels he is giving up less of himself in order to achieve this broader application.

Some famous people whose EIGHT character confronts a NINE destiny are:

George Jay Gould               Van Heflin
Laurence Housman               Alan Bates
Francisco Franco               Paddy Chayefsky
Aleksei Kosygin                E. M. Forster
Tom Jones                      Allen Ginsberg
Elvis Presley                  Alger Hiss
Rock Hudson

## THE 9 VARIATIONS OF DESTINY TO THE NINE CHARACTER

THE *9* CHARACTER IN RELATION TO THE *1* DESTINY

This is a strong combination which gives much promise for an outstanding and original contribution to a worthy cause of broad concern. It is the individual himself who supplies the expansive vision on worldly matters and it is the prodding of his fate which pushes him into new fields where leadership and pioneering spirit are so obviously necessary. The individual on his own may prefer to wander and circulate rather than to pin point himself in one decisive direction or commitment as the circumstances of his fate will demand. It is destiny which takes this choice out of his hands. A karma in NINE would ease the acceptance of this single stand in one direction. A karma in ONE would depersonalize the contribution so the individual himself need not actually be as involved in the movement which centralizes around something he stands for or represents. An example of this would be a movement which ralied around a piece of writing rather than the author himself.

Some famous people whose NINE character confronts a ONE destiny are:

| | |
|---|---|
| Raymond Chandler | Shirley Booth |
| Sir Francis Chichester | Truman Capote |
| Rudy Vallee | James Hilton |
| Joe E. Brown | Pres. William McKinley |
| Alan Arkin | Bess Truman |
| Harold Lloyd | Pierre Salinger |

Remember that all of these individuals are NINES who confront a ONE destiny but they may not all be the same type of NINE as modified by their respective motivation drive and personality image.

## THE *9* CHARACTER IN RELATION TO THE *2* DESTINY

This combination is quite in keeping with the qualities symbolized by both numbers; therefore, there is a willingness for the individual to adapt himself to the demands of his fate. This individual will take a long time to finalize his position or values in life, but he will be well prepared to follow the path which destiny provides even though that path may imply many sacrifices. A karma in NINE makes the life style much more personalized and possessive. A karma in TWO places the direction in life more on a theoretical than an actual basis.

The individual may be a much stronger advocate of certain attitudes than he is an example of them.

Some famous people whose NINE character confronts a TWO destiny are:

| | |
|---|---|
| Mrs. Charles Payson | Katherine Hepburn |
| Roy Arthur Hunt | Sen. William Proxmire |
| Leonid Brezhnev | Dr. Benjamin Spock |
| Hazel Scott | Bud Fisher |
| Ray Charles | Sen. Vance Hartke |
| George C. Scott | |

## THE *9* CHARACTER IN RELATION TO THE *3* DESTINY

This is a very impressive combination for achievement in the arts where selfless spirit is considered to have enhanced the artistic merit of the expression. Whole schools of artistic criticism are built around this criteria of selfless (theoretically pure) creative effort. The result is supposed to be less because it was "me" who did it than to have captured a universality of expression as though "everybody" somehow had contributed their share. The individual would prefer to generalize but fate will require a more specific response which is really what brings the matter (or essence) to life at all. The character has talents for wide, easy, objective circulation and the fate provides excellent opportunities for skillful, persuasive salesmanship and an assured market for his more personal (and even prejudicial) opinions. A karma in NINE would increase the willingness to personalize all forms of expression (which the Nine on its own resists). A karma in THREE would give the individual some concern as to exactly how he could best express what he feels must "come out".

Some famous people whose NINE character confronts a THREE destiny are:

| | |
|---|---|
| Bernadette Devlin | James Mason |
| Salvador Dali | Bing Crosby |
| Eddy Arnold | Conrad Aiken |

Arthur Vining Davis
Fritz Thyssen
Robert Vaughn
Dana Andrews
Niels Bohr
Sen. Leverett Saltonstall
Alan Leo

Sloan Wilson
Ruth Montgomery
Sen. Barry Goldwater
Roy Chapman Andrews
Robert Millikan
Sen. Strom Thurmond

## THE *9* CHARACTER IN RELATION TO THE *4* DESTINY

This is a combination which gives much promise of practical achievement in matters which have broad public interest. The individual may on his own prefer to broaden his views and perspective but fate will demand that he always focus this on some realitic, down-to-earth project which can put his sense of charity to test. The potential value of this pattern is the degree of broad understanding which this individual can contribute to very disciplined, useful work projects. A karma in NINE would provide less day dreaming and more cold realism. A karma in FOUR would depersonalize the FOUR demands so the individual would feel that it is sufficient for him to provide the vision and let others do most of the actual work.

Some famous people whose NINE character confront a FOUR destiny are:

Ed Sullivan
Larry Rivers
Roberta Peters
Trini Lopez
Babe Ruth
Ingmar Bergman
Edwin Land
Elliott Gould

Carol Reed
Anne Bancroft
Kaye Ballard
Loretta Young
Rachel Carson
Le Corbusier
Harold Wilson

288

# THE *9* CHARACTER IN RELATION TO THE *5* DESTINY

This is a compatible combination of qualities which gives much promise of effective direct action which is still based on broadly, comprehensive views rather than just on the spot snap judgments as the life style might appear. The individual is assured of a broad and active life which will cover much ground and provide a good deal of personal excitement and adventure. The individual's natural talent for depersonalized circulation is readily adaptable for the sudden intrustions which fate will supply that cause him to radically change direction or try totally different solutions than have ever been tried before. The talents of the character naturally make the individual tolerant and open minded about almost anything so the rash opportunism of the destiny is more likely to fall on fertile ground. A karma in NINE would heighten the individual's response to sudden changes in direction. A karma in FIVE would theorize on the innovations rather than push the individual into a more actual, full spirited participation.

Some famous people whose NINE character confront a FIVE destiny are:

William Rockefeller
Max Baer
Ralph Abernathy
Georgia O'Keeffe
Gene Littler
Sosthenes Behn
Harry Guggenheim
Aristotle Onassis
Dean Martin

Dean Martin
Tony Perkins
Rosalind Russell
Sen. Mike Mansfield
Luther Burbank
Linus Pauling
Stokely Carmichael
J. Gaither Pratt

# THE *9* CHARACTER IN RELATION TO THE *6* DESTINY

This is a combination which is fortunate for the individual because he is assured of not only a broad understanding of life (which he already has) but an opportunity to put this vision into constructive group action which generally meets with social acceptance and personal gratitude for his contribution. For many people in life there is neither immediate acceptance of their contribution (whatever it may be) or much personal gratification for a job well done. This pattern, however, overcomes these two common stumbling blocks and insures a fair measure of social pleasures as well. A karma in NINE would obscure the individual's vision but personalize his group commitments. A karma in SIX would place the individual's application to group values on a more theoretical than actual basis.

Some famous people whose NINE character confronts a SIX destiny are:

| | |
|---|---|
| Juan Trippe | Cary Grant |
| Henry J. Kaiser | Broderick Crawford |
| Whitney Young | Mary Astor |
| Jesse Jackson | Greta Garbo |
| Steve Allen | Sandy Dennis |
| Jim Nabors | James Thurber |
| Tom Smothers | Dorothy Kilgallen |
| Buckminister Fuller | Angus Wilson |
| Twiggy | Albert Einstein |
| Michael Caine | Joe Pepitone |

# THE *9* CHARACTER IN RELATION TO THE *7* DESTINY

This combination is likely to lead the individual on a long journey to a distant and unfamiliar area (or field of application) which may seem to others as sometimes imposing sad and isolated conditions. The individual himself will not feel this to be so as he discovers the strange situations into which life leads him to be immensely rewarding in non-worldly ways which only he can fully appreciate. The character itself has talent for making comprehensive broad contacts with all kinds of people while the opportunities of the destiny tend to isolate him with matters of specialized interest which give added depth to his already broad understanding of life. A karma in NINE would restrict the individual's vision so that he may be quite unaware of the true use of his talents. A karma in SEVEN would lessen the spiritual gratification with accomplishments and make his life seem even more strange because he resists the very patterns which actually tie the whole thing together. He will persistently miss these subtle factors which are interwoven throughout all his experience.

Some famous people whose NINE character confronts a SEVEN destiny are:

Queen Elizabeth II
Chet Huntley
David Susskind
Joey Bishop
Paul Anka
William Kunstler

Martha Raye
Maxwell Anderson
Sen. Tom Eagleton
Sir Julian Huxley
Tricia Nixon
Carl Payne Tobey

# THE *9* CHARACTER IN RELATION TO THE *8* DESTINY

This is a very strong combination where the individual is given ample opportunity to prove the worldliness of his philosophy in matters that call for the violent and forceful implementation of judicial positions. In spite of himself the individual is involved in action which forces him to take sides whether he wishes to or not. In this combination, however, the outcome is likely to be broadly comprehensive and an expression of justice touched with compassionate tolerance for others. A karma in NINE would heighten the individual's acceptance of judicial roles. A karma in EIGHT would confuse the individual as to exactly wherein his own contribution could function best.

Some famous people whose NINE character confront a EIGHT destiny are:

Harry Sinclair
Queen Wilhelmina
Lee Trevino
Tony Curtis
Joan Crawford
Lee Remick
Marlene Dietrich

Leonard Woolf
Sir Bernard Lovell
Pres. Millard Fillmore
Rev. Oral Roberts
Rev. Martin Niemoller
Edgar Cayce

# THE *9* CHARACTER IN RELATION TO THE *9* DESTINY

This combination is indicative of what is called in some circles "an old soul" who has been around many many times before. They are blessed with a natural maturity (far beyond anything they could have acquired just from this life alone) which in this combination will on occasion be pressed into active participation with some cause or movement when and if the circumstances are "just right". In this case (perhaps more than in any other pattern) the individual himself is more likely to be the judge of just when and how he will respond because many claims on his attention may leave him quite unmoved. On the other hand he may feel called to rise to an occasion wholly out of proportion to what normally would be expected under the circumstances. He can magnify a situation greatly beyond what it seems to others. This sense of potential as related to primal human instincts is what gives NINES their power, influence and effect over large masses of people which can prove both helpful and destructive. A karma in NINE would depersonalize the NINE quality where the individual responded to his calling more on a theoretical basis than a more whole hearted total support.

Some famous people whose NINE character confronts a NINE destiny are:

| | |
|---|---|
| Constantine Brancusi | Babe Didrikson |
| A. P. Giannini | Erich Fromm |
| Michael Collins (Astronaut) | Burt Lancaster |
| Malvina Hoffman | Al Jolson |
| Henry Moore | Shirley MacLaine |
| Jerry Herman | Moira Shearer |
| Joan Sutherland | Edmund Wilson |
| Dame Myra Hess | Sargent Shriver |

# Chapter IX

# EVALUATING YOUR OWN FATE
## AT A GLANCE

Evaluating your fate at a glance is a little misleading in that, even after you know the method, you must learn to THINK NUMBERS and apply your BEST JUDGMENT to that which is clearly indicated.

What I mean to convey is that the number pattern for evaluating your fate at a glance is very simple. You may forget the complexity of WHO YOU ARE as challenged by the SPECIFIC OPPORTUNITIES PROVIDED BY YOUR DESTINY. You may forget how talented you are, or how many serious handicaps you have in your perspective towards life. You may forget, for the moment, whether you like yourself or whether you particularly enjoy what seems cut out for you. You may also forget whether you fully understand the underlying significance of your way of doing things or the direction in which you are headed.

All you need think about in this evaluation is your FATE (which is a life time orientation) and the separation of your fate into 4 periods of time during which you are challenged to assume SPECIFIC ATTITUDES OF MIND towards any and all the opportunities which fate will provide. To refresh your memory about where the FOUR MAJOR PINNACLES OF TIMING come from, refer to Chapter VI. They are:

FIRST PINNACLE is the digit of the month added to the digit of the day of birth. THIS IS THE REQUIRED ATTITUDE UNDER WHICH *YOUR LIFE STARTS OUT.*

SECOND PINNACLE is the digit of the day added to the digit of the year of birth.

THIRD PINNACLE is the digit of the first pinnacle added to the digit of the second pinnacle.

Together the SECOND and THIRD PINNACLE comprise the 18 years of the *MIDDLE PRODUCTIVE STAGE OF LIFE.*

FOURTH PINNACLE is the digit of the month added to the digit of the year of birth. This is *HOW YOUR LIFE ENDS UP.*

At a glance you can tell how your life starts out, the quality of the middle productive years when you are supposedly at your mature best in top performance and how you finally end up.

The principle on which this comparison of ATTITUDES towards OBJECTIVES is based is the compatability or incompatability of the number vibrations TO EACH OTHER and not primarily to the quality of the FATE itself or to you as the individual involved although personal preferences or dislikes of certain activities will have much to do with your gratifications.

## HOW YOUR LIFE STARTS OUT

This single number vibration by itself perhaps tells more about your life style than any other number in your life. The behavioral psychologists have always placed heavy importance on early environment and the life long effect this has on the developing child. In number analysis this vibration is the primary conditioning quality of all experience up to ages 27 to 35, depending on the fate number itself (see Chapter VI). As already explained in Chapter VI we are subject to many subdivisions of timing (personal vibrations of the year, month, etc. down to the individual demands of each day) but the primary conditioner of this long introductory period to our life is symbolized by the number of our FIRST PINNACLE. This tells exactly how your life starts out.

IF YOUR LIFE STARTS OUT ON ONE you are presented with immediate demands for aggressive self-assertion in order to develop independence and self-reliance. Everything in your life from the very beginning is an up hill struggle all the way. There will seldom be anyone to help you, but on the other hand there will seldom be anyone leaning on you to hold you back in the way of responsibilities. There is therefore a certain degree of freedom inherent in a ONE beginning. This is a period when you are encouraged in every possible way to think of your own interests first. While there may be periods when you seem far in advance of the crowd as a leader or advance man, the implication here is not of personal responsibility. You aren't really tied to something. You can cast things off if you make up your mind to. The real responsibility during this period is for the individual TO HIMSELF. This is a period for developing the character and sense of personal integrity. In evaluating whether things are right or wrong for you during this period you must always refer the matter back to YOUR OWN self-interest. You will be prohibited by fate from easy reference to others since just when you need this self-assurance you are likely to be alone or entirely on your own. In order to develop in the individual this ATTITUDE OF ONENESS life will present you with a continual series of situations where others are in fact trying to dominate you. The desired reaction, which fate is trying to develop and strengthen, is to encourage you to strike back and assert your own domination over the situation. In early childhood this is likely to be just a holding operation and not an effective domination or control over others. But even from the beginning the infant will be building up resentments within himself until such time as he can strike back and seek the freedom he senses he needs. To him this domination is suffocating and not something he can accept or resign himself to. No one who starts his life on a ONE vibration is likely to ever forget those ingenious ways in which he fortified himself to resist all those things which pushed him around. This is a strong and good start in life and reflects an individual who generally deserves much self earned credit.

IF YOUR LIFE STARTS ON TWO you are initially held back in everything important you try to do. You learn early in life the value of patience, watchful waiting and biding your time until the right door opens up. In the meantime you have plenty of time to develop your sensitivities and carefully observe all the infinite details around you which most people are too busy to notice. Life encourages you to be gentle, quiet, unassuming, docile, compromising, considerate and kindly because, when you are, then things tend to flow your way in abundance. But if you try to behave in an opposite fashion, then nothing seems to work right. No one who starts his life on TWO is ever likely to forget the value of PROPER TIMING. When you are carefully observant and intuitively keyed to the natural rhythm of time, this can prove more effective in solving the problems of life that all the other talents combined. There is little profit in doing the right thing at the wrong time. It will never work out. But when the time is just right, then everything else seems to fall into place automatically. Everyone who enters life on TWO learns all of this from the beginning. Early childhood is, however, apt to be a series of up and down situations like a storm tossed sea. There is also that sense of dying in some respect only to awaken to the prospect of being reborn in a new image. Anything connected with TWO carries this implication of re-birth. This can at the time prove very upsetting.

IF YOUR LIFE STARTS OUT ON THREE you should experience what might be called the ideality of childhood by being able to indulge yourself freely in most of the things that seem most appropriate to childhood. There should be a marked lack of responsibility over others. You should enjoy an enviable amount of freedom to develop your sense of imagination and spirit of play. You should gradually acquire a sense of synthesis by being able to fit various things together in a composite whole which has a pleasing and decorative effect. To learn this effectively one has to have free time just to play around and experiment with whatever captures one's eye at the moment. Starting life on THREE denies an early maturity or concern for the serious matters of life and that is the way it is supposed to be for these fortunate individuals. To be otherwise would spoil the fun, charm, enthusiasm and decorative value for these people. No one who starts life on a THREE is ever likely to forget the delights of his childhood and the utter lack of concern for what tomorrow might bring, for his entire concentration was on the happy consumption of today. A karma in THREE does not change the freedom opportunities that are there but it does make it harder for the individual to make full use of them for he resists the appreciation of THREENESS.

IF YOUR LIFE STARTS OUT ON FOUR you will experience a limitation, restriction, discipline and rigidly enforced routine which places heavy accent on all material and practical considerations. In a sense this denies a real childhood altogether since the individual is expected from the start to shoulder his share of the work load and to pay in return for whatever life provides. He is never permitted to forget the obligations which he owes to life. Nothing will come easily in this child's life. Everything must be earned and paid for in full. Truth, facts and hard core reality are all under heavy accent here. The early years may be harsh and cruel. No one who starts life on a FOUR is ever likely to forget those difficult early times and the necessity for denial, discipline and careful budgeting which life harshly imposed. One may be spared the more difficult forms of material hardship because even children of wealthy parents are also born into a FOUR beginning cycle, but still for all effective purposes their parent's wealth does not relieve them of the tone of restricted circumstances. Also, it should be pointed out that one's parents do not constitute the total environment to which the child is subject. Two children in the same family may have very different beginnings which is only partly attributable to the parents themselves. The parents may also treat each child quite differently without realizing how they do this. If one of these children has a ONE beginning then the world which he faces presents exactly the type of challenge which will encourage him to respond in a ONE fashion. And for the other child which has a FOUR beginning the world which he individually faces will encourage him to respond in a FOUR fasion. And this is so even when the two children share the same family circle. Each of us reacts to a distinct set of circumstances according to our own number patterns regardless of how this may appear to others. Only we are truly aware of what exactly constitutes that challenge which is confronting us. A karma in FOUR would make it more difficult to accept or cope with the harsh demands made upon you. Anyone with a FOUR karma is not as hardy or robust or resistant to the effects of privation as he might appear. A karma in one of these cycles of time does mean that the KARMA IS LESS TROUBLESOME DURING THAT TIME PERIOD and that even though the individual may offer some resistance in accepting that role or attitude, it WILL BE EASIER FOR HIM TO DO SO DURING THIS CYCLE OF TIME. It is correspondingly easier to adjust to one's karmic problems during a period of time which matches the karma, but this is mostly effective when confronting the longer durations of time as such (as during the FOUR MAJOR PINNACLES). It does not work that way on shorter periods of time such as personal year vibrations, personal months or days although

299

the need to do something in that direction may be more pressing.

IF YOUR LIFE STARTS OUT OF FIVE you will participate in an above average share of adventure, excitement, sudden changes and intrusions into your life. This prepares you at an early date to be adaptable, innovative, restless, adventuresome, speculative and used to courting danger. Much of what captures your immedaite interest can in some way become a test of competitive skills or physical aptitudes as you learn to place great store on all sensory stimulation which activates the five senses. No one who begins life on FIVE will be likely to ever forget the thrill and excitement of his early adventures including an early introduction to sexual matters. The FIVE challenge here is likely to leave a state of unrest and insecurity which may enhance or agitate other aspects of the life style. In any event the individual does learn to cope with sudden changes early in life and to improvise with what he has to "make do" until he can be rescued or find his way to more solid ground. With the FIVE beginning in life one is naturally more prone to consider that everything is constantly in a state of flux and that life in general is pretty much what you make it to be by your own ingenuity. Of course, everyone tends to regard life for others as more or less similar to how they are challenged to see it. This is simply not true, of course, as each of us is being specifically conditioned to a distinctly individual response pattern according to our own destiny. But most people can't see this or even conceive that it is true because, after all, all they know is what they themselves experience. Most people have little talent to project or empathize themselves into a situation from someone else's standpoint. Certain people, however, are gifted in this respect and they intuitively grasp these differences. A karma in FIVE would reduce the adaptablility of the individual to his life style.

IF YOUR LIFE STARTS OUT ON SIX you will from the beginning feel and consider yourself to be a closely knit member of a group where each must assume some degree of responsibility for other members. You are seldom likely to strike out on your own because of how this will effect the group. Everything in your life tends to be more a matter of how it effects the group you belong to than it does you individually. Your values at this point are in no way individualized (to yourself), but they are highly indicative of the hopes and aspirations which the group holds collectively. The individual is assured and supported in his early life by this sense of

300

belonging and the easy social exchange which he enjoys. The challenge during this beginning period is to string along together as a cooperative family unit. No one who begins life on SIX is likely to ever forget the sense of belonging. Even though there may be other problems whatever they are they could be shared with others. Unless the SIX falls on another pinnacle as well there will never agains be such a sense of protective security such as experienced in this beginning cycle of life. A karma in SIX makes all of this seem less important even though at the time it is bound to be comforting.

IF YOUR LIFE STARTS OUT ON SEVEN you will from the beginning suffer a sense of isolation from the main stream of life. Since this is the life style that immediately confronts you, you are likely to accept this as perfectly natural if not the most ideal form of existence. You will have plenty of time to spend by yourself in introspective contemplation. You as an individual may be so constituted as to be ideally suited for something quite different, but since this is your initial fate you will accept it and explore the mysterious implications as life gradually unfolds for you. Your associations in early life will not be among ordinary, average people for you are destined to start life in a special world which is not so much make believe as it is a sincere consciousness of "other factors" which ordinary people may not experience at all. No one who begins life on a SEVEN vibration is ever likely to forget the hidden value which comes from following the indirect or round about approach. Most people tend to proceed directly toward their objective, whatever it may be. They see it, they decide they want it, they go for it. But under the SEVEN attitude one learns to walk around the matter and look to see what is on the other side for they instinctively know there is an unseen side. It takes this instinctive knowledge of the "unseen" to start the ball rolling in directions which are circuitous, oblique, double visioned and intuitively inspired. The rewards for this behavior are seldom immediate, but the individual learns to wait for the final outcome when most things seem to find a place of their own. It is this sense of completeness, which was never initially considered, that more than makes up for the shortcomings of the SEVEN's present situation. They sense that with a little manipulation here and a little modification there that the whole pattern can assume something quite distinctive and rather rare. A karma in SEVEN encourages one to act in peculiar ways without reaching the desired state of awareness where patterns are more easily recognized or the implied reality beyond ordinary things becomes compelling.

IF YOUR LIFE STARTS OUT ON EIGHT you will from the beginning be forced to make important decisions not only for yourself, in matters far beyond your maturity, but for those around you who instinctively rely on your superior judgment. You must, from the earliest possible age, learn to confront important matters with a view to altering the factors so the situation becomes not only efficient but profitable to you in some way. Money is always a subject of consuming interest, either too much of it or too little or awareness of all the ways in which money affects everything you seem to do. Even as a child you are required to know the price and exchange value of material things. You should be introduced early in life to ways where you can prove your executive abilities and efficiency in ordering others around and telling them what to do. Sometimes it is difficult for others to understand how an untrained and inexperienced child can have such skills, but inadvertently they tend to fall in with the schemes which you vividly outline. No one who begins life on EIGHT is ever likely to forget the importance of money as it might effect their whole scheme of things. A karma in EIGHT would develop a person who might learn the price of everything and the value of nothing. EIGHT on any of the cycles of time constitutes a challenge to "cash in" on programs which have reached their harvest point. Those with a EIGHT karma seem to be more effective at accumulating money than those without (see Chapter XII on the number patterns of multimillionaires and observe how many of them have EIGHT karmas. This is because the responsibility and care of vast wealth accents the "curse" of money aside from its possible advantages).

IF YOUR LIFE STARTS OUT ON NINE you will from the beginning be called upon to face life with an emotional maturity and a comprehensive philosophy far in advance of what might be expected from one of your age and experience. You are able to reflect this depth of character through intuition rather than by rational deduction since you would hardly have been able, at this stage of your life, to have already experienced these matters in order to arrive at such mature conclusions. The NINE vibration, symbolizing as it does the termintion of programs, is not exactly an ideal tempo on which to begin life because the individual's experience tends to confirm what he already knows rather than to point up the advantages of a new beginning. Most of his experience will only repeat what he has already subconsciously gathered from the past. Knowing the final answers before you have even started (like starting to read a book from the last chapter first) tends to remove the anticipation and enthusiasm from life. This individual is old and weary before he even starts. Obviously there is some real purpose in having him go "once more around", but it can be a discouraging start. Everyone who begins life on NINE is acutely aware of what he brings with him from the past and this awareness will always haunt and sadden him as he contemplates the apparent futility of repeating the same lessons over and over again. Whatever he does in this life may seen pale by comparison to the richness of his subconscious. As pointed out in Chapter VI all those individuals who enter life on NINE are on UNIVERSAL TIMING. Their personal timing always matches the exact date itself, which puts them in tune with the totality of experience going on around them, as opposed to the specific time pattern which any one of us may be facing. Being on the universal has its advantages and its disadvantages. It depends on what use you can make of this awareness. If you are unable to capitalize on this awareness, then it will probably sadden you. If you can add it to your own aspirations, then it will carry you further than ordinary (non-universal) people would be able to go. A karma in NINE would be like drawing a curtain between the individual and his subconscious where he continued to function as programed but was unable to fully comprehend his reason or motives or be as able or as prepared to draw on his subconscious memories.

## THE MIDDLE MATURE YEARS

How life starts out under the first pinnacle lasts to age 27 (for those with a NINE destiny) to as long as age 35 (for those with a ONE destiny). Immediately following the first pinnacle are the 18 years of the MIDDLE MATURE PERIOD under the SECOND and THIRD pinnacle (with 9 years under each).

We all begin life in the vibration of our destiny number. If your destiny number is FIVE your first year of life is a FIVE year. If your destiny number is EIGHT your first year of life is a EIGHT year. But we all end our first pinnacle on a NINE year and all the following pinnacles (major cycles of timing) begin for each of us on a ONE personal year.

The possibility for the FIRST MAJOR TURNING POINT IN OUR LIFE PATTERN IS THE START OF THE SECOND PINNACLE. I say possibility because in some cases the number doesn't change. The tempo of the first pinnacle may continue through the second and sometimes thereafter as well, but for most of us there is a turning point in our life at this time.

Just how radical this turning point may be depends on the compatibility or incompatibility of the qualities symbolized by each of the numbers involved. If the numbers on the first and second pinnacles are contiguous, then there is indeed a radical change in the life style, where the atttiude which guided the individual as he faced every important matter in his entire life experience up to that point of time, must be drastically adjusted to reflect the new attitude which will be required of him for the following 9 years.

This also pertains to the transition between the second and third pinnacles. What is pertinent here is how the third pinnacle number relates to the second pinnacle number which it follows. It does not matter, directly, how the third pinnacle number may relate to the first pinnacle which is now 9 years in the past.

If there is a basic compatibility between the number on one pinnacle and the number following, then there is no drastic alteration in the life style. What follows is a natural outgrowth or extension of what went before. It is fortunate, but comparatively rare, if one's whole life style follows this general rule.

These two 9 year cycles which we call the MIDDLE MATURE YEARS (for a total of 18 years) come at a time when supposedly we have reached our greatest productivity and we should therefore be able to capitalize on our best opportunities.

The middle mature years would fall as follows:
FOR THE ONE DESTINY age 35 to 53
FOR THE TWO DESTINY age 34 to 52
FOR THE THREE DESTINY age 33 to 51
FOR THE FOUR DESTINY age 32 to 50
FOR THE FIVE DESTINY age 31 to 49
FOR THE SIX DESTINY age 30 to 48

FOR THE SEVEN DESTINY age 29 to 47
FOR THE EIGHT DESTINY age 28 to 46
FOR THE NINE DESTINY age 27 to 45

In evaluating this middle period try to consider the two pinnacles together. Do not add the numbers together, but appraise the productivity in terms of two periods where the individual is able to operate for 9 mature years under one attitude and then a following 9 mature years under another attitude. The kind of questions you might ask yourself are, what kind of thing could this individual produce working under these conditions? The number on the pinnacle determines the required attitude which necessarily promotes the product'on of that type of product. And how does this compare with the over-all destiny challenge? Is this period a constructive step in that direction or an apparent detour or set back?

You must always remember that the individual started out in life in a specific tempo and since that was all he knew or was able to experience up to that time, even when the new pinnacle becomes operative there is a carry-over of habit which is never quite forgotten (especially with that long introduction to life). This carry-over is less important in the transition from the second to the third or the third to the fourth as the individual has now come to see that life indeed does change and nothing is designed to go on forever.

The first judgment is whether the middle productive period is an improvement and advance over the START OF LIFE or a decline and step backward. This judgment is to be made in terms of the over-all destiny challenge and NOT THE LIKES AND DISLIKES OF THE INDIVIDUAL HIMSELF (Motivation, Personality and Character).

Because of the vast number of patterns resulting from all the possible combinations of the destiny with the pinnacles, it is impossible to explain here each of them in graphic detail. It is hoped that in time you will be able to do this for yourself as you learn to THINK NUMBERS.

The reader is advised to return to Chapter V and review the description of his own destiny challenge. Then compare this with the description of how he entered life at the beginning of this chapter. This would be step (1) in evaluating the destiny at a glance.

Step (2) would be comparing the first possible turning point with how the individual started out in life under pinnacle one with the beginning of the middle mature years under pinnacle two. For this read the section on the start of life as though this were the second pinnacle.

In general the transition from one pinnacle to another is a step up in the ladder of human awareness if THE NUMBERS ADVANCE IN PROGRESSION FROM ONE TO NINE. There are advantages, however, when there is an advance of 2 or more digits at a time. An advance of only 1 digit accents the contradiction of contiguous numbers where the lessons to be learned under one number are just too close and contradictory to the lessons that were learned on the contiguous number.

To appraise the contrast of the pinnacles as they follow each other — or for that matter any cycles of time you may be studying — reread the descriptions of the start in life as though that is the pinnacle in question and so on throughout any succeeding cycles.

## THE NUMBERS ON THE PINNACLES

Number ONE on the Start Of Life is always a good beginning for anything that might follow. Number ONE on any subsequent pinnacle, however, is never as desirable because it signifies the necessity for a new beginning which indicates that much of what went before may have to be discarded or junked because it can't be used to solve what must be faced in the future. However, if the vibration on the START OF LIFE is totally out of keeping with the destiny number itself, then number ONE falling on a subsequent pinnacle indicates that time as the period in one's life when the individual will effectively start in the direction of his destiny. Under these circumstances (where the opening cycle was out of keeping with the destiny), it would be more desirable for ONE to fall on the second pinnacle in the beginning of the middle mature period. If it falls on the third pinnacle it would tend to throw out the value of the second pinnacle since a new start would have to be undertaken at that time. If ONE falls on the fourth pinnacle then the individual is not so much a late starter as one must undergo a complete revamping of all his prior programs in life and most of his middle mature years would also seem somewhat wasted. No experience in life is ever really wasted, but it is more fortunate when one experience can build on another rather than having to return to grass roots scratch. It is obviously undesirable and unfortunate to be required to start all over again at the close of life (in the fourth pinnacle) just as it is somewhat unfortunate to start life on the NINE of psychological endings. Number ONE is therefore best when it falls on the first pinnacle, or possibly on the second, but correspondingly less favorable on the third and especially so on the fourth and last pinnacle.

Number TWO on the Start of LIFE is a hold back as though the individual were not yet in the best possible format to face the task that lies ahead. He may have to undergo some drastic changes (rebirths) before he can appear in the proper light. Any time period under TWO is an excellent time for gathering raw material to be worked on later. It is also an excellent time for having revealed to you what may have been overlooked before. The high potential of TWO is an acute and sometimes painful or tragic revelation. Sensational events often occur in people's lives when the timing registers TWO (or ELEVEN). The individual at this time is apt to take a fall or make an abrupt turn since TWO reflects a contra or opposite position from where you were before. Number TWO on a subsequent pinnacle after the first signals a "time out" period for reparis and/or nourishment. It would depend on how far one has come and how active the life style has been as to just how welcome this "time out" period will be. It would generally not be favorable on the third pinnacle as this would be wasteful of one of the valuable middle mature cycles. It is generally quite unfavorable on the last pinnacle as it could mean being turned "out to pasture" before one's time. If the life has been very active and aggressively productive up to then, TWO ON THE FOURTH PINNACLE OFTEN INDICATES A BLOWN FUSE OR NERVES BEING GROUND DOWN TO THE BARE EDGE. While TWO time indicates the possibility of celebrity status or sensational attention of some sort it is generally unproductive unless it relates closely to the quality of the destiny and the life style up to that point has laid the ground work for celebrity status as a final achievement.

Number THREE on the Start Of Life is a relaxed, happy, carefree beginning but it is also a suspension from a more active confrontation with the broader realities of life. In any of the creative arts it is always beneficial but correspondingly less so when starting out in most other fields. The individual retains his childhood far beyond its normal span (if say, age 15 might be considered the top span for acting like a child). Number THREE on any of the time cycles always indicates conditions of comparative ease and freedom from responsibility so when it occurs the individual should be particularly released from most practical worries which would indicate that there is some independence from normal money concerns. It would be fortunate to have the THREE occur as early as the second pinnacle PROVIDING IT IS NOT SUBSEQUENTLY FOLLOWED BY A REVERSAL TO HARD TIMES. It is more logical to have it fall, however, on the third or fourth pinnacle where it can be considered particularly fortunate because it means the close of life is less of a hassle and the individual is somehow relieved of the normal concern for everyday survival that faces most people. If the destiny challenge is particularly demanding, when THREE time comes up it would denote that the main struggle was over. The individual may become even more outspoken, critical and opinionated (which might in some cases be the very way to finally put his project across) but generally speaking THREE time is not for open combat or a heavy concentration of battle wagons. Apparently the necessary time for that would have passed. From here on, it calls for the light, persuasive touch applied with imaginative flair and decorative flourish. This may not be in keeping with the destiny or what the individual himself prefers, but it is the color of the winning ticket for the rest of the show.

Number FOUR on the Start Of Life is a difficult beginning but a sound and realistic one. It should provide a firm foundation for anything that might follow providing the harshness and discipline have not embittered the individual. Almost any number that would follow FOUR on the beginning would be an improvement, but it would be more constructive if it were any number greater than FOUR, ONE, TWO or THREE at this point would not be as constructive. Ideally all pinnacle patterns should progress upwards, NOT BACKWARDS. Standing still (working and reworking the same expression style) may be desirable, except in FOUR where it is apt to become too much of a difficult situation. FOUR on the third or fourth pinnacle is correspondingly less favorable, particularly to end up one's life style when one's age and physical conditions are less responsive to life's hardest work demand. Even if one's whole life has been a matter of ease and comfort, it generally makes little sense to end up on such a harsh note as FOUR, because by then it is too late to do much about it unless the destiny is also FOUR.

Number FIVE on the Start Of Life is certainly an exciting beginning but one may have to initiate a more substantive approach later on. The sooner this comes the better, preferably on the second pinnacle; otherwise it is correspondingly delayed again if on the third and fatally so if on the fourth and last pinnacle. This judgment should be qualified, of course, if the destiny itself is FIVE. No number is really too late on the pinnacle when it matches the destiny, but it is desirable to have one's introduction to this attitude come as early in life as possible and this is exactly what the pinnacles reveal — "when" and "what" action is going on in the individual's life. Number FIVE on a pinnacle denotes an abrupt change or direction in the life style from whatever has been going on up to then. This generally comes in the nature of an outside intrusion into the individual's affairs. It can be welcome or unwelcome depending on how the individual rates his life up to then. If, under the prior pinnacles the individual has not been able to effectively come to terms with the over-all challenge of his destiny, when the FIVE time comes up there should be accelerated changes to suddenly take off in at least a different direction. The individual may have to speed up considerably in order to make up for lost time but FIVE time should provide a short cut which makes this possible. As already stated, FIVE on the final pinnacle is generally unfavorable because it indicates that the individual may have gotten substantially off the track and he must now, at this late stage in life, frantically scratch around and substitute for what might have been. In any event it divorces the rewards of later years from the earlier period when ideally one should grow out of the other.

Number SIX on the Start Of Life is somewhat of an obstacle because it burdens the childhood with responsibility for others and at the same time over-emphasizes the protective shell of group support which may be difficult to overcome in later life. SIX is a good deal more favorable when falling on any pinnacle subsequent to the first. In the life of a woman, who was happily dedicated to domesticity, SIX on both the middle mature cycles would seem quite natural. It could, however, indicate an overdependence on the family unit or the care of older relatives. SIX on the final pinnacle would be especially indicative of this. However, SIX on the final pinnacle is a favorable vibration for the close of life as it indicates a closeness of associations whether actually related by blood or not. It is the opposite of a social withdrawal from life.

Number SEVEN on the Start Of Life is somewhat of a handicap but many famous people have gone on to make their mark in life apparently spurred by some inner resolve that was developed at this time. The isolation imposed by SEVEN time gives plenty of opportunity for analyzing all the possible approaches one might undertake and sizing up what others are making of their lives. Out of this introspection the individual should realize in exactly what direction he himself should proceed. People who start life on SEVEN are far less likely to stumble later on. SEVEN time falling on subsequent pinnacles may indicate some type of misfortune where (as in TWO time) the individual is forced into some sort of retirement from the main stream of life. This can be productive in special ways (like research) when related to certain destiny patterns (as to the SEVEN itself) or the NINE providing there is still time (under another pinnacle) to put to use the insight one gains during this SEVEN time. SEVEN is generally unfavorable as a vibration on which to end life as it denotes a lonely isolation which some people might prefer, but it throws the individual entirely on his own inner resources which at that point in life may have worn a little thin. This might be an indication of some pronounced eccentricity coming to the fore. To close life on this note would certainly not be welcomed by those dedicated to an active physical life or one strongly bound to social commitments or to a life conditioned to high productivity or extensive contacts of any kind. SEVEN time definitely symbolizes the recluse and seclusion.

Number EIGHT on the Start Of Life does start everything off with a bang. The problem is to have a follow up (under a subsequent pinnacle) which would still provide forward opportunities and not a slacking off into assignments of lesser rank. As the first pinnacle lasts until the late twenties (and for some into the early 30's), EIGHT at the beginning fairly well establishes the individual's attention on "super efficiency" and securing the most profit from every situation. Anything that follows is likely to be an anti-climax or a disappointment because it doesn't live up to financial expectations. The EIGHT generates so much power and steam that it is difficult to step down to ordinary levels. The relationship to the second pinnacle number is

310

the most important because this is the first major turning point. If there is going to be a difficult change of direction in the life style it would be far better to come here than later in life. The most abrupt changes would be indicated if the second pinnacle was ONE or FIVE. TWO or FOUR would indicate a loss of power and influence which might be hard to take. THREE might indicate sufficient success to take a prolonged vacation. Numbers above FIVE would only require some modification of the energy thrust into other fields of application but not an indication that most of what had been accomplished up to then might have to be discarded. EIGHT on either pinnacle of the middle mature period is strongly indicative of commercial success and appropriate rewards, especially if the attitudes up the then had paved the way for this type of "cashing in". Ending life on EIGHT is also favorable providing the life style has, again, provided for a build up where EIGHT time would be considered a crowning achievement. If the life ends on EIGHT time with no prior orientation in this direction (either by reference to prior pinnacles, the fate itself or the individual's own make up) then EIGHT at the end of life is apt to be a frantic desperate last effort to restructure a life time of serious mistakes.

Number NINE on the Start Of Life is a good beginning for any number vibration which may follow in a subsequent pinnacle of timing. The NINE does, however, postpone the individual's necessity for coming to a more immediate confrontation with the challenge of his fate (unless it is also in the NINE vibration). This may be less important if the fate number is SIX or above as the NINE beginning establishes a broad foundation for the future application of any of these qualities. It is more of a set back if the fate number, however, is ONE through FIVE because the demands of each of these vibrations are much more personal in application and the individual has correspondingly less need for this broad foundation of worldly understanding. In fact it could be a handicap when one must put aside this philosophical detachment and get down to brass tacks. The transition from the first to second pinnacle is likely to be less surprising when following NINE (on the first). Any change at this time may indeed be welcome as though at last one can get on with the real business at hand. NINE time on either of the middle mature cycles may act as a suspension of activity or forced retirement where the individual is required to divest himself from certain attitudes, modes of behavior, personal contacts or family ties. The necessity here at NINE time is to stop what one has been doing, cut loose and broaden out — literally "quite work and go fishing". NINE, the symbol of endings, on the fourth and final pinnacle is a natural condition which ideally follows an active life. It specifically points up that the main hassle is over, there is little you can do about things at this point and you might as well make the best of what you have to put up with. This could however, provide a real opportunity for full maturity even though at the sunset of life.

If the number on any of the pinnacles of timing MATCHES YOUR MOTIVATION, then it is a period in your life when YOU SHOULD ENJOY WHAT YOU ARE DOING.

If the number on any of the pinnacles of timing matches YOUR PERSONALITY then it is a period of your life when you should BE ABLE TO DO THINGS EASILY because it is a talent YOU CAN DO INSTINCTIVELY.

If the number of any of the pinnacles of timing matches YOUR CHARACTER then it is a period in your life when YOU SHOULD MAKE DEFINITE PROGRESS because what is called for as an attitude of mind is EXACTLY WHAT YOU ARE BEST QUALIFIED TO DO.

If the number on any of the pinnacles of timings matches YOUR DESTINY then it is a period in your life which SHOULD PROVE HIGHLY SIGNIFICANT even though it may take everything you can muster to meet the challenge.

If the number on any of the pinnacles of timing is ONE OF YOUR KARMAS, then the effect of this karma is far LESS TROUBLE-SOME at this time and you seem to easily acquire a more constructive attitude in this direction. It is as though the karmic condition during the span of the pinnacle were temporarily suspended.

\* \* \*

# CRCS Books

**THE ANCIENT SCIENCE OF GEOMANCY:Living in Harmony with the Earth** by Nigel Pennick $12.95. The best and most accessible survey of this ancient wholistic art/science, superbly illustrated with 120 photos.

**AN ASTROLOGICAL GUIDE TO SELF-AWARENESS** by Donna Cunningham, M.S.W. $6.95. Written in a lively style, this book includes chapters on transits, houses, interpreting aspects, etc. A popular book translated into 5 languages..

**THE ART OF CHART INTERPRETATION: A Step-by-Step Method of Analyzing,Synthesizing & Understanding the Birth Chart** by Tracy Marks $7.95. A guide to determining the most important features of a birth chart. A must for students!

**THE ASTROLOGER'S GUIDE TO COUNSELING: Astrology's Role in the Helping Professions** by Bernard Rosenblum, M.D. $7.95. Establishes astrological counseling as a valid and legitimate helping profession. A break-through book!

**THE ASTROLOGER'S MANUAL: Modern Insights into an Ancient Art** by Landis Knight Green $10.95, 240 pages. A strikingly original work that includes extensive sections on relationships, aspects, and all the fundamentals in a lively new way.

**THE ASTROLOGICAL HOUSES: The Spectrum of Individual Experience** by Dane Rudhyar $8.95. A recognized classic of modern astrology that has sold over 100,000 copies, this book is required reading for every student of astrology seeking to understand the deeper meanings of the houses.

**ASTROLOGY: The Classic Guide to Understanding Your Horoscope** by Ronald C. Davison $7.95. The most popular book on astrology during the 1960's & 1970's is now back in print in a new edition, with an instructive new foreword that explains how the author's remarkable keyword system can be used by even the novice student of astrology.

**ASTROLOGY FOR THE NEW AGE: An Intuitive Approach** by Marcus Allen $7.95. Emphasizes self-acceptance and tuning in to your chart with a positive openness. Helps one create his or her own interpretation.

**ASTROLOGY IN MODERN LANGUAGE** by Richard Vaughan $12.95, 336 pages. An in-depth interpretation of the birth chart focusing on the houses and their ruling planets— including the Ascendant and its ruler. A unique, strikingly original work.

**ASTROLOGY, KARMA & TRANSFORMATION: The Inner Dimensions of the Birth Chart** by Stephen Arroyo $10.95. An insightful book on the use of astrology for persoal growth, seen in the light of the theory of karma and the urge toward self-transformation. International best-seller!

**THE ASTROLOGY OF SELF-DISCOVERY: An In-Depth Exploration of the Potentials Revealed in Your Birth Chart** by Tracy Marks $8.95, 288 pages. Emphasizes the Moon and its nodes, Neptune, Pluto, & the outer planet transits. An important and brilliantly original work!

**ASTROLOGY, PSYCHOLOGY AND THE FOUR ELEMENTS: An Energy Approach to Astrology & Its Use in the Counseling Arts** by Stephen Arroyo $7.95. An international best-seller, this book deals with the use of astrology as a practical method of understanding one's attunement to universal forces. Clearly shows how to approach astrology with a real understanding of the energies involved. Awarded the British Astrological Assn's Astrology Prize. A classic translated into 8 languages!

**CYCLES OF BECOMING: The Planetary Pattern of Growth** by Alexander Ruperti $12.95, 274 pages. The first complete treatment of transits from a humanistic and holistic perspective. All important planetary cycles are correlated with the essential phases of personal development. A pioneering work!

**DYNAMICS OF ASPECT ANALYSIS: New Perceptions in Astrology** by Bil Tierney $8.95, 288 pages. Ground-breaking work! The most in-depth treatment of aspects and aspect patterns available, including both major and minor configurations. Also includes retrogrades, unaspected planets & more!

**A JOURNEY THROUGH THE BIRTH CHART: Using Astrology on Your Life Path** by Joanne Wickenburg $7.95. Gives the reader the tools to put the pieces of the birth chart together for self-understanding and encourages creative interpretation by helping the reader to think through the endless combinations of astrological symbols.

**THE JUPITER/SATURN CONFERENCE LECTURES: New Insights in Modern Astrology** by Stephen Arroyo & Liz Greene $8.95. Talks included deal with myth, chart synthesis, relationships, & Jungian psychology related to astrology. A wealth of original & important ideas!

**THE LITERARY ZODIAC** by Paul Wright $12.95, 240 pages. A pioneering work, based on extensive research, exploring the connection between astrology and literary creativity.

**LOOKING AT ASTROLOGY** by Liz Greene $7.50. A beautiful, full-color children's book for ages 6-13. Illustrated by the author, this is the best explanation of astrology for children and was highly recommended by SCHOOL LIBRARY JOURNAL. Emphasizes self-acceptance and a realistic understanding of others.

**NUMBERS AS SYMBOLS FOR SELF-DISCOVERY: Exploring Character & Destiny with Numerology** by Richard Vaughan $8.95, 336 pages. A how-to book on personal analysis and forecasting your future through Numerology. Examples include the number patterns of a thousand famous personalities.

**THE OUTER PLANETS & THEIR CYCLES: The Astrology of the Collective** by Liz Greene $7.95. Deals with the individual's attunement to the outer planets as well as with significant historical and generational trends that correlate to these planetary cycles.

**PLANETARY ASPECTS: FROM CONFLICT TO COOPERATION: How to Make Your Stressful Aspects Work for You** by Tracy Marks $8.95, 225 pages. This revised edition of HOW TO HANDLE YOUR T-SQUARE focuses on the creative understanding of the stressful aspects and focuses on the T-Square configuration both in natal charts and as formed by transits & progressions. The most thorough treatment of these subjects in print!

**THE PLANETS AND HUMAN BEHAVIOR** by Jeff Mayo $7.95. A pioneering exploration of the symbolism of the planets, blending their modern psychological significance with their ancient mythological meanings. Includes many tips on interpretation.

**PRACTICAL PALMISTRY: A Positive Approach from a Modern Perspective** by David Brandon-Jones $8.95, 268 pages. This easy-to-use book describes and illustrates all the basics of traditional palmistry and then builds upon that with more recent discoveries based upon the author's extensive experience and case studies. A discriminating approach to an ancient science that includes many original ideas!

**THE PRACTICE AND PROFESSION OF ASTROLOGY: Rebuilding Our Lost Connections with the Cosmos** by Stephen Arroyo $7.95. A challenging, often controversial treatment of astrology's place in modern society and of astrological counseling as both a legitimate profession and a healing process.

**REINCARNATION THROUGH THE ZODIAC** by Joan Hodgson $6.50. A study of the signs of the zodiac from a spiritual perspective, based upon the development of different phases of conciousness through reincarnation.

**RELATIONSHIPS & LIFE CYCLES: Modern Dimensions of Astrology** by Stephen Arroyo $8.95. Thorough discussion of natal chart indicators of one's capacity and need for relationship; techniques of chart comparison; using transits practically; and the use of the houses in chart comparison.

**SEX & THE ZODIAC: An Astrological Guide to Intimate Relationships** by Helen Terrell $7.95, 256 pages. Goes into great detail in describing and analyzing the dominant traits of women and men as indicated by their Zodiacal signs.

**THE SPIRAL OF LIFE: Unlocking Your Potential with Astrology** by Joanne Wickenburg & Virginia Meyer $7.95. Covering all astrological factors, this book shows how understanding the birth pattern is an exciting path toward increased self-awareness.

**A SPIRITUAL APPROACH TO ASTROLOGY: A Complete Textbook of Astrology** by Myrna Lofthus $12.95, 444 pages. A complete astrology textbook from a karmic viewpoint, with an especially valuable 130-page section on karmic interpretation of all aspects, including the Ascendant & MC.

For more complete information on our books, a complete booklist, or to order any of the above publications, WRITE TO:

CRCS Publications
Post Office Box 1460
Sebastopol, California 95473
U.S.A.

# ASTROLOGY, PSYCHOLOGY,

## AND

# THE FOUR ELEMENTS

*An Energy Approach to Astrology &
Its Use in the Counseling Arts*

## Stephen Arroyo

$7.95

This book deals with the relation of astrology to modern psychology and with the use of astrology as a practical method of understanding one's attunement to universal forces. It clearly shows how to approach astrology with a real understanding of the energies involved, and it includes practical instruction in the interpretation of astrological factors with more depth than is commonly found in astrological textbooks. Part I was awarded the 1973 Astrology Prize by the British Astrological Association as the most valuable contribution to astrology during that year.

## PART I: ASTROLOGY & PSYCHOLOGY

Part I thoroughly explains how astrology can be the most valuable psychological tool for understanding oneself and others. Analyzing the scientific, philosophical, and intuitive dimensions of astrology, it is oriented toward the layman with no astrological knowledge, astrology students and professionals, and those engaged in any form of the counseling arts.

## PART II: THE FOUR ELEMENTS
## AN ENERGY APPROACH TO INTERPRETING
## BIRTH-CHARTS

Part II deals specifically with the interpretation and practical application of astrological factors based on the actual energies involved (air, fire, water, & earth). It presents a dynamic application of astrological knowledge that clarifies and illuminates traditional techniques and meanings by placing them in the perspective of understanding the vital energies inherent in all life processes.